MUSIC ASYLUMS: WELL
IN EVER

Music and Change:
Ecological Perspectives

Series Editors:

Gary Ansdell, Director of Education, Nordoff Robbins Music Therapy, UK
Professor Tia DeNora, Department of Sociology & Philosophy, HuSS,
University of Exeter, UK

Series Advisory Board:

Kenneth Aigen, Temple University, USA
Jane Davidson, University of Western Australia
Timothy Dowd, Emory University, USA
Lucy Green, Institute of Education, UK
Lee Higgins, Boston University College of Fine Arts, USA
Raymond MacDonald, Edinburgh University, UK
Mercédès Pavlicevic, Nordoff Robbins, UK
Even Ruud, University of Oslo, Norway
Brynjulf Stige, University of Bergen, Norway
Henry Stobart, Royal Holloway, University of London, UK

Music and Change: Ecological Perspectives, is a cross-disciplinary, topic-led series for scholars and practitioners. Its aim is to explore the question of how, where and when music makes a difference. If music is a dynamic ingredient of change, what are the processes and mechanisms associated with music's powers, and how can ecological perspectives help us to understand music in action? Book proposals are welcome in any of the following areas: healthcare, social policy, political activism, psychiatry, embodiment, mind and consciousness, community relations, education and informal learning, management and organizational cultures, trauma, memory and commemoration, theories of action, self-help, conflict and conflict resolution, the life course, spirituality and religion, disability studies, palliative care, social criticism, governance, resistance, protest, and utopian communities.

Forthcoming titles in the series:

How Music Helps in Music Therapy and Everyday Life
Gary Ansdell

Musical Pathways for Mental Health
Gary Ansdell and Tia DeNora

Music Asylums:
Wellbeing Through Music in
Everyday Life

TIA DeNORA

University of Exeter, UK

LONDON AND NEW YORK

First published 2015 by Ashgate Publishing

First published in hardback 2013

Published 2016 by Routledge
2 Park Square, Milton Park, Abingdon, Oxon OX14 4RN
711 Third Avenue, New York, NY 10017, USA

Routledge is an imprint of the Taylor & Francis Group, an informa business

British Library Cataloguing in Publication Data
A catalogue record for this book is available from the British Library

The Library of Congress has cataloged the printed edition as follows:
DeNora, Tia.
  Music asylums : wellbeing through music in everyday life / by Tia DeNora.
    pages cm. – (Music and change : ecological perspectives)
  Includes bibliographical references and index.
  ISBN 978-1-4094-3759-8 (hardback) – ISBN 978-1-4094-3760-4 (ebook) –
ISBN 978-1-4724-0032-1 (epub) 1. Music therapy. 2. Music–Social aspects. I. Title.

  ML3920.D37 2013
  781'.11–dc23

                                                                    2013007769

ISBN 13: 978-1-4724-5598-7 (pbk)
ISBN 13: 978-1-4094-3759-8 (hbk)

Contents

List of Figures and Tables

Figures

Tables

Preface

This book is the first of a three-volume set, the outcome of a six-year interdisciplinary study of community music therapy. The research focused on mental health and wellbeing within the context of a centre supporting people with mental health challenges and involved collaboration between the centre, Gary Ansdell and Sarah Wilson from the music therapy charity, Nordoff Robbins and Tia DeNora at Exeter University.

The set of books was inspired by the idea of a triptych – a three-panel painting where the first and third panels fold inward to reflect upon the main, centre panel. Two complementary books by DeNora (Volume 1) and Ansdell (Volume 2) represent the two 'side panels'. They aim to develop a grounded theory of music as a medium of wellbeing in therapy and everyday life (arenas which, the authors show, cannot be fully distinguished from each other). This topic is addressed from the complementary perspectives of the two authors' professional and theoretical backgrounds – as a sociologist and music therapist respectively. A third, co-authored, volume forms the main panel, refracting and further developing understandings and perspectives from the two side-panels.

In Volume 1, *Music Asylums: Wellbeing Through Music in Everyday Life*, DeNora considers how music offers forms of asylum. Music 'asylums' may offer respite (from pain or distress) but they can also involve collaborative transformations of social worlds. The book draws upon DeNora's work as a cultural sociologist with a long-standing interest in music in action.

Volume 2 presents Ansdell's complementary perspective, drawing on his 25 years of experience as a music therapist and researcher. *How Music Helps in Music Therapy and Everyday Life* suggests an ecological framework for understanding the key continuities between the specialist area of music therapy and people's more everyday experiences of how music promotes wellbeing.

Volume 3, *Musical Pathways for Mental Health*, is co-written by Ansdell and DeNora. A wide range of methods of data collection and analysis are used in this case-study to explore how collective musical activity helps the participants of a community music therapy project at a centre supporting people with mental health challenges forge pathways into greater wellbeing.

Acknowledgements

Most books take time to write, but this book was longer in the making than any other I have so far produced. In part, the delay was due to the fact that it is one of the outcomes of a longitudinal community music therapy research project (BRIGHT), which I describe in Chapters 5 and 6. The BRIGHT work began in 2005 and is one of the longest-running practical and research projects of its kind. (The practical arm and its music therapists Gary Ansdell and Sarah Wilson won the Royal Society for the Promotion of Health Award in 2008.) Because of the time period and because the field of music therapy and music and health was still relatively new to me when I began this work, there are a good many people to thank.

My interest in everyday musical activity and health was initially sparked at Exeter by two of the early PhD scholars in our SocArts research group, Susan Trythall and Kari Batt-Rawden. Sue, who arrived in 2002, was the first-ever SocArts researcher to develop an interest in music and health through her work on music in hospitals (Trythall 2006; Batt-Rawden, Trythall and DeNora 2007). Kari came to Exeter through an introduction from Professor Even Ruud of Oslo University and the Academy of Music in Oslo to investigate everyday musical engagement as a resource for lay techniques of health promotion.

A special thanks is also due to Even Ruud who invited me to Oslo in 2004, which turned out to be a bit of a watershed moment for me. There, I not only met Even but many of the group of Nordic scholars whose work has been central to the perspectives I develop here, in particular: Trygve Aasgaard, Lars Ole Bonde, Randi Rolvsjord, Marie Skånland, Brynjulf Stige and Gro Trondalen. Through these scholars (and the Nordic MUCH Network) I have met many others who have also helped in various ways. Among these, Stephen Clift, Susanne Hanser, Nigel Hartley, Jan Sverre Knudsen, Vigo Krüger, Lars Lilliestam, Hanne Mette Ridder, Karette Annie Stensæth, Lisa Summer (who kindly read an earlier draft of Chapter 6), Gunnar Tellnes and the late Tony Wigram have inspired me with their work and conversation. (With Scandinavia in mind, I also want to thank K. Olle Edström, through whom I have come to know the unique group of socio-music scholars in Gothenburg University, in particular Lars Lilliestam and Ola Stockfelt.)

It was also in Oslo that I first met colleagues at Nordoff–Robbins, London, now good friends and the closest of research collaborators: Mercédès Pavlicevic, Simon Procter and, of course, Gary Ansdell, my partner in Ashgate's Music and Change book series and co-author of volume 3 of our 'book triptych' on music, health and wellbeing (of which this is volume 1).

Thanks are also due to Paul Atkinson and the Cardiff Group on Ethnography, Arts and Craft, Georgina Born and Tom Rice for their comments on an early version of part of Chapter 5; David Clarke, Eric Clarke and Giovanna Colombetti, for their comments on an earlier version of Chapter 6; Jane Davidson; Eduardo de la Fuente, who was a discussant for an earlier version of Chapter 6 at a Plenary Session on the Aesthetic Shaping of Society, at the International Sociological Association Congress in 2010; Lucy Green; Nigel Hartley; Antoine Hennion; David Inglis; Raymond MacDonald, who revealed that he was the anonymous critic who read the penultimate version of this text in full for Ashgate; Lisa McCormick, who was a Fellow in SocArts in 2011–12; John Meehan; Simon Mills; Rii Numata; Thomas Regeslski, for comments on an earlier version of Chapter 7; William Roy, for comments on an earlier version of Chapter 5; Anna Lisa Tota; Tony Walter, Sarah Wilson, whose exemplary work at BRIGHT is inspirational; Dana Wilson-Kovacs; Robert Witkin; the ESRC-supported Arts and Health Seminar Group; the AHRC Network, Being in the Zone; and all the participants at BRIGHT with whom I have spent many pleasant hours involving music, talk and tea-drinking since 2006.

Early versions of chapters were given as talks at the following conferences and university departments: Music Faculty, Oxford; Musicology, Gothenburg University; Distinguished Visiting Professor Lecture, Haverford College; Center for Cultural Sociology, Yale University; keynote, International Society for the Philosophy of Music Education, Helsinki; keynote, Finnish Musicological Society, Turku; keynote, International Sociological Association Conference, Gothenburg; keynote, European Sociological Association Research Networks on Arts and Culture, IAUV Venice; keynote, European Sociological Association, University of Geneva; keynote, Manchester SEMPRE Conference on Music, Identity and Spoken Interaction; keynote, Manchester Conference, Turning Personal (thanks especially to Carol Smart and Jennifer Mason); keynote, Keele Symposium on Interdisciplinarity and two keynotes at the St Christopher's Hospice International Symposia on Arts and End of Life Care.

At home in Exeter, I wish to thank the ever-growing research family otherwise known as SocArts, with whom I share the focus on 'music in action': Sophia Acord, Rita Gracio Alberto, Kari Batt-Rawden, Arild Bergh, Pedro dos Santos Boia, Elizabeth Dennis, Sigrun-Lilja Einarsdottir, Pinar Guran, Trever Hagen, Mariko Hara, Simon Procter, Craig Robertson, Sarah Smith, Ian Sutherland and Susan Trythall.

Finally, and because it too often goes without saying, I want to extend the deepest of thanks to my husband Douglas Tudhope, companion and critic (constructive), with whom I have been having, effectively, the same conversation for more than 30 years.

And last, thank you to my copy editor, Mark Newby, indexer, Hazel Young, and the impeccable editorial team at Ashgate – Heidi Bishop, Publisher for Music Studies, Gemma Hayman, Senior Editor, and Emma Gallon, Assistant Editor. It has been a tremendous pleasure to work with you and Ashgate, where the old-fashioned values of scholarly publishing are alive and well.

*

An earlier version of Chapter 5 was published as 'Music Space as Healing Space: Community Music Therapy and the Negotiation of Identity in a Mental Health Centre', in Georgina Born (ed.), *Music, Sound and Space* (Cambridge: Cambridge University Press, 2013), pp. 259–76. © Cambridge University Press, reproduced with permission.

An earlier version of Chapter 6 was published as 'Practical Consciousness and Social Relation in MusEcological Perspective', in D. Clarke and E. Clarke (eds), *Music and Consciousness: Philosophical, Psychological and Cultural Perspectives* (Oxford: Oxford University Press, 2011), pp. 309–26. By permission of Oxford University Press.

For
Jessie, Joan, Doug and Alan

And in memory of
Ranken, Shirley and John

Not only is the self entwined in society; it owes society its existence in the
most literal sense.
Theodor Adorno, Minima Moralia

Introduction

This book is about music, healing, health and wellness. My purpose is to develop a grounded theoretical account of how music can be understood to create conditions conducive to wellbeing and what if anything might be special about music in this regard. In the chapters that follow, I describe how music, as a specific form of cultural activity, can be practised in ways that offer what I shall speak of as 'asylum'. I use the term 'asylum' to denote respite from distress and a place and time in which it is possible to flourish. By 'flourish' I mean the ability to feel as if one is in the flow of things, to be able to feel creative and to engage in creative play, to enjoy a sense of validation or connection to others, to feel pleasure, perhaps to note the absence, or temporary abatement, of pain (Ansdell and DeNora 2012). I suggest that the general topic of music and wellbeing is one of the most important we can investigate within socio-musical studies, yet it raises tantalizing questions.

At the level of lived experience, we may feel that we know the answers to these questions, but when pressed we may find ourselves unable to put into words just what it is about music that seems to help. Perhaps the fact that music can elide words is part of the problem, and perhaps this elision is linked to what it is that music can do in relation to health promotion. To be sure, the idea of music as a medium that speaks directly, in ways that do not require language, is as global as it is ancient, and the idea that music is 'medicinal' is often an everyday matter of fact in so-called non-Western places. But even in Western culture, where so-called serious music is typically deemed to be autonomous from functions, tasks and daily routines, music is frequently linked to healing and wellbeing. Thus, there would seem to be something specifically musical about music's powers, something that exists and happens outside of or beyond text and, indeed, beyond representation. To the extent that there is this something, and to the extent that it is ineffable, then perhaps text is an awkward medium for describing what it is that music can do.

At the Keyboard Circa 1800 and 2003: Trying to Make Things Better

Consider Beethoven, in the guise of early nineteenth-century music therapist, according to an anecdote relayed by Felix Mendelssohn. Visiting Milan in 1831, Mendelssohn called upon the Baron and Baroness von Ertmann, close friends and patrons of Beethoven. (The baroness, Dorothea, was a leading pianist of her day. Beethoven called her his 'Dorothea–Cäcilia' due to her gifts as an interpreter of his works.) Mendelssohn wrote to his sister, Fanny:

> [Baroness Ertmann] told me that when she lost her last child, Beethoven at
> first shrank from coming to her house; but at length he invited her to visit him,
> and when she arrived, she found him seated at the piano, and simply saying,
> 'Let us speak to each other by music,' he played on for more than an hour,
> and, as she expressed it, 'he said much to me, and at last gave me consolation'.
> (Mendelssohn c.1861: 207–8)

In our own time too music can make things better, nowhere more clearly illustrated
than in music therapy. For example, here, in a second scenario, also involving two
people and a keyboard instrument, circa 2003:

> Pam hits the xylophone hard with the beaters and throws them towards the
> piano, which they hit, causing the piano strings to vibrate. She shouts 'This
> fucking life!' and becomes very upset. (The therapist [Gary Ansdell] later finds
> out that the outburst was caused by her seeing the letter names on the xylophone
> spelling out abusive messages to her from an internal voice.) Immediately after
> the blow-up the therapist encourages Pam to come to the piano, to sit beside him,
> and encourages her back into musical engagement again. She begins playing a
> few notes on the top of the piano, which leads into a short piano duet and then
> into shared singing with the therapist. Pam takes over the singing herself after
> a short time (accompanied by the therapist on the piano), becoming involved
> and expressive. The music seems to take her somewhere else. After the music
> cadences she sighs and says 'That's better!' The entire episode has lasted just
> over four minutes. (Ansdell et al. 2010)

In both of these examples of 'live' musical participation, music can be seen as
a way of being together. And, in both, music is much more than the 'production
and consumption' of meaningful organized sound. Beyond the production–
consumption dichotomy, again in both of these examples, musical activity involves
postures, mutual orientation, para-musical action (talk, movement, gesture and
ancillary activities such as sitting together in Beethoven's lodgings or in a music
therapy studio). It also involves materials and objects – pianos, xylophones, beaters
– which may themselves be imbued with connotations, personal or historical
and cultural (for example, the piano may be understood as 'the instrument my
father played' or as a posh instrument, the xylophone is associated in popular
and classical musical culture with skeletons and the musically macabre). Even
when musical engagement involves listening to recorded music and so-called
passive consumption, it is a highly active affair, one that is often about creating
a lifeworld or habitat for action. (I have described this activity in some detail
elsewhere, suggesting that the idea of music consumption as 'listening' is overly
dependent upon a late nineteenth-century notion of the silent, rapt and physically
still audience [DeNora 2000; see also Clarke 2011: 204].)

Because music is always music-plus, and because that 'plus' is added locally,
'in action', it is probably misleading to attempt to describe what might count as

'the music itself'. As Clarke observes, 'music, then, is an endlessly "multiple" environment in which to perceive and act' (2011: 205). Yet, as Clarke and Clarke remind us, there is something specifically musical about music such that to engage in musical activity is substantively different from engaging in, say, woodworking, bridge or animal grooming (2011: xix). Before describing the key questions and themes around music and wellbeing, it is therefore worth taking a moment to ask about music's specific qualities. I will suggest that the answer to this question involves five interrelated aspects of what music is.

What is Musical about Music?

First, along with theatre, dance, poetry and literature, music unfolds over time. To a greater and perhaps less subtle and more forceful degree than poetry or prose, music can entrain through rhythm and pulse and thus structure embodiment (as made explicit when people move to music, whether as dance or more mundane forms of choreography [DeNora 2003: 136; Korczynski 2011: 92, 97]). Because it is rhythmically organized, music can also align individual and potentially inchoate or unruly bodies into shared time. Music thus involves communicative synchrony, and making music together both requires and facilitates intimate and often precise forms of communicative coordination and, thus, bonding (Trevarthan 2002): music provides, in other words, an intensive way of literally being together in time.

Second, as I shall describe throughout this book, much music is portable and thus flexibly introduced into settings through user-friendly technologies such as harmonicas, guitars, portable music devices such as radios, televisions, iPods and MP3 players and loudspeaker systems. Music has the capacity to be a highly unobtrusive medium (invisible, potentially accessible with the flick of a switch, the turn of a dial) and thus – as has been shown in research on music in the retail sector, in clubs and in exercise classes – music can be a stealthy art, potentially insidious. Conversely, music has the capacity to be imposing, to fill a space with conspicuous objects and literally cause bodies to vibrate – giant pipe organs, grand pianos, harps, bass viols, tubas, bagpipes and drums, for example.

Third, music is most often experienced and described in physical terms. It is a medium that, in Western cultures, but also elsewhere (though by no means always in the same ways), is often associated with embodied practice, spatial relations and the sense of touch. At the level of production, music often requires physical action (acoustic/embodied technique). As the two examples of people at keyboards that I presented earlier highlight, music is rendered through physical handlings (Barthes' 'grain of voice' and, beyond it, the bowing arm, tongue, fingers, feet in some cases, forearms, lungs and lips are integral to so much of musical production) and these handlings are responsible for the shape of the sound envelope, musical timbre, volume and pitch (for example, singing a low note involves relaxed vocal chords, playing the acoustic guitar loudly involves plucking the strings with more force, fading out on a note on the violin involves a gradual decrease of pressure on the bow).

Fourth, and linked to the fact that music is rarely denotative, music can be severed from words and visual images. Because music is a flexible and highly mobile medium, it is highly amenable, indeed, susceptible, as Tota argues, to 'contamination', at times in ways that can subvert music's seemingly conventional connotations, its stylistic and generic characteristics (2001). For example, music's connotations can be sometimes irrevocably transformed as musical scores and snippets of musical works transmigrate from their initial pairings and contexts to new contexts of presentation and use (for example, Mahler's Fifth Symphony in Visconti's *Death in Venice*, as Tota describes [2001] but also the delineated meanings [Green 1997] that arise when music is performed [McCormick 2009] and as its performance is framed).

Fifth and finally, as a function of music's pairings or transmigrations, music is closely associated with memory and forms of emotion experience (my/our music, my/our memories). Music thus can and is called upon to refresh memory, to occasion social action and to calibrate feeling parameters and feeling styles at the individual level – as a technology of self – and at the collective level – as a matrix for public memory, commemoration and emotion.

How Musical is Wellbeing?

Throughout this book, I will turn to examples of musical activity as it can be seen to mediate and transform and to the ways in which this mediation process involves specifically musical aspects of musical activity. These first two examples (Beethoven; music therapy), roughly 200 years apart, both involving couples at keyboards, highlight how music can be transformative ('that's better', 'gave her consolation'), how it helps in the short term, over an hour or in a matter of minutes. But music also works over the longer term of months or years, and increasingly researchers have described how sustained musical practices can contribute to better quality of life. This work describes how music can help in the face of medical adversity (Aasgaard 2002), with the management of chronic pain (Batt-Rawden 2006; Dileo and Bradt 2009; Hanser 2010; Mitchell and MacDonald 2007) and the symptoms of mental illness (Ansdell 1995; Ansdell and Meehan 2010; Erkkilä et al. 2011; Talwar et al. 2006). More generally, it shows how music can afford narratives and meaning (DeNora 2000; McDonnell 2010; Streeck 1996) in ways that foster coping (Bonde 2005; Daykin and Bunt 2009; Ruud 2002, 2005, 2008, 2010), that consolidate identity (MacDonald, Hargreaves and Miell 2002) and that strengthen communal ties (Pavlicevic 1997; Pavlicevic and Ansdell 2004; Stige et al. 2010).

That music might perhaps at times replace the need for pharmacological and/ or medical interventions – avoiding side-effects and at a fraction of the cost – is an obvious asset. It is therefore understandable that at least some people wish to believe in music's effectiveness. Yet the idea that music can make things better has, historically speaking, been a contentious idea, one that retains a certain amount of mystery and superstition. Around the world and within Western culture, music has often been linked to sorcery, religious practices, faith healing, practical magic, New Age spirituality and charlatanism. A glance at the history of music in medicine highlights the multifarious range (and often dubious reception) of musical healing in Western culture (Gouk 2000; Horden 2000; Winkler 2006). Within that history the idea that music can be harnessed in ways that benefit mental and/or physical health has been regularly asserted, to the point that, as Penelope Gouk has observed, the idea that music can heal has become a literary convention (2000). The (perhaps extravagant) discourse of music's powers – magical, curative, transformative – can be found in Tarantism, in Mesmer's use of the glass harmonica as a method of priming his eighteenth-century subjects for animal magnetism, and in the controversies around the glass harmonica itself (did the instrument cause the nerves to deteriorate and lead to insanity if taken in too great a measure? [DeNora 2013b]). Its roots extend to Aristotle's belief that music in the mixolydian mode would, 'make men sad and grave' (*Politics* 8:5), Boethius' discussions of music's influence on the human psyche, the Baroque doctrine of the affections (D minor was linked to blood, the spleen and 'womanlyness' according to Schubart's 1806 *Ideen zu einer Aesthetik der Tonkunst*) and the related notion that music could influence both body and morals (Sarjala 2001). In more modern times, the discourse of music as a powerful influence on mind and spirit lives on in the moral panics associated with jazz, rock 'n' roll, punk, rap or any other 'dangerous' genre, in discussions of the 'Mozart effect' and in some versions of the idea that music stimulates the brain. Thus, the trope of music's powers – whether in relation to healing, cognitive enhancement or moral orientation – is alive and well and often overshadows more theoretical and explanatory questions about the processes of musical healing, the 'how' questions concerning music and its purported functions at the level of experience.

How Wellbeing is Musical

The literature on music and health has so far been short on accounting for music's mechanisms of operation. If music does things in relation to wellbeing, then what does it do and how does it do what it does? While well-constructed randomized clinical trials may persuade us that music works, the question remains, 'but how?' (Maratos, Crawford and Procter 2011). While the search for music's 'active ingredients' is now well underway, it is too often unduly constrained by its confinement to music, mind, brain and individuals. That focus sidesteps questions about practice, others, institutions, collective patterns of action and belief, inter-subjectivity, embodiment and the material world. Moreover, too often when the 'power of music' trope is deployed, it does not consider the question of music's ontology (What is the musical object? Can it be understood as a stimulus? What are its boundaries? How stable or interpretively flexible are musical objects?) The 'power of music' trope also tends to beg the question that music's reception is between musical objects and individuals who engage in musical processing. Increasingly within the associated literatures, those individuals are reduced to brains.

While serious work in the neuro-scientific study of music has been articulated with a focus on real-life musical experience, helping us to understand, for example, how shared emotional experience in relation to music is facilitated by neuro-processing (McGuiness and Overy 2011), there is also a great deal of literature that tends to overplay the focus on 'music and the brain'. As Tallis has suggested, these neurological discourses are in some ways reminiscent of nineteenth-century phrenology's attempt to align psychological states with physical function (2011), but, and to the extent that the same brain regions provide the locus for very different cognitive and perceptual functions, it may not possible to reduce cognitive and sensory processing to brain regions. Meaningful experience, by definition, transcends the physical brain.

We are not, in other words, mere brains. At the risk of sounding like a paraphrase of the song 'Dem Bones' ('the back bone's connected to the neck bone/ the neck bone's connected to the head bone, O hear the work of the Lord!'), the brain is connected to the mind, the skull, the blood, the nervous system, the bones and the body. The brain is, as I shall describe, connected also to the person, to other people and their history, to language and learning, memory and association, habit, culturally constructed values, convention, physical interaction, occasions, situations, shared experience, custom, climate, diet, air quality, electro-magnetic current and many other things that linguistically we deem to be 'outside' of individuals. It is this totality of connection that we should include in our attempts to understand what music is and how it works.

Considering this totality, and considering how it is often elided by the focus on brain and mind, I will suggest in what follows that the topic of music and wellbeing is one that urgently requires a social and ecological paradigm, a paradigm that understands music and musical activity as embodied social practice and understands that practice as responsible for what we come to understand as music's health-promoting properties. This ecological focus has implications also for how we think about what music is, what kind of an object it is and how we ought to incorporate that object into health-promotion practices. I will therefore suggest that it is vital to move beyond perspectives in which music is seen as a simple stimulus, an adjunct, tool or application for medical ends. On the contrary, I shall suggest that it is in music's role as a cultural practice and as a meaningful and shared practice that we can identify its active ingredient for wellbeing. I believe that the time is ripe for building (grounded) theoretical accounts of how music actually works as part of social ecology. I also believe that such accounts can enrich cultural sociology, in particular by addressing the question of how culture works.

To this end I shall develop an account of how illness, health, the body, mind, culture and agency are intertwined. This is a tall order and, described in the terms that I have just employed, it is also rather vague. As I hope to show, such a project can be made more specific. To that end, what follows is organized in two main parts. First, in Chapters 1 to 3, I build a (sociologically informed) foundation for an ecological theory of music and wellbeing. I move, in Chapter 1, from the constructed nature of health and illness to its temporal and culturally mediated features, pausing to consider mind–body interaction and illness as a collaborative, cultural and relationally produced fact. In Chapters 2 and 3, I consider the ways in which health and illness – intertwined and linked to social settings and situations and experienced as wellbeing, flourishing and ability to play – are linked to opportunities and materials for seeking asylum (as defined above) or places where and how to be well. In Chapters 4 to 6, I pursue that theme by examining musical forms of asylum, their creation, social relations and their micro-political consequences. Then, having examined music as it can be seen to 'do good', I turn, in Chapter 7 to an age-old issue, seeking to rethink how and what we count as 'good' music. I suggest that musical aesthetics is in need of (simultaneously) fine-tuning and broadening and that, taking a cue from Blacking, goodness in music, 'is inseparable from its value as an expression of human experience' (1971: 31). Such a stance aligns music's evaluation to ethical action and thus to ecological politics. It is also less concerned with what counts as good than with how goodness is produced. Great music, perhaps, is music that offers opportunities, even *in extremis*, for being well and being together. Thinking about music in this way, I suggest in the Conclusion, enriches our investigations of how music helps. It also provides a fully fledged understanding of health humanities, one in which music is not an accompaniment or adjunct to medicine but rather an equal partner in the performance of wellbeing and in ways that can transform what it means to speak of 'care'.

Chapter 1
In Sickness and in Health:
Defining the Ecological Perspective

In *Anna Karenina*, Tolstoy wrote that happy families are all alike but that each unhappy family is unhappy in its own way (2004: 1). As with happiness, health is often assumed to be an unproblematic state, the absence of disease, something easily assessed and universally unvaried. By contrast, the forms of suffering associated with illness are seen to be diverse. In this book, my aim will be to challenge these assumptions. I will suggest that health and illness are not opposing conditions but are fused together in complex ways and experienced as multi-dimensional degrees of wellbeing. I will also suggest that this experience takes shape or is figured in relation to things outside of individuals, ecologically, and in ways that amalgamate people, practices, culture and things. One of those things, as I will describe in some detail, is music.

To lay the groundwork for this project and to consider specifically music's role in relation to health and wellbeing, in this chapter, I consider illness as it is manifest in everyday life. To that end, I will introduce a perspective that conceptualizes health and illness as a pragmatic, temporal and ecological production. In describing this production, I will also dispense with the mind–body dichotomy implicit in so much of our everyday discourses of health/illness. Thus, and taking my cue from the World Health Organization's motto, 'There is no health without mental health', I will develop the argument that the seemingly specific case of mental health can be used as a case in point for health in general, the idea being that consciousness and orientation mediates illness (identity and symptoms) and that bodily symptoms interact and can be altered in relation to mind ecologically conceived. This perspective is by no means equivalent to the suggestion that, 'a broken leg is a state of mind', but it points to ways in which we may learn a great deal about health/illness in general by considering mental illness from a socio-ecological perspective.

More specifically, and to foreshadow the theoretical line I shall be developing, the social phenomenon of mental illness and the seemingly inextricable mind–body–culture entanglements attendant with it, offers support for a non-reductionist, anti-mechanistic focus on health and illness. This anti-reductionist focus in turn offers real potential for novel and, arguably, more sustainable means by which to address illness/wellness. To what extent, for example, might the so-called myth of mental illness be but the tip of a much larger phenomenon, namely, the myth of individualized and mechanistic conceptions of health and illness writ large? To broach this question, and primarily for readers unfamiliar with the literature on health/illness as construction, I begin with a brief review of the fundamentally social and emergent character of health and illness.

The Cultural and Technical Mediation of Health and Illness

The very terms, 'health' and 'illness' are elusive. While it seems to be a universal fact that human beings exhibit physical symptoms such as congestion, immobility or fever, how these conditions come to be experienced, identified and treated is culturally specific. The cultural specificity of health/illness is, moreover, consequential for our experience of being well or ill and for the quality of social arrangements that surround this experience: for example, socially distributed opportunities for inclusion, exclusion and care. So, for example, diseases are eradicated and curtailed in relation to cultural–technical interventions – drugs and antibiotics, surgery and sanitation, but also bio-feedback and belief – and in relation to social decisions about where our health priorities lie and what should receive attention, when and how.

Medical historians chronicle the paths of diseases as they rise, fall and are reconfigured across time and place. It is no longer possible, for example, to be diagnosed with green fever or puerperal insanity nor, to my knowledge, is there a medical model of cancer in our time that invokes the idea of blood letting to release the 'morbid humors' (Diamandopouls 1996; Kardinal and Yarbro 1979). Women are no longer burned at the stake for exhibiting symptoms that are today associated with hysteria or epilepsy (Chodoff 1982; Risse 1988). Conversely, prior to the 1970s, 1980s and 1990s, there was no Lyme disease, no AIDS, no West Nile virus. There were, to be sure, people who suffered from symptoms associated with all of these maladies as there were (and are) people suffering from symptoms of maladies at one time unknown or that today continue to exist in the dappled world between official recognition and disavowal – ME or myalgic encephalopathy is a striking example (Wallace 1991).

Tracing the careers of diseases in these ways thus highlights the complex processes by which categories of diagnosis, prognosis, etiology, treatment and cure are configured within medical classification schemes. It also highlights the processes by which these schemes are linked to institutional practices of health provision. These processes are of course interrelated with a host of mediating factors and the history of medicine offers numerous cases where this shaping is contentious and – most interestingly – knowledge-based. In the nineteenth century, for example, puerperal insanity was the subject of rival knowledge claims between two groups, both with vested interests and both concerned to secure authority and economic dominion (Marland 1999, 2004). On the one hand, midwives advocated keeping the patient at home and thus out of the grasp of the then-emerging specialists in 'mental alienation' (early psychiatry), on the other, mental alienists advocated relocating the mentally unwell to lunatic asylums and, thus, under their own auspices.

In the twenty-first century, the factors that mediate definitions of health and illness most often include techniques and technologies, research funding priorities, lobby groups, policy cultures, systems of belief, discursive categories and iconic depictions in the media and the arts. Other factors include a widening raft of powerful players adjacent to the medical-industrial complex – health maintenance organizations, pharmaceutical companies and insurers. In relation to these factors, the medical, paramedical and non-medical, the economic, the technical and the socio-cultural are often so mutually inflected that disentangling them is impossible.

Moreover, in our time, perhaps as never before, new categories of disease are emerging. This emergence is both symptom and cause of a medicalized culture in which increasing numbers of human conditions are pathologized (Conrad 1987, 2007). Some observers link this trend to what they call, 'disease mongering', the widening or the boundaries of treatable illness so as to generate new markets for medical goods and services (Moynihan Health and Henry 2002). But the growth of medical conditions is also fuelled by the fears and desires of healthcare consumers, a process bolstered by a 1985 FDA ruling permitting direct-to-consumer 'ask your doctor' drug advertisements (Herzberg 2008; Menand 2010), internet search engines and the plethora of on-line advice for the 'worried well'. Indeed, at least one study has suggested that doctors are more likely to prescribe a medication if the patient requests it (Kravitz et al. 2005).

Most recently, medicalization has been further propelled by biometric technologies in ways that are transforming the practice of medicine (Clarke et al. 2010). At the heart of this transformation is an issue that deserves sociological attention: the emergence of so-called personalized, predictive medicine and its reorientation of the temporal conceptualization of illness and disease.

Personalizing Medicine?

In the nineteenth and twentieth centuries and earlier, the medical gaze focused upon illness as it became manifest through pathological matters. The gaze was, in other words, retrospective, in response to and dealing with, the onset of illness and with the aim of cure or palliation. Rarely was it concerned with health conditions that might occur. By contrast, in the twenty-first century, a trend has emerged that shifts the temporal focus of the medical gaze. What was retrospective is now also in part prospective, a focus linked to and facilitated by the development of new 'predictive' technologies, in particular genetic screening and, most recently, neuro-imaging. These new technologies are, moreover, personalized: individuals' unique bio-markers are interpreted as probability indicators of the risk of contracting one or another form of illness in the future. These bio-markers are also often used to assess individuals' degrees of receptivity to particular drug therapies. This personal, prospective approach, along with its associated technologies, is increasingly hailed as an emerging new paradigm in medical science and clinical practice (Issa 2007; Hobson 2009). A journal devoted to the subject was founded in 2004 (*Personalized Medicine*) and new, public–private partnerships devoted to bio-marker research are on the rise (Cooper 2012). Increasingly, moreover, personalized diagnostic technologies are marketed for over-the-counter sales drawing predictive clinical authority into the domestic sphere and the culture of everyday life. The push is accompanied by bullish economic rhetoric – in 2009 the core segment of the personalized medicine market – medical devices and diagnostics – was estimated at $24 billion annually and predicted to rise by 10 per cent a year until 2015 (PricewaterhouseCoopers LLP 2009). Despite the fact that, in 2011, growth has slowed (Tufts Center for the Study of Drug Development 2011), there is, nonetheless, much at stake here of a non-medical nature.

It is worth pausing to consider the significance of the term 'personalized' in 'personalized medicine' and beyond the realm of mental health. The term is not used, for example, to indicate a concern with the lived experience or biographical contingencies of individual patients. Rather, it refers to the collection and use of unique biological information – the individual's biological 'fingerprint' (the discourse is important here) as revealed by biometric scans. The courses of action implied by this information are in turn relatively generic – pharmaceutical and/or surgical. So, to take one of the more dramatic (and least complicated) examples, if it discovered that a patient has the genetic mutations BRCA1 and BRCA2 associated with breast or ovarian cancer, she may be advised to undergo preventative surgery. Similarly, the quality and quantity of protein enzymes are being used to tailor courses of drug therapy for other cancer patients. At the same time, as some observers have noted, personalized medicine does not involve so much a form of individual bespoke tailoring as a more coarse attempt to differentiate between rough treatment groups, a kind of 'small, medium or large' form of allocation for drug therapy (Hedgecoe 2004).

While, on the one hand, the science of personalized medicine may add some nuance and precision to diagnosis, treatment and prevention of disease (or at least this is the aspiration); on the other, it can sidestep many other features of health and illness such as patients' behaviour, beliefs, aspirations, socio-economic circumstances and – critically – the physical and social environment. In this sense, personalized medicine furthers a medical model of disease and, in the process, can be subject to critique. This critique throws into relief the politics of medicine (Hedgecoe 2004; Rothstein 2003), in particular the way in which the social relations of illness are narrowly conceived when viewed through the lens of personalized medicine. Within the personalized medical purview, expert clinicians, technologically assisted, provide accurate diagnoses, perform medical procedures and/or prescribe effective pharmaceuticals, to patient-recipients, who are sometimes counselled by specialist counsellors about the risks associated with bio-markers, drug therapies, clinical procedures and, sometimes, social and socio-biological practices (such as, in certain situations, whether or not to procreate).

Beyond the professional–lay relations associated with the medical model, there is yet a further set of relations that is also unduly narrowed by predictive medicine. This is the set of relations between illness and those who have it. To consider this set of relations is to consider the ontology of illness itself. If, on the one hand, illness is genetically preordained, if it is intracellular, independent of and latent in the patient, then there is or can be little or no mutual influence between the patient, her/his disease and her/his biological makeup. In its extreme form, personalized medicine transforms illness into a statistical probability: illness becomes an intrinsic and preordained statistical trait of the organism and in the organism. If, on the other hand, one maintains that environmental factors are also involved (in the oft-quoted words of Judith Stern, 'all illnesses have some hereditary contribution. Genetics loads the gun and environment pulls the trigger'), then (and depending upon how the term 'environment' is defined) illness is never entirely distinct from the consciousness and lived experiences of those whom it afflicts, and biological determinism is insufficient as an explanation and basis for treatment options. Thus strongly biologically determined perspectives constrain ontologies of health and illness in ways that preclude more nuanced and perhaps more empirically accurate accounts of how we become and stay healthy and/or ill.

Much hinges on the focus on bio-markers, avenues are closed and avenues are opened. The bio-marker focus closes pathways into critical theory and the critical history of science and technology, in particular on perspectives that seek to investigate connections between illness and (a) the environment (environmental pollutants, toxins and stress factors), (b) the economy (social class and illness), (c) agency (can individuals be empowered in their own healthcare beyond merely choosing from medical menus or opting in or out of tests and procedures?), (d) socio-cultural conventions (are there ways of arranging social life in which illness conditions might be transcended?) and (e) faith (is there any way that incorrigible belief [in something] can be beneficial or harmful to health?). Turning its back on these questions, the focus on bio-markers opens new avenues to enhanced medical authority, specifically to a materialist conception of illness, whether physical or mental (for the distinction between them is diminished), as independent from culture and as immured from contingency. The aetiology of illness, it is implied, is linked to chromosomes, biochemistry and an individual's preordained chances. According to this aetiology, the pathways to treatment are prescribed: when illness manifests itself (when the trigger is pulled), it is best dealt with through resort to the latest advances in the medical and pharmaceutical arsenal. Thus, locating illness inside individuals has important social implications. It absolves all others from a shared – communal, moral – responsibility for the social distribution of illness and health. Simultaneously it elides alternative responses to diagnoses and illness identities (for example, one might decide, for various reasons, to live with a condition, diagnosis or risk). Linked to these forms of narrowing, the treatment pathways associated with predictive medicine implicitly also prescribe and endorse an ontological stance. Matter triumphs over mind, culture and environment and in a way that reasserts biology as destiny, but this time with destiny cast as something science and technology can at least in part redirect.

Still Crazy After All These Years?

Nowhere, arguably, is the burgeoning paradigm of personalized medicine more prevalent than in psychiatry (Singh and Rose 2009: 202–3). Articles devoted to correlations between particular genetic bio-markers and mental disorders such as schizophrenia, bipolar syndrome, ADHS and antisocial behavior have multiplied since the early 1990s. More recently, work on neuro-imaging techniques has highlighted correlations between psychiatric disorders and features of brain function. As a report on the research in *Science Daily* described it:

> According to previous research, normal interaction between the amygdala and the VMPFC may underlie the proper adaptation of levels of the stress hormone cortisol on a daily basis. These levels do not vary as widely in people with major depressive disorder; future research may now be able to clarify the mechanism that underlies this aspect of depression. It could also examine the possibility of using measurements of activity in the amygdala to predict the effectiveness of treatments for depression such as cognitive behavioral therapy. (Society for Neuroscience 2007)

Similarly, the *Director's Blog*, on the National Institute for Mental Health website describes the drive toward prospective diagnosis:

> As NIMH research increasingly reveals the brain circuitry for various forms of mental distress, our hope is that we can look forward to a classification system validated by a deep knowledge of both the genetic risks and neural basis of mental illness. This approach could transform not only diagnosis but treatment. We know from studies of neurologic disorders, such as Parkinson's disease and Huntington's disease, that behavioral signs and symptoms are late manifestations of the underlying brain disorder. Imagine the impact of identifying the neural basis of schizophrenia or mood disorders before the onset of disabling behavioral symptoms so that clinicians would regularly intervene to preempt psychosis or depression. (Insel 2010)

This screening boom and the arguments in favour of mandatory screening have been met with criticism from within the psychiatric field (Lehrman 2006). In relation to mental health conditions the ethical issues linked to these developments are urgent. For while the illness status of mental disorders remains hotly contested even within psychiatry itself (see below), individuals identified as at risk (prior to any onset of symptoms) may (perhaps unnecessarily) be subject both to drug treatments (at pre-symptomatic stages) and to social stigma still sadly associated with treatment for mental health concerns (Singh and Rose 2009: 204).

The adage, 'don't fix it, if it isn't broken' might seem applicable here, since drug therapies often bring with them new problems in the form of side-effects and counter-indications. While such side-effects might be acceptable and, indeed, but a small price to pay (by whom and for what reasons is of course an issue), there are some further, and serious issues at stake, namely the reality status of mental illness – even in the most real and serious of cases. For these reasons, it is evermore urgent that interdisciplinary expertise is pooled to consider, from as many angles as possible, the complex and often contradictory ways in which the ontology and aetiology (the reality status and causes) of mental illness are, have been and might be conceptualized. This investigation needs, moreover, to consider conceptions of mental illness in terms of their impacts and prerequisites across a variety of domains, social, economic, technical, ethical, institutional, political and cultural.

Conceptualizing mental illness has, since 1957, been dominated by the *Diagnostic and Statistical Manual of Mental Disorders*, or DSM. A highly contested tome, the DSM illustrates the social, cultural and technical mediation of disease categories over time and place. Various 'illnesses' have been dropped from DSM over time – homosexuality being perhaps the most notorious example. But other currently well-ensconced categories only emerged in recent times (bipolar syndrome in 1980, for example) and debates continue over the aetiology/causes and reality status of various categories within DSM (Alloy et al. 2005).

Indeed, the most current published version of DSM (American Psychiatric Association 2000) is now undergoing wide-ranging process of revision and debate. The new DSM (DSM-5) is scheduled for release in 2013. The full first draft was released in 2010 (American Psychiatric Association 2010). In the decade between the revised edition of DSM-IV and 2010, two critical and related trends have emerged, both in relation to growth of interest in and publicity for predictive medicine's focus on bio-markers. Both of these trends have been noted by a number of highly established, internationally prominent, psychiatrists (one of whom was at the time the president of the American Psychiatric Association [see Kirsch 2010; Sharfstein 2005]). The first trend is that, according to some of the proposed criteria for DSM-5, a growing number of so-called normal conditions are being hailed as psychiatric conditions – shyness, for example, as 'social anxiety disorder' and cigarette addiction as 'nicotine use disorder'. The second, and related trend, is that these disorders are medicalized and treated, increasingly, with drugs (paxil or seroxat the recent drug for 'shyness', for example). In short, the explosion of new kinds of mental 'illness', combined yet again with a growth in screening practices of personalized medicine, adds up to an exponential growth in new cases. In 2004, the World Health Organization's Global Health Observatory Data suggested that there were nearly 200 million cases of mental disorder worldwide (WHO 2004). In 2010, they estimated the number as nearer 450 million (WHO 2010). The fact that cases of mental illness have been on the rise since the economic crisis of 2008 is of course an important part of this global picture, as is the fact that mental illness rates are highest in countries where income inequality is high (Wilkinson and Pickett 2007), and I will return to these socio-economic, ecological conditions below. Unlike mining for minerals, where supply exists independently of demand or exploration, mental health is a different sort of phenomenon, at once more speculative and the kind of phenomenon (unlike copper or diamonds) that can expand in direct proportion to the attempts to locate it – beneath the surface of seeming health. An important question thus arises about the validity of diagnostics by bio-markers and their associated predictive measures.

This question is currently being raised as much from within the psychiatric community as outside it. As the NIMH *Director's Blog* described the state of play in 2010, the diagnostic science of biomarkers is both incomplete and imperfect, confounded by the co-presence and often inextricable relationship of one or more conditions:

> A recent report in *Nature Genetics* reminds us of the challenges to classifying mental disorders. A meta-analysis of the largest sample of its kind to date has implicated genetic variation on Chromosome 3 with both bipolar disorder and depression. This follows hot on the heels of a study last summer that similarly linked bipolar disorder and schizophrenia to the same common variants in DNA sequence. Add these new genetic findings to the non-specificity of previously identified mutations, such as DISC-1 or the 16p11 deletion. And consider the absence of specific biomarkers or treatments, the high prevalence of co-morbidity, and the clinical heterogeneity of each disorder and you can see why diagnosis continues to be one of the most confounding aspects of both research and practice in psychiatry. (Insel 2010)

Thus, if bio-markers are contested and if there is clinical heterogeneity (individual variation in terms of how a condition is manifest), then the (biological/ pharmacological) treatment pathways associated with these markers are also subject to question. Beyond these uncertainties, however, lie further good reasons to reconsider and reassess the value of bio-markers in relation to the conditions that we classify as mental illness. For example, the idea that mental disorders are, in fact, illnesses (that is pathological conditions such as cancer or bone fractures) has been subject to protracted interrogation and critique, by work in the sociology of health and illness, by anti-psychiatry activist movements, by patients themselves and, more recently, by critics of drug therapies for mental conditions. While the standpoints of each of these groups may of course also be questioned and while those questions in turn imply a host of other issues about fitness to judge, such as: 'Can mental patients know whether their drugs are helping or hindering?' 'How should we weigh the evidence, pro and con, that the administration of anti-psychotic drugs leads to fewer psychiatric readmissions?' (Leucht et al. 2012). 'Do sociologists push constructivism because it is a discourse that buttresses their occupational niche?' 'Do physicians promote pharmacological forms of treatment because of the ways they are lobbied?' 'Do for-profit pharmacological firms advocate their products to make money?' 'And, as some have argued, is the fact that pharmacological regulation is nowadays biased in favour of commercial interests, with governmental regulatory agencies increasingly funded by commercial contributions?' (Abraham 2008). Despite these caveats, considering the perspectives of different groups provides additional vantage points from which to consider medicalized representations and – importantly as I describe at the end of this chapter – develop worked examples of how mental/physical illness and wellbeing may be understood in socio-ecological perspective.

The Myth of Mental Illness

In 1961, the psychiatrist Thomas Szasz published the now classic work, *The Myth of Mental Illness*. The book drew a distinction between physical and mental types of illness, suggesting that the former, unlike the latter, were defined according to pathological (that is, cellular, molecular) criteria and that diagnoses of the latter, therefore, were associated with considerable imprecision. To be sure, there have been studies that have highlighted the difficulty and ambiguity involved in diagnosing mental illness, despite the best intentions of psychiatrists. For example, in a real-life version of Kesey's *One Flew Over the Cuckoo's Nest* (1962), David Rosenhan's social experiment, 'On Being Sane in Insane Places' (1973), described how his normal graduate students presented themselves at the local mental institution where, after claiming (on Rosenhan's instructions) that they were hearing voices, otherwise acted normally. The students were duly diagnosed as schizophrenic and admitted to the mental institution. Once there, the students' every act and utterance served only to further the psychiatrists' incorrigible assumptions that their clients were mentally ill. Eventually, Rosenhan himself had to intervene: the hospital would not release the students. The point of this research was not to debunk psychiatry but rather to highlight the power of institutionally situated decision-making, that is perception and judgement that is nested in patterned and pre-given sets of procedures, risk assessment matrices and incorrigible assumptions (such as that one does not ordinarily expect hoax-cases to arrive on the hospital doorstep).

Szasz's work in the early 1960s thus highlighted an important unscientific feature of mental illness and its diagnosis – ambiguity. He suggested that mental illnesses (that is, diseases of the mind, as opposed to diseases of the brain) were recognized through normative arrangements rather than pathological procedures. The reality of mental illness was, he claimed, established through how communities of practitioners used conventional practices to arrive at consensus about the ontology of mental illnesses. These practices produced reliable (capable of being repeated, generally agreed upon) diagnoses but not necessarily valid diagnoses.

Szasz's work has been and is highly controversial, though both its admirers and detractors regard it as part of the canon of works on psychiatric critique, a canon that also included the works of R.D. Laing and Michel Foucault. Szasz's work can and has been read as demonizing psychiatrists as a category (notwithstanding the fact that Szasz was, himself, a psychiatrist). There are, however, subtler problems with Szasz's conception of mental illness (or rather his defense of its mythic status), namely, that it places undue emphasis on personal responsibility, as illustrated in his 1960 essay 'The Myth of Mental Illness':

The notion of mental illness thus serves mainly to obscure the everyday fact that life for most people is a continuous struggle, not for biological survival, but for a 'place in the sun,' 'peace of mind,' or some other human value. For man aware of himself and of the world about him, once the needs for preserving the body (and perhaps the race) are more or less satisfied, the problem arises as to what he should do with himself. Sustained adherence to the myth of mental illness allows people to avoid facing this problem, believing that mental health, conceived as the absence of mental illness, automatically insures the making of right and safe choices in one's conduct of life. But the facts are all the other way. It is the making of good choices in life that others regard, retrospectively, as good mental health! (Szasz 1960: 118)

Szasz rejects biological determinist aetiologies of mental illness as metaphoric and imprecise. He points instead to a holistic conception of mental illness, understood as a result of social conflict and mental health as a result of 'good choices in life'. While his work could have been connected to a fully social and fully complex conception of health and illness, it is linked instead to a libertarian conception of individual responsibility. Because of its libertarian tendencies, Szasz's work has been critiqued, notably, by advocates of medicalization who read him as not only out of date but inhumane:

The disease model of mental illness is now so central to American medicine and culture that the most common response to Szasz – aside from utter disregard – is typically something like: 'Just look around – anguished teenagers, depressed adults, distracted children. Only a fool would believe that mental illness is a myth.' Indeed, to the modern psychiatric mind, rejecting the legitimacy of mental illness is not just an error but an act of inhumanity, leaving the sick without the hope of a cure. The Szaszians of the world are not just fools but monsters. (Oliver 2006: 70)

As is often the case, polarized debate can serve to highlight missing middle ground. In this case Szasz's libertarian conception of mental health as social reductionism (personal responsibility), on the one hand, and the advocates of medicalization as biological reductionism (the bio-markers that load the gun), on the other, between them show what has been missing from the debate, namely the supra-individual factors associated with being well, and this returns us to critical theories not only of mental health and illness, but of ability, disability and, most fundamentally, to a fully social understanding of the self. To illuminate some of these factors (interpretation, ritual, material cultural arrangements, cooperatively produced identities and the role of belief and trust), I will discuss recent reconsiderations of drug therapies and their effectiveness before moving beyond the 'mind over matter' perspective to set health/illness in full ecological context.

Drugs: How do They Work, What do They Do?

The idea that mental illness is pathological and that it can be alleviated, or at least managed, through drug therapies is not new. The point is that drug treatments for mental illness have burgeoned since the 1960s, but are drugs in a general sense the best and/or only way to address mental disorder? When and how, for whom and with what? And if drugs do help, if people report that they 'feel better' in response to drug therapy, what are drugs' active ingredients, the mechanisms by which drugs effect a change in health/illness state?

The official wisdom is clear: modern psychiatric drugs offer a chemical ameliorative: they can be used, if not to cure, then at least to manage the debilitating symptoms of mental illness.

> Psychiatric medications treat mental disorders. Sometimes called psychotropic or psychotherapeutic medications, they have changed the lives of people with mental disorders for the better. Many people with mental disorders live fulfilling lives with the help of these medications. Without them, people with mental disorders might suffer serious and disabling symptoms. (NIMH 2008: 1)

> Most cases of major depression can be treated successfully, usually with medication, psychotherapy or both. The combination of psychotherapy and drugs is very effective in treating moderate to severe depression. The medications improve mood, sleep, energy and appetite while the therapy strengthens coping skills, deals with possible underlying issues and improves thought patterns and behaviors. (Chew, Hales and Yudofsky 2009: 133)

Of course, as all of the official sources are quick to add, drug therapies are associated with various side-effects ranging from trivial to, in a small percentage of cases, severe. Thus drug therapies pose compromise solutions to the problem of mental illness – the client has to accept, for example, urinary difficulties, dry mouth or eyes or drowsiness in return for alleviation of other symptoms.

In recent years, some critics have spoken of the trend toward, 'toxic psychiatry' linked to the mass-prescription of Prozac and other psychiatric drugs (Breggin 1994; Glenmullin 2001; Greenberg 2010; Kramer 1997). Meanwhile, though, prescriptions continue to rise. In 2009, a report documented the number of Americans on antidepressants rose 75 per cent between 1996 and 2005, from 5.84 per cent to 10.12 per cent (Olfson and Marcus 2009). The drugs, one might conclude, must be effective if they are so widely prescribed and consumed. Yet, the debates continue, and they continue to be reframed. They have shifted from concerns about the side effects of psychiatric drugs and have begun to focus on a more fundamental issue – effectiveness, around which a maelstrom of knowledge-based controversy currently rages. In what follows I am emphatically not suggesting that the use of drugs for all mental health issues be abandoned, here, now and as policy. To do so would be dangerous and irresponsible. I am, however, suggesting that over the medium and longer term, scholarly and clinical debate should consider the growing and often powerfully argued critique of pharmacological applications as the best, dominant and future strategy for the management of mental health, indeed for health and illness writ large. Consideration of current critical perspectives is, moreover, useful for considering the mind–matter or body–mind relationship.

Rethinking the Placebo Effect

In *The Emperor's New Drugs* (2010), Irving Kirsch reported on 15 years of research involving meta-analyses of antidepressant drug trials. His aim was to investigate recovery rates associated with the taking of placebos (non-active sugar pills). In an initial study Kirsch and a colleague examined 38 clinical trials involving 3,000 research subjects (Kirsch and Sapirstein 1998). They considered three categories of clinically depressed patients who took part in drug trials: those who took nothing at all (who were in clinical trials for psychotherapy but were on the waiting list: the control group), those who took placebos and those who were given anti-depressants. The aim was to compare placebo effectiveness rates with anti-depressant effectiveness rates and both with rates of spontaneous recovery (no pill, just the passage of time). They found that anti-depressants, psychotherapy and placebos produce significant changes in the symptoms of depression, and that all three strategies were linked to more improvement than no strategy at all (Kirsch and Sapirstein 1998: 10). Kirsch and Saperstein concluded that engaging with some form of therapy, whether drugs or talking, was better doing nothing at all. Importantly, they also found that taking a placebo was also better than doing nothing at all.

Their more surprising finding, though, was that while there was a sharp difference in recovery rates between placebos and doing nothing, there was a 25 per cent difference between taking an anti-depressant and a placebo. Thinking about this difference in reverse, the placebo was 75 per cent as effective as the anti-depressants, or as they authors put it, 50 per cent improvement could be gained by taking a placebo (Kirsch and Sapirstein 1998: 11). Kirsch and Sapirstein then returned to the data to control for the diversity of drugs, testing the hypothesis that perhaps some of the drugs in their overall statistics were effective and others less so. They found that even when controlling for specific type of anti-depressant, the placebo effect remained constant.

Kirsch and Sapirstein's next step was to explore and account for the 25 per cent difference between the recovery rate associated with the active drug and the placebo. They hypothesized that, because anti-depressants are associated with side-effects, subjects taking the anti-depressants were able to 'break blind' (that is, come to know they were being given the active drug because they were experiencing side-effects) and their awareness or belief that they must be taking the real drug contributed to its effectiveness. Put to the test using active placebos (that is, placebos that produced side-effects similar to the anti-depressants being tested) and comparing the effect of this active placebo to the inert ones (no built in chemicals to mimic side effects of the real drug), the benefit of the anti-depressant compared with the active placebo became insignificant, and 'the more side effects that depressed patients experience on the active drug, the more they improve' (Kirsch and Sapirstein 1998: 21).

In *The Emperor's New Drugs*, Kirsch described the complex issues surrounding unpublished clinical trials, trials that drug companies 'withheld from public scrutiny' (2010: 21–2), obtained using the Freedom of Information Act. These studies had been discarded (legitimately) on methodological grounds, according to a complex rationale known as 'assay insensitive' in which a new drug, an old (and previously proved effective drug) and a placebo are compared. If the difference between the placebo and the two active drugs is not significant, the study is disregarded on the grounds that the methods used to measure effectiveness must not have been sensitive enough to register the proven effectiveness of the old drug. Belief in the earlier established finding is retained as a shield against new and potentially contradictory findings (the idea being that something must have gone wrong with the trial procedure since the older drug was proven effective and should have been effective if the trial methodology was correct). The RCT (randomized controlled trial) process then begins anew, with different criteria and techniques for registering the difference, until, eventually, a significant difference is found.

Kirsch's book offered a critical polemic – written by an insider – against the massive rolling out of drug therapies for depression, taking into account as he saw it, the various forms of harm associated with anti-depressants – physiological, in terms of side-effects and long-term effects, and economic, in terms of the costs associated with drug development, marketing and insurance. He concluded by offering his preferred alternatives, namely cognitive behavioral therapy (CBT) and exercise, underlining the economic argument that even psychotherapy costs less than drugs. I shall return later on to comparisons between CBT and music as quite different cultural strategies for addressing – and conceptualizing – mental illness.

Rethinking Mind–Body

While, as I observed earlier, there are clear dangers in too rapidly dismissing drug therapy from psychiatry's toolkit for depression, and while it would be highly irresponsible to recommend that clients immediately cease taking their medications, Kirsch and Saperstein's work gives pause for thought. Their work on the placebo effect calls, I suggest, for a thorough-going reconsideration of the interconnections of mind and body, and the interconnections between, on the one hand, mind–body and, on the other, nature–culture in the form of environment. These issues have been given impetus by a more general re-evaluation of the placebo effect (Finness et al. 2010; Howland 2008a, 2008b). To the extent that this is so, it is possible to entertain a very different, and much more holistic, conception of health/illness, mental and indeed physical. Such a conception calls into question any precise distinction between mental and physical conditions, a point underscored by Kirsch's consideration of the expectancy effects arising from interactions between belief and somatic state. In a rich range of examples from the laboratory and clinical practice, Kirsch describes the placebo's 'dark twin', the 'nocebo' or negative mind–body effects that can arise from sheer belief – skin rashes or upset stomachs, for example.

Outside of the laboratory or psychiatrist's office, anthropologists offer yet more extreme examples of nocebo effects, most notably voodoo rituals where death occurs, or so it is claimed, after a spell has been cast. More mundane examples of placebo effects include alternative pain management techniques such as aroma therapy, bio-feedback and the myriad ways in which individuals seek to transform body perception and bodily capacity through interactional and cultural procedures such as dance, yoga and exercise. In all of these examples there are interconnections between belief, social practice and physical embodied phenomena. These interconnections highlight some of the ways in which the cognitive, symbolic and aesthetic framing of an illness condition and its meanings can prime and trigger embodied sensation and embodied response.

A similar perspective was articulated compellingly in some strands of the sociology of health and illness in the 1970s and early 1980s. Peter Freund, for example, described how:

> The core assumptions of 'holism' in medicine emphasize the need to look at the whole patient – not separate mind and body or the context in which the patient is found. Pain, for instance, is neither organic nor 'all in the mind' but psyche and soma influencing each other, in a complex interrelationship. Stress and tension may induce muscular spasm, which aggravates and prolongs pain and other symptoms in many illnesses; physical distress further induces stress and tension. (Freund 1982: 30–31)

It is instructive to follow Freund as he outlines a holistic perspective for physical illness (which he regards as the 'harder case') since that perspective in turn opens a number of avenues for rethinking mental illness. In particular this perspective highlights illness as an open-ended, flexible identity, as affected by mind–body issues, as embedded in physical and environmental ecologies (proximity to pollutants, for example) and, above all, as the product of social ecologies and situated interaction: in short as a core topic for critical inquiry. Within this perspective, the distinction between mental and physical illness is blurred, and, contra to current trends that seek to stabilize our understanding of mental illness as pathology (as biologically determined and thus associated with probabilities for prognosis that are adjustable through personalized drug therapies), this perspective does the opposite: it suggests that illness, either physical or mental, can be caused, modified and sometimes cured through means that extend beyond the purview of mainstream medicine and that extend into a realm where mind and body are interlinked. The constituent ingredients of illness and recovery, therefore, include a healthy dollop of belief. But is there more yet to health and illness than mere mindedness?

Beyond Belief: A Critical Theory of Health/Illness as Practice

Considering examples of coronary disease and hypertension, Freund suggests that conditions such as these are associated not merely with attitudes or beliefs (for example, a fear that one may be developing coronary disease or a joyful and relaxed belief that one is truly well). They also correlate with specific and recurrent practices that can both establish and exacerbate health/illness conditions. Some of these practices are addressed in full by mainstream medicine – diet and exercise for example – but others are subtler. They may elide conscious thought, and they are not necessarily visible to an untrained eye. (These are precisely the sorts of practices that I will be describing in Chapters 3 to 6.) They may take the form of micro-patterns of behaviour, clusters of little and often-invisible sub-conscious or non-conscious practices, such as those be associated with stress and distress. They include such things as compensatory habits (eating patterns, the use of stimulants and depressants, nervous ticks, inefficient breathing, compulsions, neurotic habits), endocrine responses, muscular and skeletal habits (slouching, tensing). Through repetition and routine, these micro-events can come to be body-modifying, laying down, on and in the body physiological parameters that may establish the somatic groundwork or susceptibility to particular conditions and developments. When they affect whole groups of individuals, they may give rise to illness epidemics.

The sociologist Mildred Blaxter has also described this process, which she calls 'sociobiologic translation', a process akin to bio-feedback, in which perceptions are translated into biological signals that may exacerbate or ameliorate disease and illness. She underlines the question of central importance, namely, the search for the specific mechanisms by which, as she puts it, 'stress can be transformed into specific disease or general susceptibility' (Blaxter 2003: 74).

While sociobiologic translations are exhibited by individuals, they are by no means individually fostered. Rather, they are embedded in socio-cultural patterns that arise from, for example, power relations, a lack of autonomy or a need to constrain one's behaviour and responses unduly, pressures at work, economic insecurity and a high degree of uncertainty. (It is worth observing that the word 'stress' is etymologically derived from 'drawing tight' and 'compressed' – see the discussion of 'room' in Chapter 3.) In this sense, illness is conceptually no different from other nature–culture interactions that affect and modify the body; for example, the historical and gendered specificity of musculature over time and across culture as described by feminist biologists (Birke 1992; Fausto-Sterling 1985) or the embodied gestures, routines and 'quasi-bodily dispositions' as Bourdieu calls them (1990: 68), that coalesce as recognizably generic styles of being in social worlds (for example, styles associated with emotion, character or personae, occasions or settings – pampered groups who go to the gym and the spa as opposed to those who find pleasure and comfort from junk food in front of the television). These practices accrue in the body which, as Bourdieu once put it, becomes a 'a living memory pad' (1990: 68). The idea here is that one may embark upon a pathway of patterned behaviors into (and out of) illness categories and that this pathway can lead one deeper and deeper into conditions and patterns we associate with illness or, conversely, health. This idea has affinities with Becker's discussion of the informal learning processes (practices, behaviours, expectations and perceptual tunings) that lead a novice marijuana smoker into the sensations associated with being 'high' (1953; I return to this study below). The drug does not do its own work, but rather its effects emerge from interactions between the drug's active ingredients and what one does so as to experience and heighten its effects. There are also resonances with what sociologists of sport have had to say about the process of becoming 'Olympic class' where years of minute practices accumulate into being able to be the fastest (Chambliss 1989).

While the idea that we can 'believe and behave' ourselves into illness has considerable potential for enriching our understanding of what promotes both illness and health, it is also a dangerous idea. It is dangerous because it can be used to promote an overly individualistic explanation of how people become ill. For example, it can be used to support therapeutic (and commercial) depictions that emphasize individuals' needs to learn how to unblock or release tensions and energies or more generally look after themselves, and as such it can be used also to support an understanding of health as the responsibility of individuals ('One must have discipline'). While individual patterns of behaviour are undoubtedly contributors to health status ('If you overeat you will probably get fat'), the focus on individuals leads away from a properly conceived, holistic perspective for health and illness. Such a focus is not holistic, because it does not consider the full range of factors that impinge on what we take to be the individual's condition and that collectively make that condition a reality (see DeNora 1991). Instead, the focus on individuals foregrounds the illnesses that they have and positions the contexts within which illness (and its recognition) arise in the background so that they become, often, difficult to perceive.

The holistic focus as developed by Freund is critical of the 'individualistic ideologies' associated with concepts such as self-healing (so much a part of many New Age techniques). Freund suggests that these conceptions of mind–body interactions fail to consider the wider contexts that constrain our bodily and mental practices. Freund points to various forms of 'body deregulation' associated with social structural demands on human beings. For example, he points to disruptions to endocrinological systems due to workplace stress and other pressures to perform or conform (for example, to preferred images – visual discourses of beauty, health, status) and to connections between emotions (feeling threatened, angered or frustrated) and social constraints (such as feeling the need to suppress signs that one is angry) that prevent the body from self-regulation.

Over the years, the question of stress and its links to illness have been the subject of some debate within the sociology of health and illness, primarily around the question of the relationship between stress and physiological illness (Newton 2003; Williams 2003). More recently, medical researchers are returning to the connections between mind, body and social experience, suggesting for example, that psychological distress is linked to premature death due to, among other things, the ways in which distress triggers cortisol which in turn engenders inflammation and leads to cardio-vascular complications (Russ et al. 2012) and examining the connections between forms of illness and workplace stress (Kivimälo et al. 2012). Thus arguments in favour of a holistic understanding of health/illness are being renewed and the paradigm sketched by Freund, insofar as it draws together emotions, physiology and social environment, is one that should be taken seriously. In particular the articulation of a perspective for health/illness as ecologically mediated and founded in external physical/social/cultural worlds and thus originating in factors outside of individual physiology is increasingly compelling. Such a perspective is however undoubtedly complex and this point requires some discussion.

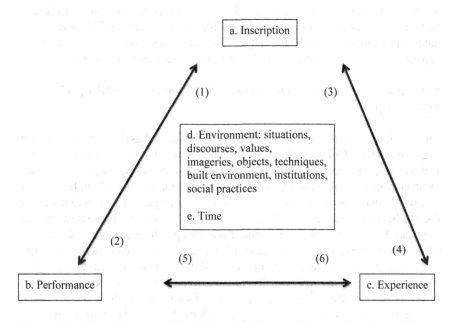

Figure 1.1   Three features of 'health' and their mutual interaction, situated in relation to social media and time

To speak of health – an identity, condition or state – as ecologically constituted is to speak of human beings and their health/illness states as 'open systems'

(Freund 1982: 31). This point is a critical one and it requires explication. I will end this chapter by describing how the ambiguity of health/illness comes to be clarified in relation to factors extrinsic to individuals and in ways that highlight individuals and their health/illness conditions as open-ended. To introduce that discussion (and using the diagram displayed in Figure 1.1), in the next section I describe the multi-faceted character of health/illness understood as an admixture of inscription performance and experience (points a, b and c in the diagram). From there I describe health/illness as contingent, taking shape in relation to things outside of individuals (point d, the environment in which points a, b and c are clarified). Finally, I describe health/illness as temporally fluctuating over intervals of time, from split seconds, to days to years (point e).

Inscription, Performance and Experience: A Relational, Fluid Concept of Health/Illness

As I have described above, in relation to mind–body and the placebo effect and in relation to holistic perspectives, health/illness is a complex phenomena. To attempt to illuminate some of these complexities, I now describe what we can think of as three interrelated dimensions of health/illness. These dimensions involve the naming or identification of health statuses and conditions, health/illness as forms of capacity and capability, and health/illness as it is perceived by those who 'have' it.

Points a, b and c: Three Dimensions of Health/Illness and Their Reciprocal Relationship

First (a), health consists of the inscriptions attributed and assigned to it, by others and by ourselves. Our condition is named. We are told by the doctor, for example, that we have an ulcer, a disability or some form of mental illness, or we are told by an alternative healer that we must dispel bad karma. Second (b) our health state involves capabilities, manifest in performance. Can I perform a function such as digest a heavy meal at night, walk up stairs or sustain a conversation with a stranger (e.g., can I walk into a post office and manage to purchase a booklet of stamps)? Third (c), our health state consists and has meaning as lived experience. I may believe my indigestion is only temporary and can be cured by herbal tea or that the voices I hear in my head are divinely inspired. I may not understand, believe or be able to cognitively process your or my doctor's instructions about what, if anything, is wrong with me and what, if anything, I should do about it. I may not perceive any problem, or conversely I may perceive something that my doctor cannot ('It's all in my mind; I'm a hypochondriac!') The reciprocal relationship between these three features of health helps highlight some key points that help to further develop an ecological understanding of health. I will now consider this relationship, after which I will consider point d (the cultural and environmental mediation of health/illness – how health/illness takes shape in relation to things outside individuals) and point e (the temporal dimension of health/illness).

First, what and how we are able to perform will be a factor that is considered when our health state is inscribed (no. 1 in Figure 1.1). If I cannot walk up a hill or a flight of stairs, that performance 'deficiency' will no doubt be a factor taken into account when my doctor assesses my condition. She or he may tell me that I have a pulmonary, cardio-vascular, arthritic or neurological condition that is 'disabling', and at a later date, if I can walk further, she or he may pronounce me 'recovering'. Conversely, the various inscriptions offered as descriptions and diagnoses of my health state may come to affect my performance of that state, as discussed above in terms of the nocebo effect. Such an inscription may, for example, 'knock the wind out of my sails' (no. 2).

At the same time, my experience may affect the status (as perceived by me, and perhaps others) of inscriptions applied to me and my health state (no. 3). For example, I may choose to disregard or not believe what I have been told by my clinician (I might, for example, seek a second opinion, or I might explain my condition according to non-clinical terms: for example, 'I'm just tired this week'). I may also simply not be receptive to or take in what I have been told ('I don't think she's taken in the implications', my physician might say), adhering to a different account, or indeed, avoid settling on any account. In this way, my experience and outlook reposition (erase, debunk) inscriptions, even if only for me. Conversely, my experience of my condition, for example my conscious awareness that something is wrong may be heightened when I am given a diagnostic label and in ways that lead me into an illness identity (no. 4). (This is an example of the nocebo effect.) I may, for example, adopt an illness identity, give up trying to achieve things that 'in my condition' I am 'unable' to do, or I might develop a heightened awareness of symptoms that, hitherto, I had not noticed that in turn condition my ability to perform. In addition my performance may be mediated by my experience of my health state and situation (no. 5). For example, I may not even realize that I am without a capacity (e.g., I never even think of, have any desire or need for climbing those stairs and so my ability to perform stair climbing goes untested). In this case, and for all practical purposes, I am not incapacitated (I do not notice my incapacity). Thus, in these first five examples, it is possible to see performance affecting inscription, inscription affecting performance, inscription affecting experience, experience affecting inscription and experience affecting performance. To complete the circle, how I perform can affect my experience of how I am (no. 6). When I attempt to use my capacity to climb the stairs, I may notice, for example, that it hurts or is more difficult than it used to be, and that might lead me to visit the doctor for an opinion about the causes of my difficulty (inscription) and a possible remedy. Thus health/illness conditions are complex and multi-dimensional. The question arises, therefore, how are these conditions configured and in relation to what? In relation to what does the admixture of inscription–performance–experience take shape?

A fully fledged sociology of health and illness explores the question of how these inscriptions, performances and experiences are constituted. Moreover, it seeks to situate these three interacting features of health/illness (point d: Environment), understanding them as emerging within social ecologies, worlds, material cultures and spaces (Clarke 2005). To speak of these worlds is to speak of matrices of discourse, value, imagery, objects, techniques, the built environment and institutions and social practices. It is in this sense that health/illness figurations are relational and emergent – their status and identity takes shape in relation to things outside of individuals.

To return to the fifth point as just discussed through the example of how I may never even think about climbing the stairs, if I have lost the ability to climb stairs, but have adapted to living on the ground floor where I am never confronted with stairs, then my inability to perform may never be distinguished and remarked upon and, within this world, I may count as able, as well. The issue of my dis/ability is, in other words, elided since it there is no contrast structure for revealing it as an issue in the first place. The point here, however, is that inscription, performance and experience are related to what my material and social world affords or does not afford. This is as much a problem about ethics as it is about arrangements. (If I am to be without disability, then you may need to live differently.)

Point d: Cultural and Environmental Mediation of Health/Illness

So far, this three-cornered model and its six forms of mutual influence has captured the complex ways in which interaction, experience and inscribed health identities interact. What it has not yet described is a second important matter, namely, how these interrelated aspects of health take shape or are figured in relation to things outside of individuals. The mutually influencing dimensions of health (performance, inscription and experience) are mediated by socially shared matters such as the physical environment (materials, pollutants, climate), discourse, objects, symbolic and aesthetic media and organizational/institutional procedures and routines. This matter must be clarified, because it highlights some of the ways in which seemingly matters of brute fact, such as symptoms (what can be performed/not performed) are simultaneously real (I cannot climb) and socially established, made manifest, magnified or diminished, in and through their place in social ecology. Health and illness are not negotiated between individuals but emerge from and are mediated through relations between individual body–minds and socio-technical worlds, as the various theories of cyborgs, assemblages and actor network have been suggesting (with varying degrees of empirical detail) now for decades.

To be sure, medical science is expressly devoted to understanding the mechanisms by which some external materials interact with bodily processes to cause or ameliorate disease (medications, prosthetic devices such as canes or spectacles, environmental pollutants). But it has left in shadow most of the ways that more mundane things standing outside specific individuals may do the same.

Outside the realm of medical science, in daily life, in activism, these questions are increasingly prominent.

For example, in areas as diverse as disability studies, the anthropology of material culture and technology, philosophy of extended mind and constructivist sociologies of culture, scholars have begun to explore how the manifestation of health states is mediated by particular and institutional configurations of the built environment and cultural practices. In these studies, an individual's health performance and experience (and therefore inscription) emerges from combinations or couplings between individuals, practices and modes of experience. There have been some excellent anthropological and historical studies that underscore this point, such as Nora Groce's, *Everyone Here Spoke Sign Language.*

In nineteenth-century Martha's Vineyard (an island off the coast of Massachusetts), there was a high incidence of hearing impairment, due to intermarriage between cousins. While hearing impairment is often a disability (more specifically, it challenges conventional patterns of auditory communication), on Martha's Vineyard, a primarily agricultural community, patterns of working life were organized in ways that did not depend upon the ability to hear sound. So too, communicative patterns (everyone speaking sign language) were such that, for all practical purposes in daily life, there was no distinction between those who could and could not hear sound. The disability and the category 'hearing impaired', while still real, were now socially, materially, technologically and culturally irrelevant, much as, in mainstream culture, our inability to be able to wave our arms and fly like a bird is not a problem. In both cases, our patterns of action and interaction are arranged such that these disabilities are neither apparent nor missed.

This example highlights how cultural and environmental features mediate ability and disability or, more broadly conceived, our capabilities to perform social and physical acts, identities and cognitive tasks. Moments, episodes, phases and lifetimes of being well can be understood as performances and experiences that are fostered by social, material and symbolic arrangements over time. The more densely these wellness performance–experience inscriptions are clustered, moreover, the better the environment is serving that performer (within a/my world, I can perform mobility and experience/describe myself in terms of wellness) and thus, the healthier that performer is. It is here that the sociology of health/illness, ecologically conceived, leads to a critical theory of wellbeing: how an environment serves an individual or group of individuals is a question about resource allocation and thus an ethical question.

The historian and philosopher Ian Hacking's concept of 'niche' captures this transient, ecologically embedded character of ability/disability and points to the ethical nature of health ecologies. Focusing on mental illness, Hacking outlines how, just as polar bears exist only in arctic climates, so too certain configurations of mental illness emerge within ecological niches that are conducive to them. The idea of niche is horticultural: in much the same ways that certain plants may establish themselves in a landscape, through repeated propagation under hospitable conditions and dying back when the climate is inhospitable, so too for forms of illness and mental health conditions. Even the illnesses that look most like diseases of the brain, Hacking argues, need to be contextualized historically. The propagation of niche-based forms of mental illness occurs, according to Hacking, because of looping, a process whereby the classification of illness comes to affect the condition; that is, when conducive features of an ecology permit or afford the successful propagation of illness types. (It is easier to develop or be diagnosed with a condition that is recognized already within an environment.)

Point e: Temporality

Finally, if we recognize health/illness as a phenomenon that is composed of interrelated dimensions of performance, inscription and experience and that takes shape in relation to the environment, symbolic and material, it is also possible to understand health/illness as a fluid mercurial and temporally shifting entity. As lived experience (Charmaz 1993), but also in terms of symptom severity and the capacity for performance, features associated with illness and disease are not unwavering over time. By contrast, they vary from day to day, moment to moment, according to cyclical or circadian rhythms. They will vary according to factors seemingly intrinsic to individuals (such as whether a tumor is growing and pressing on a nerve, levels of hydration, temperature, blood pressure or oxygen), but they will also vary according to a host of factors extrinsic to individuals such as when a medication was last given, the individual's position (sitting up, propped up, lying down) and many psycho-social matters to do with motivation, distraction, pleasure and engagement. They will also vary according to the individual's relation to the built environment (for example, someone with respiratory problems may be less ill when the air pollution levels are low, more ill if she or he needs to climb stairs). In short, even when the overall trend of health state is downward, as in the case of those who are gravely ill, there will be phases of ups and downs within that trajectory. Thus, as the environment changes, so too do health/illness states.

The point about fluctuation is that this intra-individual variation may be as great or greater than the variation between well and ill individuals, depending upon how it is defined and experienced. There is, in short, health within illness and illness within health. Moreover, and in ways that challenge simple notions of health as the absence of illness, there are states of health/illness that go unrecognized: it is not possible to know the extent of sub-clinical illness within populations where disease or illness is not associated with signs that are clinically recognized or detectable. These forms of not-quite-health may be serious and yet they slip past notice. Neither clinicians nor individuals themselves may know they exist or, if they do, that knowledge may be subliminal and fleeting ('There's that pain in my shoulder again' or 'I don't eat X, Y, Z because it gives me dyspepsia.')

In sum, illness, whether depression, heart disease or the common cold, is multi-dimensional, temporal and open-ended. It is open-ended because it takes shape in relation to things outside of individuals and beyond the individual's internal physiological and biological composition, and, because it is figured in relation to various factors external to individuals, it is inevitably temporal, in flux, potentially variable. Returning now, to the WHO motto with which I began this chapter – 'There is no health without mental health' – it might be possible to say, 'all health/ illness is mental/physical, cultural and situationally varied'. Thus, in an almost roundabout way, we have also come back to the point at which Szasz intervened in debates abut mental illness when he concluded that mental illness might be best understood as 'problems in living'. For Szasz, those problems, culturally mediated, manifest themselves as symptoms of disease (1961: 262). By contrast, the treatment Szasz proposed was not (exclusively) medical but rather, social and ethical. It highlighted a focus on communication, judgement and the allocation of resources:

> Although powerful institutional forces lend their massive weight to the tradition of keeping psychiatric problems within the conceptual framework of medicine, the moral and scientific challenge is clear: we must recast and redefine the problem of 'mental illness' so that it may be encompassed in a morally explicit science of man [*sic*]. (Szasz 1961: 262–3)

A concept of mental illness recast as a problem for the human sciences is of course the key theme that underpins Erving Goffman's classic study, *Asylums*. In the next two chapters, and to prepare the foundation for thinking about music as a medium of wellbeing, I describe how this theme points to a focus on the ecologies in which health and illness identities are made manifest. That focus is, I will suggest, of paramount importance in Goffman's work, though it is sometimes overlooked when readers focus unduly upon his concern with the self. By contrast, I shall argue, self is only the figure, the thing we produce from a much more nuanced holistic matrix of things that come to be allocated and perceived as figure versus ground. Moreover, the acts by which, as Goffman sees it, the self is preserved *in extremis*, involve something beyond the self: they are actions whereby the ground and the figures afforded by that ground are cast and recast and in ways that enhance and diminish the lived experience of health and illness on a daily basis. The question remains then, just how collaborative (and with what dynamics) is this casting process? And how is it linked to how we are able or unable to find forms of asylum or places of and for wellbeing in everyday life? As I hope to show in the next two chapters, our seemingly individual states of health/illness are collaboratively achieved.

Chapter 2
Learning from Erving Goffman, Part I: Agency and Culture

Why Goffman and why now, 50 years since *Asylums* (1961) was published? The first answer is simple and grounded in reception: *Asylums* remains a primary text for the study of the self, mental health and the everyday life of 'total institutions'. An almost instant classic, the book's influence has been felt across a wide range of academic and applied areas including psychiatry, where it was an impetus for the deinstitutionalization movement in mental health around the world during the 1960s and later (Borus 1981; Stroman 2003), and where it continues to be read and revalued half a century later (Mac Suibhne 2009, 2011). But there are other good reasons to reread this work. One of these is that *Asylums* offers a platform for developing an ecological theory of wellbeing and thus a theoretical basis for understanding how music helps to promote wellbeing. I develop this thought in the next two chapters.

First, in this chapter, I consider the relationship between culture and agency in Goffman's work, tracing its development from *Presentation of Self in Everyday Life* (1959) to *Asylums* (1961) with a nod to the work that led up to *Asylums* (1957a, 1957b, 1957c). I suggest that the gap between culture and agency and public and private evident in Goffman's early work was bridged in *Asylums*. This bridging not only illuminates the plasticity of culture, agency, public and private and thus identity and wellbeing within social worlds, it also connects the ideas I have presented in Chapter 1 (health/illness as multi-dimensional, relational and temporal) to the reconceptualization of asylums that I will describe in Chapter 3 and the idea of the music asylum to be introduced in Chapter 4. I pave the way for the idea of the music asylum in Chapter 3 where I disconnect the concept of asylum from its physical location (villages, neighborhoods, buildings, campuses, towns) and/or groups of personnel (psychiatrists, family, friends, communities, groups) and attempt to recover the original meaning of the term (shelter, safe space, place for living and flourishing, room in which to create, play and rest). As I will describe, asylums take various forms and are produced and sustained in various ways which inevitably exist in tension and thus affect the ebb and flow of resources within socio-cultural health/illness ecologies.

Too General in Perspective?

Asylums: Essays on the Social Situation of Mental Patients and Other Inmates is sometimes misread as a report of fieldwork in a mental hospital. However, the hospital, or 'Asylum with a capital A', was, for Goffman, but one species of a more general phenomena, the totalizing institution: 'a place of residence and work where a large number of like-situated individuals, cut off from the wider society for an appreciable period of time, together lead an enclosed, formally administered round of life' (1961: xiii). According to Goffman, total institutions take one of five forms:

1. institutions established to care for people who are incapable but not considered harmful to the public (e.g. homes for the elderly);
2. institutions that care for people who are incapable of caring for themselves and who are seen as a threat to the community albeit not an intentional one (e.g. mental hospitals);
3. institutions explicitly devoted to incarcerating those who are dangerous and where care for inmates is not the primary purpose (e.g. prisons);
4. institutions set up for occupational reasons that involve sequestering of personnel (e.g. the military, boarding schools); and
5. institutions that provide retreats from the world linked to an organizational or contemplative task (e.g. convents).

With this typology Goffman sought to address, as he put it, 'the general characteristics of [total institutions]' (1961: 5). For Goffman, the mental asylum was of interest as much for general lessons about the structures of the self as it was for the particular study of mental health and mental hospitals. This conceptual tilt toward the general has been the target of criticism over the years, beginning in the 1960s (Levinson and Gallagher 1964: 18–23), and it is worth considering, since it opens up key issues that concern Goffman's conception of subjectivity, identity and social experience, and these are of course important, if we are to develop an ecological theory of wellbeing.

The criticisms launched against *Asylums*, in particular during the early phase of its reception history, dwell upon Goffman's tendency to overlook the unique features of totalizing institutions devoted to the care of those deemed mentally ill. This elision in turn blurs the distinctions between inmates of different types of total institution. There is, as one recent commentator put it, 'an abstract quality to Goffman's assertions' (Mac Suibhne 2011: 1).

The critics do, at least in part, have a point. The experience of self-effacement in, for example, a convent differs considerably, for example, from that in a mental hospital. In the former, self-effacement, the renunciation of one's former and more worldly self is linked to a new self-identity and one associated with social approbation – one is, for example, honored or gratified to wear the habit, just as one might be honored to wear a cap and gown at a graduation ceremony. The uniformity imposed is, therefore, more self-enhancing than self-effacing. The adoption of new customs (the uniform, the gown) and the associated acquisition of a new institutional identity is, moreover, voluntary. Similar points could be made with regard to other forms of total institution, such as the military. Thus, Goffman's critics suggest, it is possible that in seeking to generalize from the particular case of the mental hospital, Goffman has diverted us from the question of specifically what is involved in being an inmate in a mental asylum.

Linked to this criticism, Goffman has been accused of presenting a researcher's point of view on the topic of being mentally ill as opposed to an ethnographic perspective devoted to understanding the experience of the hospital and mental illness of mental health service users themselves (Fine and Martin 1990: 93). As one critic bluntly put it, 'Goffman in reality has proffered the researcher's point of view, even though he claims it is the patient's viewpoint' (Weinstein 1994: 274). (I will suggest below that this criticism is partially unfair since Goffman's neo-Durkheimian project centred upon the production order of identity, namely, how scenes are put together, and not on the validity of participants' narrative accounts which in his perspective are understood as, themselves, cultural products and thus part of this scenic activity.)

Why, then, did Goffman follow this generalizing strategy, or, more specifically, what explanatory advantages did such a strategy offer, given that it is also associated with the kind of shift away from members' accounts as just described? There are at least two (not unrelated) ways of answering these questions.

The first is the most familiar. It considers *Asylums* as an exercise in sociological irony. Goffman the ironist is of course a well-known figure in social theory: one *British Journal of Psychiatry* editorial spoke of his 'mordant wit' (Mac Suibhne 2011: 2; see also Burns 2002; Fine and Martin 1990). In *Asylums* this irony can be said to take the following form: contra to the humanitarian conception of the mental hospital as a non-threatening, sequestering space for people with mental distress, asylums are, in fact, repressive institutions. As a total institution, the asylum is responding, at least in part, to a market demand for help with problematic members of families and other organizations and to an occupational project linked to professional claims and the politics of expertise (Abbott 1988). The asylum's institutional practices and its built environment unwittingly exacerbate inmates' suffering, because they interrupt or otherwise curtail their attempts at self-presentation by curtailing their access to the kinds of resources that self-presentation requires. Asylums interrupt the self, and these interruptions feed back into a negative spiral whereby further attempts to restore the self are read (by those in charge) as pathological, that is, tautologically as symptoms of illness.

The second answer to the question of why Goffman focused on generic features of total institutions through the case study of a mental hospital involves a subtler replaying of the first. While it takes account of the aforementioned irony, it sets that irony in the context of Goffman's fundamentally sociological project concerning the self and the morality of the interaction order as a local production order (Fine 1979, 2010; Rawls 1987). It also serves as a riposte to suggestions that

Goffman's work presents a cynical vision of action, that it is overly individualistic or that it ignores inequality and institutional constraint (in particular, see Rawls 1987, where Goffman is also defended against these criticisms).

It has been suggested that all of Goffman's work is, to varying degrees, concerned, as Branaman has put it, with '(1) production of self (2) confined self (3) nature of social life and (4) frames and the organization of experience' (1997: xlv). But in the work that followed his 1953 University of Chicago PhD dissertation, 'Communication Conduct in an Island Community' (later published as *The Presentation of Self* [1959]), the critical and moral strand in Goffman's work is brought to the fore. It is not a coincidence that this period also marks the start of Goffman's investigations into mental health, or, more accurately, identity politics, with three essays published in 1957 at the end of his time as a postdoctoral researcher in the Laboratory of Socio-Environmental Studies (1954–57, funded by the National Institute of Mental Health) and, of course, *Asylums* itself (Goffman 1957a, 1957b, 1957c, 1961).

The nature of this critical turn and with it the defence against the accusation of cynicism is linked, I suggest, to some notable differences in how the figuration of the person and with it the nature of public and private (and the culture–agency nexus) is conceived in, on the one hand, *The Presentation of Self* and, on the other, *Asylums*. It is this difference, I will suggest, that opens the door to a consideration of wellbeing and social ecology.

In *The Presentation of Self*, the focus is upon impression management, face and deference. Within this focus, culture is a tool (prop, persuasive media) or a constraint (script, ideal, expectation). Alongside this focus on management, Goffman draws a distinction between the front- and back-stage regions of activity, highlighting the latter as the spaces and places where one can, as it were, let one's guard down. As examples, Goffman offers the waitress who returns to the kitchen from the 'front-stage' of the restaurant floor, or, equally tellingly, the rehabilitation of objects (the butter from a dining table remoulded and sent out for further duty to the next set of diners). Back-stage is, in short, the space and place where things that do not conform to presentational ideals can both relax and be retouched or mended before their next public performance. Back-stages are less places of play than of privacy; they are also residual and ancillary to what happens out front. Goffman spoke of these spaces as regions protected by 'barriers to perception' (1959: 109).

By the time we come to the essays in *Asylums*, however, the hidden regions of the self are something more. As I will argue, their significance for wellbeing becomes immense for, unlike *The Presentation of Self*, *Asylums* shows us how it is possible for cultural practices and values to flow from seemingly back-stage or private regions to the front or more public realm. This point is critical: the very framing of what is public and what is private (which is what counts and does not count as cultural) becomes increasingly prominent in *Asylums* and is linked to the politics of identity, in particular to the classification and differentiation of the well from the ill.

To put this slightly differently, in *Asylums*, Goffman explores explicitly the moral economy of selfhood, namely, the politics of symbolic production of the self and the opportunity distribution posed by this politics for personal (or so-called, inner) experience. The stigmatized, mortified self of the mental patient is, Goffman shows, a self caught in the crossfire between what others deem as publicly acceptable (competent) presentation work and private aberration. The mentally unwell self is a self that is figured as, to some important extent, operating outside culture, and, tragically, someone for whom the situation of the hospital is inhospitable, exacerbating an already alienated and dysfunctional relationship to cultural resources. Thus, with *Asylums*, Goffman enriches his focus on culture, which becomes an ethically and politically charged media for living. Whereas in *The Presentation of Self*, culture is a list of rules and a repository of goods that mediate or afford self-presentation, in *Asylums*, culture is the means for our ceremonial constitution of ourselves and our relations. This critical take on culture in Goffman is later clarified, in *Relations in Public* for example, where cultural materials – physical and symbolic – are equipment for living, that is, not merely presenting oneself to impress. These things are, he says, 'made available to a populace in the form of a claimed good while-in-use' (Goffman 1971: 29). As his career progressed, it would seem, Goffman came to see culture as a modus vivendi.

Thus, and in contrast to his take in *The Presentation of Self*, in *Asylums* Goffman highlights the situated distribution of resources (including social credibility), not merely for impressing others but for the more existential and socially fraught project of identity figuration. To take the most obvious example, the back-stage regions are removed or severely curtailed in total institutions and in ways that exacerbate being able to live and self-present. It is here that we can begin to see how *Asylums* articulates an incipient ecological theory of culture and an explicit theory of cultural mediation, one that is cued by its subtitle ('Essays on the Social Situation of Mental Patients and Other Inmates'). Understood in this way, inner experience, the personal and, indeed, health status and the sense of wellbeing are all conceptualized as products of concerted action, a form of action and commitment to the interaction order that taps various resources that are available within real-time action settings. Thus *Asylums*, not only exonerates Goffman of the charge of cynicism. It also draws out into relief the mutually constitutive relationship between agency (what actors do, what they imagine, what they wish and will, what they are able to do) and culture (the media for and within which actors do, imagine, wish, will, are able). In short, *Asylums* closes the gap between agency and culture that had been apparent in *The Presentation of Self*. To clarify this important point (which leads into the health ecology concept), it is thus worth comparing Goffman's handling of the culture–agency nexus in *The Presentation of Self* and in *Asylums*. This comparison will prepare the ground for the re-conceptualization of the asylum concept in Chapter 3, which will in turn pave the way for an aesthetic ecological theory of wellbeing through music in Chapters 4 to 6.

The Culture and Agency Nexus

In *The Presentation of Self*, Goffman introduced his characteristic dramaturgical perspective. This focus is directed to the strategies used by social actors as they seek to impress one another through various forms of self-casting, what we might call self-impersonation or the adoption of personae in action. The means for this impersonation are, as Goffman describes in *The Presentation of Self*, cultural. Actors take up pre-existing lines of action (scripts, scenarios), mobilize materials (props) and align themselves with typified characters (roles). Culture is the medium through which an individual impersonates her/himself and thus maintains face (positive self-image perceived by others and by self) and avoids mishaps (1959: 56).

It is perhaps easy to see how this vision lays itself open to the charge of cynicism as described above (and thus an individualistic conception of social life and social action), and it is perhaps unsurprising that this charge has been the subject of some commentary in social theory (Chriss 1995; Habermas 1984: 90–94; Manning 1989; Rawls 1987: 143). But one might counter that the more serious charge is a theoretical one that also helps to highlight the shifting conception of the culture–agency nexus in Goffman's work. That charge goes as follows: *The Presentation of Self* is individualist. It focuses on the individual actor as she or he moves from front- to back-stage in the attempt to impress and influence others. As such it deflects attention from the actor's relational connection to the ground (relational as in the sense I described at the end of Chapter 1) and thus it deflects attention from the ways in which individuals (and selves) are themselves figured socially, ecologically. This point now requires further development.

In *The Presentation of Self*, for example, we see actors who deploy the available tools for impersonation. These actors are concerned with performance evaluation, how well or skilled they/others are in cultural appropriation. For a medical professional, for example, a stethoscope is a prop that signals status (professional, medical) and as such it is a potential resource for achieving deference (from patient to doctor). To take another example, a tailored suit might be worn by a manager to signify seniority, affluence and perhaps taste and lifestyle within an organization (and thus as a resource for potentially maintaining authority/power). In these examples, performance is akin to Garfinkel's notion of 'passing' (1967) or being able to lay claim to an identity category and with it attendant social relations and practices. (For example, Garfinkel describes the intersex person, 'Agnes', who manages to pass as a 'natural, normal' female through forms of culture appropriation, in her case, by adopting garb such as twin-set sweaters and pearl necklaces and learning how to cook, thereby enjoying the rights and privileges associated with being hailed as feminine.)

In these examples, however, there is no explicit appreciation of how performance is not only about seeking official/public recognition for the achievement and successful deployment of pre-existing criteria (of professional or gender status) but is simultaneously seeking to perform (through performance) the meaning of the criteria against which the performance is being judged. There is, therefore, no mechanism for conceptualizing innovation and change, and thus there is an implicit quietism in Goffman's *Presentation of Self*. The focus is on 'successful' and 'unsuccessful' performances within which cultural criticism is reduced to the task of ranking (degrees of good and bad performances). It misses how, for example, the tailored suit as just described, might be worn in an innovative or even ironic or satirical way (for example, without a necktie or with a T-shirt or with the sleeves rolled up) or indeed, might have been thrown on haphazardly but deemed to be chic. In any of these cases, the wearing may redefine sartorial standards within a particular organization, setting or milieu. (And as others follow the example, a new trend, and standard, emerges and new practices of relating may be linked to this trend.) Here agency is interdependent with a cultural code and 'presentation of self' is cultural politics. That is to say that agency is not merely the enactment or realization in practice of pre-existing codes, rules, ideas or images but rather that what we do is simultaneously oriented to general notions and clarifies those notions (I redefine our understanding of sartorial elegance through how I wear my clothes, for example). Within the more restricted notion of agency as enactment, cultural materials (the suit, for example) are materials for impression management, tools: they are not understood, as others have so ably argued that they are, as mediators in their own right (DeNora 1997, 2000; Hennion 2007; Pinch 2010). As Pinch observed, 'the "interaction order" studied by Goffman but never explicitly analyzed, is embedded within, mediated, and staged by material circumstances and mundane technologies' (2010: 419). It is for these reasons that critics of interactionism in its various guises often suggest that interactionism suffers from an individualistic bias. What I have been suggesting so far is that Goffman's *Presentation of Self* may have suffered from that bias but that the vision he put forward in *Asylums* does not.

In *The Presentation of Self*, actors seemingly have open access to cultural forms. There is no allusion to the ways that mounting (and succeeding in) a particular performance is conditioned by features of the setting where it takes place – personnel, networks, perceptions, informal knowledge systems and prejudices, local instantiations of general procedures, skill, knack, embodied culture, materiality and, in general, relations between people and things. Nor is there any allusion to the ways that these features of settings are differentially distributed, not equally available or deployable by all. To return to the sartorial example, one might be considered by relevant observers to have dress sense and look good in this or that tailored suit but nonetheless not have sufficient economic resources to purchase such a suit. Or one might have the money and might purchase and wear the suit and yet not be deemed to wear it well, that is, not be recognized as possessing the attributes associated with wearing something well. ('The money spent on that suit is simply wasted with her figure!'). Related to this issue, there is no conceptual mechanism in *The Presentation of Self* for describing how opinion may change, how one might make a switch from 'wasted on her' to 'actually that looks good – in a different kind of a way' and how that change will affect the stock of cultural resources and criteria for valuation in these seemingly micro-public spheres. (I return to these issues in Chapter 7, where I consider the idea of 'goodness' in relation to musical aesthetics.)

To be sure, in *The Presentation of Self*, Goffman notes the injustice associated with differential reception when he suggests that social situations are 'organized on the principle that any individual who possesses certain social characteristics has a moral right to expect that others will value and treat him in an appropriate way' (1959: 13). He does not however elaborate on how in social life things are rarely this fair. Thus the same performance is not the same performance because it is contextualized or framed (locally) in different ways through the act of perception. These differences in turn are noted by performers whose performance histories can and often do themselves become, recursively, conditions of action next time. ('I don't have the kind of figure to get away with wearing a dress like that, so I will stick to this type of outfit.') Through this recursive process (akin to Hacking's notion of 'looping' [1995: 351]), actors develop 'form' over time and in relation to reception contexts and cultures, so for example, one becomes known as the 'shy one', the 'bright one', the 'fat one' and so on, as one is, effectively, backed into a cultural corner. (Does one assume a jolly attitude more often after one grows fat, for example, simply because it is easier to play to the expectations of others or because assuming a different demeanour may seem to others incongruous with one's body shape and thus meet with confusion or censure? ['From the way she acts, she must think she looks like Sophia Loren!']). Between *The Presentation of Self* and *Asylums*, I suggest, there is a shift, a move from a focus on successful performance to a more critical focus on the politics of performance and in particular the background resources that afford forms of performance. This moves from a concern with figure to a concern with ground. It highlights some of the ways in which the dramaturgical parallel, drawn in *The Presentation of Self*, between, on the one hand, the figure of the actor on or behind the stage and, on the other, the action within everyday life and social institutions is imperfect. It is thus worthwhile to attend to the reasons why this parallel conceals as much as it reveals about culture and agency.

First, as Atkinson has observed, Goffman's understanding of the source domain for his dramaturgical metaphor, the theatre, was in fact sketchy, begging the question, moreover, of just what in fact the theatre is:

> In developing his metaphor, and in using the dramaturgical model as an analytic lens through which to examine everyday life in general, Goffman was in danger of basing his explanation on an unknown quantity. In the absence of any detailed ethnographic work in the theatre by himself or by others, Goffman had relatively little evidence to go on. Theatrical performance itself and the organization of theatrical work therefore remain an unexamined resource in Goffman's dramaturgical analysis. Recognizing the absence of the theatre from Goffman's analysis throws analytic attention back towards the *theatrical* itself. In

a sense, therefore, Goffman's sociology of everyday life serves to emphasize the continuing sociological neglect of practical theatrical work. (Atkinson 2010: 5)

Second, and as has already been implied, everyday life involves aspects that are not typically found in theatre and in ways that highlight the significance of play in everyday life. For example, an actor in everyday life may be like a theatrical actor, but her or his performances involve much more than reciting lines and/or mobilizing props. Casting, in other words, is much looser. A social actor may play no fixed character, may not know that she or he is playing a particular character or may be suddenly recast; she or he may play more than one character in the same scene and, indeed, simply staying in character may be difficult. Acting in daily life may, moreover, involve more turbulence than in the theatre: actors may constantly need to negotiate and renew their roles in the wake of crosscurrents created by the simultaneous performances of others. The nature of the play, the plotting of a course is uncertain, the destination possibly unknown (being charted for the first time, being repeatedly re-determined). As I described earlier, in everyday life, unlike in the theatre, audience response can redefine plots and indeed supplant whole scripts. Finally, unlike the characters played by actors (who are fictions), actors playing characters (in any realm, including the theatrical stage) may experience actual sensations that extend beyond character and that impinge upon its form – nervousness or other affective states. One's lip may tremble while one is attempting to perform in the role of a stiff-upper-lipped character, but the (fictional) character's lip only trembles when the author writes it or the actor makes it so. In short, the possibility of newness and playing with roles is an ever-present feature of social action and to a much greater degree than in the theatre. Indeed, social action may involve considerable play and tinkering with norms, images, scripts and ideals. This play, while important on the theatrical stage, is of even greater importance in daily life (Melucci 1996), and, as I shall describe below, it is a vital component of making the spaces of action habitable and conducive to action.

The 'Playing Self': Culture-in-Action and the Possibility of Innovation and Change

For Goffman, a self is an identity constructed out of an interlacing of different possibilities and stances. A self is also an identity that is reliable, representable to self and to others across time and situation. ('I am – this kind of – woman/ man'.) That identity is often indexed by words such as 'character', 'style', 'personality' and 'persona', but it is also the result of practices of self-constitution and maintenance, 'technologies of the self' in Foucault's sense. 'Self', then, is a kind of broker in social meetings, whether between strangers, between familiars and between those in the middle ground, acquaintances (Morgan 2009), because it offers a promissory form of identity. To have a self, and thus to be a person, is to offer others a form of regularity through a reliable style of action, patterned characteristics, values and taste commitments, and communicative modes. This regularity in turn offers a stable basis for cooperation and action in concert: a kind of 'you can count on me' and 'here is what we might do together'.

As such, the concept of self has a strong moral component (to present a socialized self to others for the purposes of collaboration) and is subject to forms of regulation. For example, the self will be enjoined to engage in self-governance, in the myriad ways Foucault described: from how one looks, to life-style choices, to the control of the body as part of the 'civilizing process' (Elias 2000). Thus, to 'pull one's self together' is to find a way of figuring the self within an environment and its various ecological constraints and affordances in ways that both take from that environment and give back possibilities for collaborative action. In the sense that the self is not in a play but is a playwright, crafting her/his and others' characters across time and space (Melucci 1996). Indeed, once the dramaturgical notion that life is like a play is qualified, and once we see that the parallels between life and theatre are imperfect, it is possible to return to the sociology of play and in ways that connect a focus on the territories of the self to a conception of culture and agency as entwined and to a more explicit understanding of mental illness as an ecologically produced identity.

To date, and with notable exceptions (Simmel 1949), sociologists have made too little of the concept of play (not merely the more familiar focus on games and game theory, but, for the purposes at hand here and, more importantly, the role of the random, of mimicry and approximation and of altered perception [on types of play, see Caillois 1961; Huzinga 1938]). Play theory tends too often to set play aside as distinct from other features of social life (often in ways that are linked to the life course and developmental theory and so understood as the province of the young) and/or as a free modality. More interesting however is play as a way of negotiating social worlds, a realm in which possibilities of difference and change may be broached in safeways, but which are simultaneously more than mere rehearsal.

In a sense, to play is to dream in the medium of action. Sutton Smith's observation that play involves 'acting out one's capacity for the future' and that play is in this regard 'the opposite of depression' (2001: 198) points to play as a medium of world-making, the creative making of self, other and situation, now, again and later. Play is also, in Kenneth Burke's phrase, a 'dramatistic negative', a 'way of indicating the negative through an affirmative action that is not clearly the same as that which it represents' (Sutton Smith 2001: 1–2). In sum, play is about much more than a feeling of flow or being in the zone or pleasure: play is about being engaged in working out the world and its relations and one's potential places in relation to those relations. Play is, in other words, about making a place in which one can be and have the possibility of play understood as potential relations and identities. As I will describe below, play furnishes the lifeworld with opportunities for action, with things (roles, riffs, possibilities, personae, scenarios, postures, action chains, styles) that one can play, replay and play over and play around with, together in ways that access forms of experience and ways of being in the world (and which, some argue, are therefore functional as they hone skills and adaptability, preparing the individual and the group to handle diverse conditions and tasks [see Feldhammer 2007]).

If play is engagement with the world, then the features of the world can be understood in the broadest sense as toys (Ball 1967). Just as dolls enable one to act out versions of the pathetic fallacy, the ascription of sentience, life and meaning to seemingly inanimate objects ('Barbi wants to go to the beach today, not to school'), toys, playthings, playmates and play-spaces more generally are the medium through which realities are brought into being and narrated. Toys are objects that enable the imaginative continuation of envisioned scenarios between people, made present, drawn into and mobilized within worlds. In the 'grown-up' world, anything can be a toy. As such, toys are not mere playthings but are deployed in ways that displace other objects (other potential toys and possibilities for action), and thus, other attempts to play at other things. It is through the playful use and deployment of toys that actors register themselves and their presence in the world to themselves and others and thus, arguably, mark out their personal territories, the range or compass of their potential for action and being-in-the-world and thus their opportunities for, and range of, agency. Because it is liminal, however, play is an important resource for (re)making the world. It exists on the edge of what is serious and what is trivial or not real, and thus play is a flexible mode of action and a safe modality for effecting change. Play can be, according to its outcome, either distraction or engagement with the world.

For these reasons, assuming that a consideration of play is important, so too is a consideration of its social relations. The playing self is a self *in situ*, a self with something to play with (in this context a virtual is no less situated than any other insofar as it makes use of cultural materials and tools or toys), a self that can play within a space. ('Here they think I'm clever, but when I was in Paris they didn't like my work.') It is here that we see how play is connected to the self's territories and, moreover, how those territories are themselves linked to the environments where play occurs. As Goffman described in *Relations in Public* (1971), the self is protected and projected through different territorial layers and realms – the body and its covering, objects and possessions, talk and information including biography (and the construction of personal biography/myth – hence the impossibility of narrative as an unmediated window into the self and its experience). Thus the self secures certain rights in relation to others and to the spaces (conceptual, symbolic and physical) between itself and others. These are themselves potential spaces for self expansion, but they are also the spaces that protect the self from encroachment, that give it the space or leeway it requires so as to remain a self and, thus, to play without threat of violence. In civil society they are therefore to be respected, as Goffman describes when he turns to the ceremonial ways in which selves are protected from being violated. Thus territories of self are places where selves can play, and play is a means for creating and maintaining territories of self. The back-stage regions which Goffman described in *The Presentation of Self* are different from these play spaces and this difference further highlights the way in which Goffman did not sufficiently consider the topic of cultural innovation in that work. The relationship between the kitchen and the restaurant dining-room is not identical to the relationship between, say, the tree-fort and the family living-room or school-room. While kitchen/back-stage is a place where one recovers, rehearses and prepares to re-enter the front-stage dining-room, the play space/tree-fort is where actors extend themselves, try out, approximate and explore new roles, poke fun at old or official identities and generally create new possibilities for action and role transition (for example, making the transition from young child to quasi-autonomous pre-teen). The tree-fort is a locally produced but distally understood place for play. The kitchen or back-stage region may be or become a place for play, but a place for play is much more than a back-stage region.

It is here that the irony of *Asylums* cuts deepest. In *Asylums*, Goffman's cultural theory took a critical – and anything but individualistic – turn. *Asylums* shows us what happens when the territories of the self (and its play spaces) are overly managed by others and thus curtailed, and, by contrast, how the focus on the social situation of the self in a total institution points up the need to consider just what the term asylum can, might and should mean. For if damage to self is both symptom and cause of mental health conditions (a loss of social functioning), and if mental conditions are treated in ways that diminish possibilities for sustainable self-maintenance, then it is necessary to consider how mental illness involves more than the treatment of brains and minds, how it may also be considered, in Szasz's term to be a 'problem in living' (1960: 113), a problem that is both ecologically emergent and morally charged. In short, might the aetiology and care of mental illness be a social problem, one that also might possibly be owned in common?

We can begin to pursue these questions by thinking about the actor's occupation, familiarity with and fit within environments (as these are understood and experienced by actors and through actions). Harking back to the discussion in Chapter 1 of how environmental materials mediate performance, inscription and experience of health/illness identities (and to the discussion of Groce's work on hereditary deafness on Martha's Vineyard), we need to ask are the venues (physical and symbolic) for the production of self allocated for actors and action hospitable to all (unlikely perhaps) and, if not, who do they favour, when and how? (Which actors are able to 'play' in these venues and what can they play?) To ask this question is to enquire about how actors are able to appropriate resources from action milieus so as to engage with (play in) those milieus.

To be sure, actors have, within milieus, certain user-requirements. At their most basic, these requirements may be physical (climate, oxygen levels, sources of nourishment and water). More complex are matters about communicative modalities such as languages, styles and accents (as Durkheim famously put it in *Rules of Sociological Method*, he was not obliged to speak French with his fellow countrymen, but if he wanted to be understood he needed to do so [1961: 2]), ambience, style of action, comportment or dress, ways of handling materials, justificatory discourses of value and aesthetics. While some of these matters may be addressed under the rubric of health and safety or accessibility (wheelchair ramps for example), most are not. Yet, much as actors vary (some climb stairs more easily than others), so too do their ecological requirements. Indeed, actors may not be aware or conscious of those requirements and yet find some action settings or some collaborators feel better than others ('I don't mind climbing these stairs because they are not too steep and wider'). At the same time, an absence of environmental conductivity is not a simple given (constraint) upon agency and the self since, within the sphere of play, conditions may be and are over-ridden as the environment is refashioned. Thus constraints are themselves indexical and subject to re-enactment in the interaction order through play (the inextricability of agency and culture as described above, the potential of play to redefine and reframe). Thus, the concept of the normal and healthy individual is itself enacted locally, as Goffman himself notes in *Stigma*, and, as such, normal and abnormal identities are jointly produced and jointly owned, indeed, institutionally fostered:

> The notion of the 'normal human being' may have its source in the medical approach to humanity, or in the tendency of large-scale bureaucratic organizations such as the nation state, to treat all members in some respects as equal. Whatever its origins, it seems to provide the basic imagery through which laymen currently conceive themselves (Goffman 1963: 7).

Thus, passing as normal is connected to how well one fits within a particular setting: the identity emerges from the interaction of actor and setting. That setting thus becomes a dynamic component of whether and to what extent one appears to be fit for action. As such, setting can be understood to be an extension of oneself (which is the converse of Goffman's original point that the self is the extension or by-product of ceremonial action in concert), and, if one finds a setting inhospitable, one may also find that it is difficult to be or pass as well (normal or above normal) within that setting. How, then, to conceptualize wellness so as to highlight its experiential and operational features, and, from there, how to theorize the aetiology of these features in ways that make them applicable and visible from within specific action locations?

How Positive is Positive Psychology?

In recent years, concepts from positive psychology have helped to highlight this issue, pursuing both the question of how health is maintained and the question of what wellbeing is, experientially and operationally, in terms of capacities. This focus, along with the critique of medicalization, has developed in productive ways within and outside of sociology, where it has led to a rediscovery of the first wave of anti-psychiatry (Scott and Thorpe 2006). The first of these concepts is 'ontological security', the sense of oneself as secure, bounded and distinct from others (Antonovsky 1979, 1987; Giddens 1991; Laing 1969). Operationally, this sense is experienced when one can act in the world, when one is no mere ventriloquist for others (Burns 2002: 301) and when one is not constantly being imposed upon, disrupted or potentially engulfed/swallowed by others. By contrast, one has or is in, to some degree, control over the world-making process. In turn this fosters a sense of belonging in the world and thus a sense of well-being, ease.

This ability to move in the world or in some medium or sphere and to find a way of operating has in turn affinities with Csikszentmihalyi's concept of 'flow' (1990). Flow, according to Csikszentmihalyi, includes operating in and on the environment (including others) in ways that are effective, that are not ultimately blocked or thwarted. This flow sensation is a characteristic of enjoyment and absorption or a good fit with one's action environment (and task at hand). It is the antithesis of anxiety on the one hand and boredom on the other (Csikszentmihalyi and Csikszentmihalyi 1988) and it is linked to the ease with which one can accomplish a demanding task.

In his work on creativity, and coming closer to Goffman's concerns in *Asylums*, Csikszentmihalyi links flow to the ability to create (and recreate), which is, of course, to be able to play as discussed above and thus to extend the territories of the self, to generate greater scope for protecting the self and a wider field of play (1996). Extending the territory of the self in this way allows the self/actor to appropriate features of the environment and modify them in ways that are pleasing, comforting or useful, that feel like they fit and that can be sustained. This fit and the ontological security it engenders can be understood to be a feature (and a cause) of wellbeing.

But how, where, with what and whom and when do we experience ontological security and flow? When can we be creative in social life and when can we not? Positive psychology tells us too much about flow as an individual experience and not enough about its social conditions. In this sense, it has been necessary but is not sufficient for understanding health ecologically. For that task, it is also necessary to know about the local spaces and arrangements where wellbeing is experienced and where it can be grown. Here, the concept of affordance, which has received considerable discussion in recent years across a range of disciplines, is useful, at least in its sociological guise (Anderson and Sharrock 1993; DeNora 2000). Its use in cultural sociology highlights how the properties of materials or other cultural furnishings, including acts and utterances, can support uses, user identities, acts and projects within social worlds. How then, is it possible to speak of environments as affording wellbeing? It is now time to address this question and to develop a theory of health ecology. For this task Goffman's *Asylums* offers a theoretical basis. It is possible, I suggest in the next chapter, to extend Goffman's concept of asylums in ways that allow us to consider asylums and asylum-seeking in everyday life.

Chapter 3

Learning from Erving Goffman, Part II: Reconfiguring the Concept of Asylum

Room of One's Own

If, as I have just suggested, wellbeing takes shape in relation to environment, then asylum can be defined as a space, either physical or conceptual, that either offers protection from hostility (a refuge) or, more positively, a space within which to play on/with one's environment, whether alone or in concert with others. The metaphor of space is Goffman's own and in *Asylums* he speaks of inmates' need for 'distance' and 'elbow room' (1961: 319). Thus asylum is both back-stage and play-space. First, it is a place where one can relax, let one's hair down metaphorically, recover from and touch up various factors of what goes on out front. It is a buffer from 'the deterministic demands that surround [workers]' (1959: xx), and thus, as Goffman notes, critical to worker control (think of the Japanese convention of the 'rage room' in corporations where workers can go to vent their anger by beating effigies of the boss with bamboo sticks). Second, an asylum is a room in which to remake features of one's world, to play in ways that foster changes in that world. In both these senses, then, an asylum is a 'room of one's own' (Woolf 1929), a space for self but also a space one can, in part, 'own', and share.

That 'room' may be physical, as in a sanctuary or safe place in one's daily territorial round (a friendly cafe, a quiet corner in a public library, a place in a park or a leisure venue), but it may also have nothing to do with walls and roofs. It may take the form of a person and being with that person (the sensations associated with love, care, affection, nurture perhaps even the mere feel or smell of another). Equally often, an asylum may be yet more ephemeral, more fluid, less dependent upon the physical features and/or patterned routines of a place or person. For example, one may create an asylum on the spot and anywhere by withdrawing into memories, by imagining images or by humming to oneself. One may, similarly, make a temporary shelter by simply changing a topic of conversation, by shifting the lighting in a room (lighting a candle) gazing out a window at the world outside. One might open a window to alter the local environment ('Let's have some fresh air in here, shall we?') in ways that may be as much about social relations and aesthetics as they are about thermostatic control. The point is that all of these examples show how materials in one's environment are used for repositioning, broaching new topics or seeing new things, making a space for dreaming, pleasure and difference, even if short-lived.

So asylums are not necessarily places constructed with bricks and mortar. Nor do they need to be of any temporal duration. On the contrary, the phenomenological experience of finding asylum may be such that even a fleeting moment can be transfiguring and in ways that enhance one's longer-lasting sense of wellness and belonging in the world (one's right to play). This point about the temporality of asylums and their phenomenological reality is worth exploring in more detail.

In Chapter 1, I described just how much temporal variation there may be within one person's state of wellness. Illness is not a homogenous and constant state but a variable from day to day, hour to hour, indeed from split-second to split-second, and this variation is mediated by factors outside individuals. Of considerable interest, then, is the question of which moments come to be taken as emblematic of illness, and this question often entails further questions about power and contested identity (Mehan 1989). As Dorothy Smith describes it, this process involves practices of 'assembling observations from actual moments and situations dispersed in time, organizing them or finding that they can be organized in accordance with the "instructions" that [a] concept provides' (2005: 11). That assembly is, one might note, a form of serious play (work in the literal but also ethno-methodological sense of preparing the semblance of a natural, normal world [Goffman 1967]). The questions arise then of how to capture and capitalize on moments in ways that maximize the self and its wellbeing and to minimize those things that detract from this wellbeing, and how to hold these in balance as part of a shared moral economy of identity?

For example, in the midst of feeling ill or, indeed, even at one's worst, there may be brief but intense moments when one encounters something in the external (or internal, mental) world that serves to refresh, recharge, alleviate. These moments may be epiphanic or transfiguring. They may be provoked by ideas, aesthetic media, visual and sensory materials or human contact and may not have much to do with medical or healthcare technologies per se. They may involve dissociation from the apparently 'given' reality (Butler 2006), fleeting insights, glimpses of beauty, momentary distractions of any kind, hearing good news, very short events (having one's face washed or hand stroked), a moment outside in a sunny spot, a cup of tea, a pleasant odour or scent, a moment of peace and quiet or even a moment or part of a day that recurs regularly (a visit, the sight of something such as sunrise or even a particular stranger who walks past the window or over the bridge at this time each day) and so on. If carefully managed, such moments can be extended and augmented in various ways, for example, through forms of anticipation, memory and retrospective talk about them ('I have to tell you about a wonderful thing I saw today'). There is, as Aasgaard wisely puts it, no one answer to the question: 'How long does a moment last' (2002; see also Adam 1990), just as there is no answer to the question: 'How long must an activity or perception last for it to count as a form of asylum?' Asylums are phenomenological realities.

They are also flexible constructions. There is, therefore, no firm connection between the concept of asylum as it is sought and found in daily life and the institution of the Asylum or mental hospital. Asylums, in daily life, including

the daily life of the mental hospital, can be quickly located, often with few or
no physical materials. In *Asylums*, at least implicitly, Goffman recognized this
displacement, the non-identity of asylums with Asylums, and this is one of his
key preoccupations in that text. For example, he speaks in varying ways of how,
within the Asylum, there are asylums from the Asylum. This recognition is evident
in Goffman's discussion of 'removal activities' or ways to 'kill time' (1961: 69),
by which he means reposition inmates in temporal structures that are not, strictly
speaking, of the asylum. Some forms of removal activities described by Goffman
are social/collective in nature, sponsored by the institution and, although distinct
from the everyday administration of the hospital, their aims and objectives are
related to the institution's official culture:

> Field games, dances, orchestra or band playing, choral singing, lectures, art
> classes, or woodworking classes, and card playing; some are individual but rely
> on public materials such as reading and solitary TV watching. (Goffman 1961: 69)

(It is worth noting in passing that Goffman does not acknowledge that these
removal activities offer considerably more than mere time-killing, as I describe
below.) By contrast, other forms of removal activity are pursued in isolation, not
merely from others (such as reading in private) but also in ways that may not meet
with official approval, such as excessive day-dreaming, over-orientation to what
is deemed to be a fictive or fantasy world (Walter Mitty) or collecting objects that
are not normally considered to be collectable (I return to this theme below). What,
then, is an actor's relation to her or his environment, and how can she or he find
asylum within a social location?

   Though, as I have just described, Goffman bundled together many types of
activities under the heading of 'removal' (basically anything that took the inmate
away from the day-to-day reality of being in a total institution), in what follows I
will suggest that it is useful to speak of removal activities in a more restricted way.
To that end, I shall speak of removal activities as those forms of asylum-seeking
activity that gain distance or offer 'room from' hostile features of the environment.
I shall also speak of forms of asylum, by contrast, that offer 'room for' or that
allow actors to intervene or make an impression upon their worlds, to refurnish
their environments, so as to make those environments more conducive to being (a
self) in the world. I will refer to these forms of asylum as 'refurnishings'.

Removals and Refurnishings

As Goffman described them, removal activities kill time. They also reconfigure
time in ways that dispel unwanted times and realities. Removals do this by
physically or symbolically relocating actors in places that are more conducive to
wellbeing. Removal, in this sense, most obviously involves a physical relocation
(leaving a place, situation or friendship group, for example). But it may also

involve mental, conceptual or perceptual relocation – getting away, blotting out, distracting. So, for example, an actor may use fantasy, meditation, displacement activity (playing a game, watching TV, reading a book, people watching, listening to an iPod [described in detail in Chapter 4]), diary or poetry writing (where the work is never shared with others) or medication/substances (food, alcohol, aroma therapy or toiletries, drugs) to assist her or his efforts to transcend or ignore a given environment.

By contrast, there are asylum-seeking strategies that remain within and play with the social environment. In many cases, these forms of asylum-seeking involve attempts to transform or build upon some feature of that environment so as to maintain the space or room for self, security, flow and belonging. These are refurnishing activities and they may involve rhetorical or political action to the extent that they need to justify the claims they make on attention, action or environmental resources. ('Blue is such a cold color, but I do love the color pink. It's so cosy and pretty, isn't it? Shall we use it in our public room?') When actors engage in any form of refurnishing, singly or together, they are acting upon and in their environments and in ways that affect those environments, whether materially or symbolically. They are recreating, engaging literally in re-creation, replenishing, refurnishing their environments in ways that, in some way, make them more habitable. Unlike removal, which is in effect a form of retreat from the environment, a giving up of space within it, refurnishing is an advance. It is about remaking, albeit perhaps in small ways, the environment, about acting in and on that environment. Refurnishing strategies can take myriad forms, from an account of a situation to the introduction of representative media (a depiction or module or portrait). These strategies may involve aesthetic interventions (playing music with the windows open) or the modification of physical settings (anything from opening a window to repainting a room to spraying graffiti on a public wall). They may involve actors' attempts to modify their own appearances (grooming, costume or body modification and actors' attempts to modify the appearances of others ('You look so nice in pink!')). The key and defining feature, indeed, the only feature of refurnishing, is that it adds to an environment something which others will encounter. Refurnishing is positive: it contributes something to the collective pot of action's conditions. Refurnishing is inevitably, then, also about claiming and taking space in a social milieu, and it may involve the perception that at times too much is being taken. Actors have many options in terms of how much, where and for whom they refurnish. They may be overly self-effacing, never attempting refurnishing; they may seek to refurnish in ways that are conducive to self-wellbeing but also respectful, indeed, facilitative for others; they may seek to refurnish in self-indulgent ways.

As an added complication, in practice, the distinction between removal and refurnishing activities is not always clear. For example, if one wears earbuds or headphones in a public space (the NY Port Authority Terminal, for example) to listen to a personal music player, one may be simultaneously engaging in removal (the privatization of public space) and refurnishing (the action may be read to signify that one has rejected the current audio environment in favor of something else). Thus removal activity, if observed as a form of symbolic action, becomes a stance and thus also a statement of rejection of the environment or some of its features and thus a call for refurnishing. So too, their classification as either one or the other is negotiable, contingent. What seems like mere diversion or distraction to one, might be world-making to another, and this cross-over may be meaningful in particular environments and circumstances. It may also be misread or overlooked.

The environment, or social space, understood in terms of the features it offers for asylum-seeking, in particular whether it is hospitable to refurnishing, is in this sense an important component in Goffman's discussion. It is central to how illness identities are determined within the mental hospital. It is here that Goffman's *Asylums* highlights the ways in which access to the resources for seeking asylum are or may be differentially structured. This point is as applicable to the inmates of mental hospitals as it is to the inmates and fellow participants of everyday life.

Resource Allocation: The Social Distribution of Asylums

Being able to seek asylum through either removal or refurnishing is by no means an opportunity readily available to all. It is linked to institutional regulations and identities that are often saturated with degrees of status and prestige. For the purposes of example, consider the hypothetical case of Miss A, a 27-year-old, unmarried, middle-ranking professional. Her forms of asylum are painting in watercolours (always flowers or cats), needlework, athletics (ballet since the age of 5), rereading the novels of Jane Austen, playing the piano (Chopin and Schubert are her favourites) and keeping her small apartment tidy. Saturday afternoons are taken up with ballet (she now coaches young dancers). Every Thursday evening she takes a piano lesson, and, on Fridays on the way home from work, she buys a small bunch of flowers, which she places in a west-facing alcove window and paints them on Sunday afternoon, when the light is at a particular angle. We know nothing about her so-called private life. All of these activities are refurnishings: they are projected into the social world both through the practice of them on site (during actual ballet or painting classes, sitting in a room with others while doing needlework, attending a book club, displaying comportment) and elsewhere (for example, when she speaks in conversation about her art class or shows photos of a ballet recital).

Miss A's refurnishing practices are proactive in the social world, even when they seem merely to reinforce that world ('Nothing challenging or contentious in, say, doing needlepoint, is there?') Moreover, her activities are part of her resourceful, self-in-interaction part of her multiple capabilities, the communicative modalities she can mobilize or claim to mobilize. When she enters a room, her balletic figure, posture and comportment are, potentially, significant to the extent that her physical stance can be matched (in Smith's sense discussed above – reading a person's conduct in accordance with the 'instructions that [a] concept provides') with various descriptors ('graceful', 'haughty', 'pretentious', 'elegant', 'feminine'). When she tells her colleagues that she cannot go out with them after work, because she has a piano lesson, she is furnishing that encounter with her priorities and commitments to an alternate use of time and telling them that her time is pre-allocated, itself a measure of the extent of her self-assemblage, her commitment also to others beyond her circle at work. When she draws her needlework out of her bag in a meeting or waiting room, both the activity and the object of work itself can be read. For example, is that flowers or birds, or, as Ray Materson's miniature embroideries made while in prison, is it a syringe and a spoon full of heroin that she is stitching (Materson and Materson 2002)? If the former, and we learn that it is a cushion cover for her living-room, we have learned that much more about how Miss A operates stylistically to furnish her world, materially, but also in terms of her sensibility and thus her history. If the latter, and we find this incongruous ('How could someone like that want a pillow cover for her living-room sofa that looks like this?'), then we have learned something about ourselves and what we think 'goes with what, how, when and where' and perhaps in the process Miss A is able to 'play with culture' (femininity, for example) and thus her self-identity, as well as perhaps something about her needlework world (who has she learned from, emulated, been inspired by, in dialogue with?). Through her furnishing activities, Miss A thus calls forth and maintains a world in which she is able to live, which is conducive to her wellbeing. By examining her aesthetic practices with the needle we have learned a great deal about how she operates and thus about the kind of world she literally stitches together, what she plays at within that world.

As already intimated, these practices come to be linked by others to attributes of identity. So, for example, Miss A is disciplined, practised, perhaps conservative, multi-talented, graceful, accomplished, deft with a needle, busy: all of which in turn form a higher order cluster of identifiers – in this case, perhaps, 'traditional' and 'feminine'. These identifiers may in turn provide the basis for bonding and bridging capital (Putnam 2000), insofar as Miss A's interests and hobbies may anchor her patterns of association with others. She may be closely affiliated with others who dance, with the local habitués of a needlework shop and with her dance class. It may be that her needlework class draws together participants from a wide range of backgrounds, all seeking to perfect their stitchery (bridging capital – she and the prison artist Materson may take part in a similar class or she may have been selected to join a masterclass with Materson). Within that group, the matter of how this stitchery should be applied (colour schemes, subject matter) may be hotly contended and yet the group bonds over the mutual appreciation of craft, dedication and technique. Conversely, her affiliation with piano-playing, for example, may fend off other potential affiliations (such as helping to prop up the bar after work on Thursday evenings because she has a piano lesson). Indeed, this is the well-recognized essence (and double-edged character) of bonding capital: ties both bind and, by virtue of binding, exclude some individuals and types of people and, to anticipate discussions to come, highlight how bonding capital may or may not also bridge people from very different backgrounds when they share an interest, Miss A and Materson, for example.

However her activities bind her to others, Miss A's pursuits have an impact upon her social space: they establish or seek to define the key values or peaks in the topology of her social world and, to the extent that they do, they make her world hospitable to her way of being. As topics, these pursuits may also furnish her mind, such that she finds herself going over in her head a certain passage of her piano piece for next week or imagining a new image to be embroidered on a pillow cover. This external/internal world then is one that easily offers her, Miss A, asylum (but is not necessarily conducive to the wellbeing of Miss B, Ms C or Mrs D) in both senses – escape, or sanctuary, and opportunities for refurnishing. The point here is that the self and personal wellbeing is nourished through the mobilization of resources that have varying degrees of legitimacy as viewed by others. The concept of asylum shows us how the use and manipulation of culture is about the preservation of self in everyday life and that is about how the background for figuration is compiled in and through action.

To be able to pursue such action, though, one must have access to further resources that enable the materials that create asylum to be appropriated. For Miss A, these resources include a piano, music and ballet lessons (and a family culture that valued and could afford such things), time, a particular body type (at least for the ballet), lots of thread, needles, scissors and linen, an embroidery hoop and, perhaps, clean, 'pretty' hands that can be displayed to advantage against the foil of needlework and on the keyboard of her piano (would cracked nails or some forms of nail decoration detract from the values associated with such work or, if combined with certain repertoire or subjects for needlework would they partially reconfigure the meaning of those pursuits?)

In this way, Miss A crafts simultaneously herself and the environment within which she operates (reflexive connection between agency and culture). This crafting involves the development and clustering of various factors into an assemblage of people and things, an actor-network perhaps (Latour 2006). The decorative hands, may in turn be read as belonging most fittingly in places where rough housework is not required. No one could reasonably ask Miss A to scrub a floor using a hand brush or attempt to bleach the grout in her shower (or could they and if so how?), though she might dust the ornaments on her mantelpiece. Her hands, embodied style and hobbies, thus afford and perhaps tacitly elicit some modes of conduct and deflect others which might literally chip away at the presentation of, for example, those delicate nails, that very gentle, feminine self.

Without the relative economic security enjoyed by Miss A, however, opportunities for asylum-seeking are or may be constrained. One might not, for example, have a choice in the matter of scrubbing floors (one's own or others'), and one might not have either time or money to afford a hobby such as ballet or piano. One might, for example, play a less expensive instrument, dance at clubs or outdoors or 'upcycling' (converting a used object into something more valuable than what it was when new). Because these activities involve more readily available (and indeed readily sustainable, democratically distributed) resources, they may garner less attention if specialness is equated with the ability to command resources (to the extent that specialness is equated with scarce resources). This is a theme I return to in Chapter 7.

Miss A would clearly score highly on a survey of cultural participation, if participation is assessed in relation to culture's conventional forms. But what counts, or could or should count, as cultural participation? Which media are acceptable, preferred or indeed even media qua media (versus wasting time or being destructive)? The answer to that question also involves setting it in context of local environments and thinking empirically about what counts in statistical terms, as participation. In their 2003 survey of cultural participation and consumption, Gayo-Cal, Savage and Warde found that there is, in the UK, a significant proportion of the population who would appear to be culturally disengaged (no participation/ preference for a variety of cultural activities and forms – music, art, literature, media, sport, leisure venues such as restaurants) – and that this proportion is far too great to be termed culturally excluded, marginal or 'out of the mainstream' (2006). (On the contrary, Gayo-Cal, Savage and Warde suggest that the culturally engaged are actually the minority.)

Gayo-Cal, Savage and Warde's work raises important questions about how these disengaged respondents might actually be spending their time. Might they be engaged in forms of cultural creation and thus re-furnishing, but forms of re-furnishing not currently captured by survey and/or interview methodology? For example, street art or graffiti (one might not willingly admit to engaging with this medium given its illegality and status [for some] as a nuisance) or hanging out and people-watching or sitting at home playing with the mobile phone or trying on clothes as a leisure pursuit or multiple forms of connectivity (texting, phoning, updating social network pages, taking part in online discussions about cultural media [Avdeef 2010]). So too, there may be other cultural pursuits one is unlikely to admit to, even if they are covered in a survey or interview (drugs and other forms of illegal activity being one example), and there may be forms of cultural practices such as samizdat, urban exploration or technological make-dos that involve some degree of covert practice (Goffman 1961; Hagen 2012; Hagen with DeNora 2011). Finally, if one is homeless or otherwise destitute, money and time may prohibit mainstream forms of cultural participation but also lead to alternative cultural/economic activities such as begging or scrounging. (There are many different ways one can ask for spare change, with different roles, discourses and communicative modalities involved.) In short, engaging these seemingly disparate activities may be world-making, expressive and a means for refurnishing worlds for asylum. In this context, the comprehensive portrait of UK cultural engagement and disengagement highlights how, in the UK, seemingly mainstream cultural forms are minority pursuits. It highlights how we need therefore need to address ourselves to what people are actually doing in the name of culture, and how these doings are part of their roles as makers (or evaders) of social worlds.

Formulating the Asylum Typology

To sum up the argument presented so far: on the one hand, asylums can be created through removal; they can offer protection against a distressing social world. As such, the asylum is a place for fantasy, day-dreaming and the recovery of personal time and rhythm. On the other hand, asylums can be created through refurnishing, and here they involve collaborative play that remakes or renegotiates social worlds. Refurnishing allows actors the latitude to be and act in certain ways, to feel at ease while so doing and to pursue various projects and trajectories that involve navigating (which is also the making of) social space/time. In both forms of asylum, individuals and groups can establish ontological security, a sense of at least partial control, opportunities for creativity, pleasure, self-validation, a sense of fitting comfortably into some space, scene or milieu, flow and focus. Where the strategies of removal and refurnishing differ lies in the relationship between actors and their environments. Actors engaged in refurnishing intervene and thus potentially affect environments: they are participatory agents who help to craft the world in which that they and others operate. Actors engaged in removal on the other hand are engaged in escaping environments that they experience negatively: they are removing themselves from noxious factors. To speak of the relationship between actors, asylums and the world of others seems to equate removal with the private realm and refurnishing with the public realm, but this equation is not quite right (I will return to this point below). For the time being, and to elaborate the differences more systematically between removal and refurnishing, I will retain the distinction between shared/negotiated versus individually located (and potentially unshared) rooms for being in the world. To clarify these distinctions, Table 3.1 contrasts removal and refurnishing along five axes: (1) what asylum is (2) how it is achieved (3) examples of techniques for achieving asylum (4) outcome of asylum-seeking activity and (5) potential risks associated with removals versus refurnishings.

The Psycho-Social Consequences of Removal and Refurnishing Understood as Ideal Types

In the case of both forms of asylum the end is the same: room or respite from irritant features of the environment, ontological security, control and creativity, pleasure, validation of self, sense of fit, flow, comfort, ease and a feeling of being in focus. The differences between these forms of asylum are linked to the strategies used for the creation of asylum. In the former, removals, actors seek to create distance from, to get away from the (irritating) world; while in the latter, refurnishings, actors seek to engage with and modify the world so as to make it more hospital, more conducive to being well and these strategies are exemplified in row three of Table 3.1.

Table 3.1   Removal and refurnishing

	Room through Removal	Room through Refurnishing
1. What asylum is	Room, ontological security, control and creativity, pleasure, validation of self, sense of fit, flow, comfort, ease, focus, temporal fit	Room, ontological security, control and creativity, pleasure, validation of self, sense of fit, flow, comfort, ease, focus, temporal fit
2. How asylum is achieved	Withdrawing from interaction and shared media; space is place for getting away from, being screened, buffered, diverted, protected	Involvement with/ manipulation and appropriation of shared media; space is place for adaptation, negotiation, innovation, expression, performance
3. Examples of techniques for achieving asylum	Fantasy, reading, sleeping, travel (relational since may enter new environment elsewhere), privately pursued craft activities (knitting, poetry writing [unshared]) solo sports, meditation, various forms of consumption (food, alcohol, drugs, consumer goods, health and beauty services, gambling, TV and radio, films, theatre, concerts)	Conversation, dress, policy-making (formal or informal, as in clubs or friendship groups), group activities (dining, sports, clubs or informal social gatherings), organized religion, participatory arts activities (choirs, bands, amateur theatricals, reading clubs), adult education classes, cookery crafts, gardening, housework and decorating, blogging and discussion lists
4. Outcome of asylum seeking activity	Respite, relief, recovery of self, time out from social spaces where one needs to perform/act; no transformation of socially shared spaces; no gain of resources for next call to act (capacity for action) in shared space with/of others	Respite, relief, recovery of self, association, more engagement with/in social spaces where one needs to perform/act; transformation of socially shared spaces; gain of resources for next call to act (capacity for action) in shared space with/of others
5. Potential risks	Alienation, atrophy of social skills and/or influence in shared space, decoupling from worlds with others, shrinking social presence ('taking too little space' or 'not able/not recognized as able to claim space')	Egotism, over-assertiveness, symbolic violence to others; dominion over some form of space or media/resource ('attention-seeking', 'talks too much' or 'is overly directive')

The outcomes of these strategies diverge in important ways. While both removals and refurnishings can create room and respite for wellbeing, the former do not transform the world (whether to make it, negatively, less irritating or, positively, more conducive, for example, more beautiful or easier to navigate). It is this transformative capacity that creates a form of sustainability by producing resources that can be used next time round. Removals, therefore, risk diminished returns since, eventually, one must re-enter the (unchanged) environment from which one initially sought respite. The social implications and social consequences associated with removal activities deserve further attention.

To the extent that they remove, such activities remain separate from that world and thus have to be pursued in, as it were, private time or time out from others. Upon return from being removed (finishing reading the book or watching the DVD, sobering up), the actor returns to a world of others that is no different and perhaps as irritating, disturbing or disabling as ever, perhaps even more so if one feels guilt, discomfort or has to catch up upon re-entry to the everyday world. Thus, a negative spiral may be formed, whereby the actor becomes increasingly distant from and debilitated in the world where she or he must act with others and increasingly prone to search for respite (asylum) outside that world. In this sense, the 'public' is a realm that involves, simultaneously, potential confrontation and potential negotiation of desegregated, shared spaces for asylum, spaces, moreover which actors can assist each other to enter and to make use of resources for asylum without isolation or sequestering.

I have now set out the ideal types of removal and refurnishing. But how do these types work out in actual social life? Is the distinction between public and private forms of asylum valid in terms of what people actually do with culture? This question prompts further development and a more nuanced conceptualization of removals and refurnishings, one that queries the removal = private / refurnishing = public dichotomy.

What is Public and What is Private in Everyday Life?

In practice, the public and the private are by no means mutually exclusive terrains (where does the public sphere end, the private sphere begin and who determines this distinction?). So too, removal and refurnishing activities are by no means necessarily distinct. (This point reminds us that we need to conceptualize cultural participation in ways that do not predefine what is and is not cultural.) One might, for example, seek to refurnish a shared space so that one establishes a 'corner in which to hide' (and so refurnishing creates a means for removal). Conversely, refurnishing activity may begin as an act of removal. Imagine, for example, a cluster of individuals at a pub who take their drinks outside to avoid the pub's background music. If additional people join them and also comment they do not care for the music, a group begins to be formed. That is, this cluster of people may begin to perceive itself as a group with a shared taste or sensibility, different from the group inside ('Look at how many of us are out here because we don't like this restaurant's background music!'). Thus what began as removal may become a statement and object lesson about how to exist within and in relation to a space or scene, and, to the extent that this translation occurs, removal is recast as a form of refurnishing.

The mutual determination of removal and refurnishing raises in turn a second issue – how small can a public sphere be? This question has recently been explored in relation to religious groups where it has been suggested that the voices that make up the public sphere may, 'come from micro public spheres that are "bottom-up, small scale" public spheres consisting of maybe "dozens, hundreds or thousands" of people' (McCallum 2011: 179, quoting Keane 1998: 170). McCallum also draws upon Gerard Hauser (1998) to describe a reticulate public sphere, 'composed of organisations, groups, movements, and circles' which in turn influence what we then speak of as a 'meso-public sphere' (McCallum 2011: 178).

As McCallum observed, Hauser is willing to consider a micro-public sphere as occurring, 'wherever two or more people "exchange views on a public concern, some portion of the public sphere is made manifest in their conversation"' (McCallum 2011: 64, quoting Hauser 1998). So, for example, the people who have come out of the pub, in the example just discussed, because they disliked its background music, may begin to comment to one another on how 'background music ought to be banned'. As such, they are acting in concert to refurnish (a part of) the world. They have discovered an alternate set of values and thus a (small) form of mutual empowerment. In this case, the social ecology of what is happening inside the pub is partially eclipsed (for these actors) in favour of a different space where these actors (but not the those who have remained indoors) feel increasingly at home. Through this small form of banding together, the wider world may be inflected in new ways and, depending upon the scope and momentum of such bandings alternative realities – new worlds – may form. Such is the stuff of counter-cultural movements.

The questions of when and where something private (an event or encounter, for example) begins and ends and what counts as private versus public activity, or indeed as a category of activity associated with the labels 'private' or 'public', are central to cultural and critical sociology. For example, what is deemed to be an intimate form of ritual interaction may be highly impersonal and de-localized (Collins 2004: 229). Conversely, the seemingly most impersonal realm of interactions between strangers or acquaintances may nonetheless contain forms of nuanced intimacy that commonsense dictates occur only between lovers or close family (Hiscock 2007; Morgan 2009). These mundane and often fleeting connections can make links between strangers in ways that not only counter isolation but – in small ways – politicize them and draw them together in ways that help to raise consciousness of social conditions (Goldfarb 2006).

The personal or intimate can be nested in the impersonal, clinical/professional and in ways that draw strangers together in often highly intimate – though not sexual – ways. When a visiting nurse, for example, shows exquisite care and courtesy in handling a client, when we speak of how he/she lovingly attends to the minute features of an elderly patient's bedsore in ways that involve situation-specific and highly personal modalities, such as tone of voice, touch, warmth or smoothness of hands and mutual disclosures, it is possible to see how private and public roles meld together in everyday practice. ('I did this for my own mother, Mrs X' she or he tells the patient, while training family members in the care and treatment of such wounds.) Here the nurse's instantiated performance of his or her craft makes use of cultural practices that exceed the formal (in this case institutional) definition of the situation; his or her performance of dressing a wound takes that task beyond the medical realm into a much more personal and private, intimate domain that transcends textbook accounts of wound dressing. Significantly in this case, however, the nurse's performance of wound dressing may also seek to, or come to, refurnish medical understanding of how to offer 'best practice': intimate involvement in a patient's particular wound may highlight the importance of bespoke attention to medical phenomena.

This last example also highlights some of the ways in which the ostensible definition of a space as public/private, impersonal/personal, virtual/real is flexible and open to inflection. This inflection may, at least sometimes, dramatically redefine the normative and aesthetic quality of social space. Thus, as with the asylum concept, so too the more general concept of social space requires re-specification. We need a concept of social space that allows us to consider how spaces are appropriated and re-appropriated, how they can be nested one within another, how they can be converted, sometimes in an instant from one sort of space to another. The same space, situation or form of encounter may take on different hues, temperatures and textures as it is figured temporally and through various techniques.

Therefore, just as the asylum concept itself had to be separated from the physical bricks and mortar of the hospital building, so too can the concepts of public and private space be separated from specific locations, institutional occasions and encounters. They are rather, I suggest, better understood and examined as malleable, indeed, often interpenetrating realms, and, thus, the status of what are deemed to be refurnishing versus removal activities are also malleable: we are back at the critical core of Goffman's *Asylums*. It is possible to consider how particular, situated understandings of what counts as a public asylum (shared negotiation of space) versus a private asylum (removal or escape from space) is achieved and modified in interaction.

As Bourdieu put it so eloquently in an article titled, 'Social Space and the Genesis of Groups', spaces are structured and become social topologies,

> because the schemes of perception and appreciation available for use at the moment in question, especially those that are deposited in language, are the product of previous symbolic struggles and express the state of the symbolic power relations, in a more or less transformed form. The objects of the social world can be perceived and uttered in different ways because, like objects in

the natural world, they always include a degree of indeterminacy and fuzziness – owing to the fact, for example, that even the most constant combinations of properties are only founded on statistical connections between interchangeable features; and also because, as historical objects, they are subject to variations in time so that their meaning, insofar as it depends on the future, is itself in suspense, in waiting, dangling, and therefore relatively indeterminate. This element of play, of uncertainty, is what provides a basis for the plurality of worldviews, itself linked to the plurality of points of view, and to all the symbolic struggles for the power to produce and impose the legitimate world-view and, more precisely, to all the cognitive 'filling-in' strategies that produce the meaning of the objects of the social world by going beyond the directly visible attributes by reference to the future or the past. This reference may be implicit and tacit ... or it may be explicit, as in political struggles, in which the past – with retrospective reconstruction of a past tailored to the needs of the present ('La Fayette, here we are') – and especially the future, with creative forecasting, are endlessly invoked, to determine, delimit, and define the always open meaning of the present. (Bourdieu 1985: 727–8)

At issue, then, is the question of how the public, or shared realm, and the private, or individuated realm, is postulated and assembled and how actors come to recognize aspects of their lives as private or public in the first place. This recognition will be linked to actors' capacities to be well, to feel secure and to be empowered within settings in time. To establish something as public (small, large or in-between) is nothing less than a bid for recognition and empowerment in everyday life.

Here we come to the crux of the issue (and the moral heart) of *Asylums*, the theme that also underscores Goffman's irony. For if the capacity for refurnishing is a means for assuring one's wellbeing, then a constraint on the opportunity to pursue refurnishing activities is a threat to wellbeing. Thus, the social structure and distribution of resources and opportunities for furnishing the world is of critical importance to wellbeing. Goffman is both clear and full of compassion when he considers the question of opportunities and resources for refurnishing and their social distribution. A key point in *Asylums* deals with the tautological situation that actors placed in totalizing situations have the most need and the least opportunity for asylum-seeking. The ironic use of the term 'asylums' in this context has been the subject of some commentary over the years (Burns 2002: 141). It highlights actors as, with constrained resources, they make do and otherwise scavenge for resources with which to engage in refurbishment:

> When a patient, whose clothes are taken from him each night, fills his pockets with bits of string and rolled up paper, and when he fights to keep these possessions in spite of the consequent inconvenience to those who must regularly go through his pockets, he is usually seen as engaging in symptomatic behavior befitting a very sick patient, not as someone who is attempting to stand apart from the place accorded him. (Goffman 1961: 307)

That this observation is ironic is linked to the fact that these attempts to make do are launched on an individual, and thus idiosyncratic, basis. If the patient who collects string were to collude with like-minded others, or if she or he were to gain attention and admiration for what she or he does from others, she or he would no longer appear quite so sick. If patients were able to organize themselves in this manner, it would be difficult to say that they had a problem in living, instead, one would need to say that they have a problem in living like we do, which shifts the identity politics from health to culture and illuminates the issue of the right to play. Thus, the sociology of mental health needs to consider the social structure of how actors do or do not adapt and coordinate with others and how this adaptation is linked to opportunities for refurnishing, playing or otherwise participating in the negotiation of one's world and, thus, selves. Mental health is a problem that perhaps should best be understood as our problem in living, and this may be linked to our need to accommodate diversity and difference.

Conclusion: The Social Consequences of Asylum-Seeking Strategies

Goffman sought to avoid prejudice concerning actors' asylum-seeking strategies. He would, had he been considering cultural consumption outside the Asylum, have been cautious before pronouncing on whether cultural activities were or were not worthwhile. He was overwhelmingly compassionate in *Asylums* ('it ... is my belief that any group of persons ... develops a life of their own that becomes meaningful, reasonable, and normal once you get close to it, and that a good way to learn about any of these worlds is to submit oneself in the company of the members to the daily round of petty contingencies to which they are subject' [Goffman 1961: ix–x]). Yet, despite his compassion, Goffman never romanticized acts such as the string-collecting he describes (as if they were merely misunderstood). On the contrary, he observed the paradoxical character of these acts.

On the one hand, such activities (notwithstanding their pathological interpretations) enable inmates to make an attempt at being culturally expressive and creative ('See my string collection? Let me tell you how I choose which string to collect'). They open up possibilities for remaking the environment and they provide an object or fetish through which to hold on to things (attitudes, memories, stances or beliefs, for example). On the other hand, when the materials that resource attempts at refurnishing are perceived by others (or by the others who are in a position to deem and pronounce) as lacking legitimacy within the social world, then the attempt to find asylum fails in ways that rebound negatively upon the inmate. 'She or he must be crazy: witness how they keep all that junk around them and on their person!'

If such activities are not perceived to be legitimate by observers, and if those observers have the symbolic or physical power whereby they can destroy inmates attempts to create personal asylum, then the political negotiation of the status of these forms of asylum (as legitimate, conventional, sanctioned) is denied and the forms of asylum imperiled or at least made insecure. Thus, unlike Miss A, who has a whole drawer-full of coloured embroidery thread, the inmate who makes a collection of string for its own sake is not engaging in a conventionally recognized hobby and the activity thus poses risks of censure and further stigma. (Though of course, as in the case of Ray Mateson, who initially obtained his thread by unravelling his socks, if the collection can be demonstrated to be part of a more complex assemblage; for example, if the inmate unravels a sock and begins to sew tapestries, and other inmates or staff or external collectors of outsider art credit that unravelling and stitching as worthy, it is possible to build a refurnishing activity out of, initially, very little and scavenged materials [for parallels, see Hagen 2012; on make-dos in underground musical culture Eastern Europe, see Hagen with DeNora 2011].)

Moreover, because of the risk of stigma that one may incur by making do, an actor may decide to relinquish the refurnishing attempts, in which case she or he also relinquishes the implicit claim to space for self that refurnishing sought to secure. She or he may decide, instead, to stick with removal activities, to make room from distress through private activities such as excessive day-dreaming, solipsistic rituals which may seem to outsiders like forms of obsession, DIY forms of body-modification and/or self harm or over-reliance upon substances such as nicotine, alcohol, food or legal/illegal drugs, with which to find room or, rather, to block out the room in which one lives.

While these practices may or may not be harmful (and many are subject to heated debate on that issue), they may be understood to be harmful in a social sense. This is to say that removal activities, by definition, do not seek to invest in the environment and thus they cannot be grown by subscription and through collaboration. Thus, they cannot become transformative actions and, when they end, they deliver the actor back to the irritating world, a world that may even seem to be lying in wait. Returning on such a basis may heighten vulnerability (actors are less equipped to protect themselves and to function in the world and with others) and place actors in danger of mortification, for Goffman the ultimate form of symbolic violence. How then to effect removal in ways that will not too readily bring with them stigma and that are also able to transform or mollify environments (removing the sources of distress rather than removing oneself from distressful circumstances) and thus make them more habitable? We are now in a position to consider music as a way of making room for being well.

Chapter 4

Music Asylums, Part I:
Disconnections, Reconnections and Removal

To speak about music as creating room, whether by furnishing or through removal, is also to speak about musically inflected space. Some of the most powerful work to date on the concept of space has come from music sociology and sound studies, in particular as those fields have examined the situated uses of sound technologies. A number of recent works have considered how musical and sonic media enable individuals and collectivities to redraw the boundaries between public and private spheres (Bijkersveld and Pinch 2011; Born 2012; Cook et al. 2009; Gopinath and Stanyek forthcoming; Rice 2010). Music and sound can change the relationship between public and private experience, and they can change the locations available for this experience. The iconic image of this change is the urban dweller, using a public transport system while privately cocooned in an iPod-facilitated, individualized sonic space wherein the private is nested in the public (Bull 2007). But music, and more generally sound, has always been used to inflect space. It was always possible for example, to whistle while you work, to sing a lullaby or a protest song. While the voice may be the mobile musical device par excellence (it is the instrument that is built in to the human body), armies have marched to the beat of a drum for centuries. So too the more general medium of sound or quasi-music such as bells, foghorns or sirens used to inflect and signify, to warn and to remind.

Thus, in some respects, music recording and playback technologies simply enhance forms of sonic dissociation and sonic furnishing that have gone on for centuries. In other respects, however, digital technologies have transformed the ways in which music comes to inflect space. First, digitization gives rise to music's ubiquity. Second, while the layering and nesting of public and private was and is always possible through pre-digital and non-musical means, through secret relationships, fantasy and day-dreaming ('I am here at work, but my thoughts are miles away') digitized music, coupled with miniaturization (iPods and iPads, MP3 players, smart phones), offers many more possibilities for musically inflecting and managing space and thus, in the process, for seeking musical asylum.

As scholars such as Michael Bull have observed, when we seek in public to renegotiate or reclaim space, that reclamation takes place primarily through auditory channels (2007: 4). (In earlier times remediating the smells of places was also much more common; for example, the scented handkerchief held to the nose or the wearing of pomanders and fragrant herbs [Classen 1994: 60].) We are rarely in a position to rearrange the built environment of, say, a shopping center or a transport hub, but we can alter its auditory features, erasing or cancelling out its soundscape and substituting sounds of our own choosing. We can, in short, remediate space through our use of personal listening technologies. This remediation, as Bull so aptly described, helps us to cope with the stresses and unpleasant features endemic to urban life. I shall suggest that these devices function in various ways that can be understood as asylum-creating, though I will also offer a critical examination of the forms of asylum they offer in light of the perspective developed in Chapters 2 and 3.

The vision of urban life that is typically evoked in discussions of mobile musicking is the idea of a landscape of strangers (Simmel 1903), architecturally cold and denuded of resources and textures. This vision is one that reappears in the work of Sennett, where urban life is envisioned as anonymous, cold and disconcerting, a 'chilly' place (1974: 9). It also dichotomizes: it poses concepts such as *Gemeinschaft* versus *Gesellschaft*, micro versus macro, personal versus anonymous, public versus private. It contrasts the warmth of, the proximate, the inclusive with the chill of the distant and the exclusive as found in airports, shopping malls and motorway conveniences. The seemingly middle ground, the world of acquaintances (Morgan 2009), is not acknowledged in this vision.

In his work on mobile musicking, Bull is quick to observe that this stark picture of urban life, which too neatly distinguishes between place (identity-linked) and space (non-place, devoid of meaning) is over-determined (2000, 2007). (It also tends to caricature classic social theory, see Inglis 2009.) By contrast, Bull suggests that such a dichotomy contributes to, 'minimalizing the subjective response of subjects to the spaces they transit through' (2007: 15). Mobile musicking, according to Bull, enables subjects to transform spaces into places (to privatize space) dematerializing and dislocating the sense of place (2007: 4).

As I have already suggested with reference to the interpenetration of private and public (and the focus on local cultures in Chapter 2), there can be other, more collaborative means by which private and public come to be mutually elaborated and, as described above, nested and translated – and in quick time. Thinking about this issue recovers spaces as perhaps not nearly so chilly (that is, as requiring the warmth that personal listening adds) as Bull, Sennett, Simmel and Augé suggest. The chill is less readily perceived if we consider public spaces in terms of their actual uses. When we do, we find – once again – that everyday life defies theoretical compartmentalization. There is a middle ground that is neither private nor public which is collaboratively produced through appropriation and re-appropriation of space. This production consists of ways of inflecting space and in a manner far removed from the sonic cocooning associated with private iPod listening.

To take a simple example, shopping centres are not, for all individuals and everywhere, anonymous, cold and soulless. For aficionados, they certainly do not all look alike. Moreover, they do not necessarily atomize. Some people and some groups love shopping centres for what they afford (which is not necessarily what they offer for sale). (Two such groups are young skateboarders, who congregate in and around mall spaces, and the elderly, who favor American shopping malls for their morning exercise because such spaces are climate controlled, safe and level-grounded places where one can exercise, push a Zimmer frame or wheelchair easily, meet friends, stop for a coffee and, importantly, feel secure.) In this sense, the individualized listening practices employed by Bull's respondents, the solitude associated with these practices, and the concern with gaining control over the rhythm of one's day, may be age-linked – the median age of Bull's respondents was 34 (see Bergh, DeNora and Bergh forthcoming).

I will return again to the 'middle' ground later on in this chapter, when I consider collaborative musical 'furnishing' activities as asylum-creating practices. For now, the point is that Bull's work has highlighted mobile listening devices as technologies for the care of self, highlighting the importance of music use to sustaining a sense of coherence and thus ontological security in daily life (Ruud 2002, 2005, 2008). Despite the fact that this work highlights essentially lonely (individualized and thus often acritical) solutions to the problem of health maintenance and health recovery (and ones that in turn augment modern Western notions of the individual and unique person [Becker 2010: 13; Geertz 1983; Taylor 1989]), it has been of enormous value, and for at least three reasons.

First, it describes the practices and personal strategies for avoiding stress and for feeling 'at home' in strange or hostile environments (Skånland 2011). Second, it highlights the importance to wellbeing of normative dissociation (Herbert 2011), namely that most individuals need time out from daily life, time in which to day-dream, meditate, trance, remember and generally rejuvenate/refresh by stepping outside normative demands and frames. Third, by showing us the circumstances under which individuals use personal listening as a form of dissociation or escape, it highlights some of the environmental factors that lead to distress. How, then, should we conceive of the asylum-creating features of personal music listening?

The Asylum-Pod

Bull's investigations highlight the iPod as both a 'gating' (protective filtering) and a 'tethering' (continual connectivity) technology. In these ways, mobile listening reduces some of the disruption caused by an otherwise polyrhythmic environment, as one encounters, as it were, too much contingency in the rough and tumble of dealing with one's environment. Put slightly differently, the iPod can be used to redefine and reclaim space (and situated meanings), making spaces more habitable, supportive, nurturing and conducive to individuals' sensibilities, tastes and courses of action. So for example, if I am listening to ambient relaxation music, I may be able to transcend what are otherwise routine responses to my environment. If I am in a crowded underground station, I may revise the meaning of what I see in this scene: the music may help me to look afresh at what is happening. My chosen soundtrack may enable me to shift role, from participant (harried, late, elbowing my way on to an underground train) to observer (*flâneur*, zen-like watcher of human flow at rush hour). The scene around me comes to be reframed (aestheticized) as a form of modern dance: a stance, it goes without saying, that simultaneously flatters and empowers me, as it converts me into a member of a highly select audience of one. 'Otherness', as Bull puts it, is negated (2007: 49).

In this example, music effects a form of displacement: it distances me from the setting within which I am and it reconfigures my role in ways that allow me to rise above (virtually) the matters taking place on the ground. In this sense, personal listening permits dissociation. (One of Bull's informants put it: 'When I plug in and turn on, my iPod does a "ctrl+alt+delete" on my surroundings and allows me to "be" somewhere else' [Bull 2007: 9].) Music has redefined the situation. I have just described how my orientation will change through this distancing and with it, very probably, my emotional orientation (I may feel more detached, calmer, more critically oriented to the scene, more observant of detail). So too, there may be changes in my embodied state. My heart rate may decrease, there may be shifts in my galvanic skin response and hormone levels, my blood pressure may shift, probably lowering. I am now, body, heart and mind, at one remove from the space (and its hitherto negative connotations).

I may also use my private soundtrack to cancel unwanted noises and sounds. On a train, ironically, this includes the sounds of other people's music – we are all recursively blocking out the sounds of our blocking out each others' sounds. I may also seek to avoid disruptive conversations, the sound of announcements and advertisements and, indeed, background music, muzak and other site-specific sonic programming. I may use my soundtrack, in other words, simply to avoid some other soundtrack and as a basic strategy with which to establish and retain control over the place where I am and may have to remain. In itself, this control is a significant feature of health maintenance and a basic feature of what makes something into an asylum in the sense that I am seeking to develop that term. Here, it may not be anything in particular about my chosen music. It may be simply that it is a way for me to show – to myself perhaps more than to others – that I am enough of an agent to be able to make such a choice. I may, for example, wear my headphones or earbuds even when I am listening to nothing, much as people have feigned sleep or reading to avoid having to engage with others nearby.

The iPod shelters, it remediates public reality, cocoons its users in the comforting fabric of self-chosen sound but, as Bull observes, simultaneously isolates and privatizes its users who 'never willingly interact with others whilst engaged in solitary listening' (2007: 50). Harking back to the potential risks associated with removal practices outlined at the start of this chapter, it would seem that the social costs of this form of asylum may be high indeed as Bull suggests:

> Sound colonises the listener but is used to actively recreate and configure the spaces of experience. Through the power of sound the world becomes intimate, known and possessed.
>
> Technology has empowered the ears – it has turned the ears from the most democratic of the senses ... to the most exclusive. This empowerment is embodied in the earphones, which supplant the uncontrollable and chaotic noise

of the street with the chosen sounds of the individual consumer. The price of technologically mediated empowerment is privatization. (Bull 2007: 21)

Personal listening affords the gaining of distance from stimuli and features of the environment that are distressing, unpleasant, depressing or otherwise disruptive. It removes its users from the presence of irritant audio data, it remediates environments through sonic- and music-led forms of perceptual recalibration and reorientation (I return to this point in the next chapter). But personal listening is also, by definition, a highly individualized solution to the problem of wellbeing.

Musical Enchantment

According to Bull:

> The aesthetic appropriation of urban space becomes one cognitive strategy as users attempt to create a seamless web of mediated and privatized experience in their everyday movement through the city, enhancing virtually any chosen experience in any geographical location at will. In doing so they create an illusion of omnipotence through mediated proximity and 'connectedness' engendered by the use of their iPod. (Bull 2007: 40)

So, for example, 35-year-old 'Jason' describes how when listening to his iPod he is able to project the lyrical content of songs on to the people he sees around him:

> I was looking at some of the people standing around me in a coffee shop, with the look of anxiety on their faces and general angst. It made me want to hug them and tell them it's OK. ... I would look at other people and they would smile at me, almost like they knew what I was thinking. ... It's almost like watching a movie, but you're in it. ...
>
> Sometimes I think I can calm people down just by looking at them when I'm listening to music. (Bull 2007: 41)

Social psychologists have shown us how music filters our perception of environmental stimuli, how it provides a mediating influence that reshapes our perceptions according to its images. As the psychologists of music have demonstrated, music can provide a frame against which other sensory stimuli come to be contextualized and perceived, for example, in the retail environment music may prime purchase behaviour (Areni and Kim 1993; North and Hargreaves 1997), in work-related scenarios music may condition workers' emotions and motivation (Pieslak 2009) or, in public spaces, music may reframe the implicit understandings of who and/or what belongs in a space (DeNora 2000). Through these forms of musical contextualization, aspects of the environment are musically mediated/

remediated and enhanced. In this respect, the personal stereo may be understood as a prosthetic mental device: it extends the capacity to fantasize and to perceive one's surroundings. Musical enhancement is, in effect, musical enchantment. It is achieved through the ways that music, when it inflects environments, provides a filter through which contextual cues come to be identified and selected. It both hones perception and reconfigures that perception in ways that take on its properties.

Non-Negotiable = Non-Shared = Alienated = Unsustainable?

But what of the social and technological bases of this enchantment? If a look on the face of a stranger is read in musically inflected ways, and if that reading is not shared by anyone else at the scene of the reading, how sustainable is such a health-promoting practice? There is, for example, no validity check (which itself is less about assuring a correct reading than a negotiation of what will count as a reading), no attempt to coordinate interpretive activity with others: the environment is 'read only' from within the iPod zone, the sonic cocoon or place of removal. Individually 'gated' users are thus an atomized group connected to individual iPods and, conversely, disconnected from each other. While this disconnection/connection may indeed help individuals cope with individual situations and recurrent problems (such as a distressing commute), such disconnection may present disadvantages in terms of its sustainability and the diminishing returns it poses for engagement with the environment and thus for the possibility of making a environment more conducive to wellbeing so that one feels less need to escape.

This extreme solipsism, a strategy for keeping the world at bay, is paradoxically experienced as connectivity. For Bull's respondent Jason, it carries him through an otherwise dreary, less emotionally laden form of experience. It is, in short, mood enhancing. As with other forms of removal activity, however, the enhanced sense of wellbeing provided by this type of asylum pod is dependent upon remaining insulated from the world outside the pod. At its most basic, this insulation may lead to dangerous forms of sensory deprival (not hearing traffic, for example) and to hearing loss associated with too high volume levels, but, beyond this, the asylum pod may under some conditions be unsustainable or costly to sustain: for example, batteries may run out and not be rechargeable or there may be no access to the web and hence no opportunity to locate music or one may have access but not the means by which to download music or share it, via a docking station, with others. A device may break, earbuds may be misplaced or such devices may simply be banned from places, such as they are in hospitals, class-rooms and many workplaces. In short, the device establishes certain forms of user-dependency.

Under conditions such as these, when music stops (or is prohibited), users are vulnerable and required to re-enter real life and perhaps with fewer skills for the negotiation of real life. There are dangers associated with relying on technology as a way to smooth one's world. But there are also missed opportunities.

Do Artefacts have Politics?

First, remaining sonically gated means that one is immured from opportunities that the environment itself might afford for pleasure, respite and, indeed, rebuilding and politicization. For example, imagine an environment full of some type of offensive noise – perhaps the sound of someone drilling, hoovering or hammering nearby, or even some form of background music that one finds, perhaps many find, irritating. Once the noise-cancelling headphones are in place, one may not know if the offending sound ceases. Conversely, while without the headphones, one may be subject to irritation, one also misses the moment of relief when the offending sound/noise stops or is replaced. But beyond this individual pleasure, one might also miss that relief as a shared moment with others (one might turn to someone in the vicinity and smile, gesture, perhaps even comment 'That's better') and as such gain a sense of empowerment – one is not alone in finding this offensive, in wanting to prevent it from happening again or one might comment on how, 'Finally they're playing some good music', and with this sense, this mini-communication, one might also feel that the environment is not so bad after all – it gave something of pleasure and thus it might not be quite such a bad place to be another time. A good experience with others, even if fleeting, can recontextualize the environment and its inhabitants in ways that galvanize actors as activists (social, aesthetic, micro-political) next time around. That recontextualization may also extend to features of the environment that were hitherto perceived as unpleasant, distressing or otherwise negative (refurnishing). It is through processes such as these, where small acts of engagement may simultaneously build skills for engagement and enhance the actor's tolerance of what was hitherto strange or distasteful (things in the real world outside of their control). As these skills and tolerances develop, so too can tastes and tolerance for tastes, such that it becomes possible to appreciate new things, including new forms of music and environmental sounds and thus develops the capacity for aesthetic engagement with the world of others. (I describe an example of how broadened tastes are linked to broadened capacities for social interaction and orientation through the case study of 'Peter', in Chapter 5.) In the gated world of the iPod (at least when the technologies are used in the ways they were designed for – see below) this form of aesthetic development is not possible.

Second, being removed from the external sonic environment also means that one is deprived of opportunities to connect ('Sorry, I didn't hear what it was you said'). If one finds, at least occasionally, features in the shared environment that offer asylum (musical or other), alienated is slightly diminished. These little moments of connection are chinks in the armour of an otherwise privatized existence, thin ends of wedges that can be driven into relations in public to foster refurnishing (reforming, reprioritizing). These small things are the cobbles from which pathways are laid into the social world and away from isolation.

One does not have to fully reject the world and seek refuge in a world of one's own making in the solitary (aesthetic) confinement in one's asylum pod. Indeed, and this point is vital to the rationale for music therapy, sometimes individuals are not able, on their own, to locate sonic resources that can make it better: simply issuing an iPod (and recommended play list) on prescription is, in this context, trivial (and potentially dangerous: 'We gave you the music that's good for you, now try to cheer up!'). On the contrary, sometimes individuals require assistance, if music is to help, and this assistance is less therapy and more a musical being with others – to make it better (Ansdell forthcoming; Pavlicevic and Ansdell 2004). It is here that musical activity with others (controlled collaborative musical furnishing or refurnishing) comes into play – socially and musically things can be achieved which, for the individual acting alone, may have been impossible, and this is where music therapy can help.

For example, reconsider the case of Pam and Gary, quoted in the preface to this book: what Pam could not do for herself, even in the presence of various musical instruments and options, was achievable in collaboration with someone else who, for a moment, was directive (in this case a music therapist). Together, they identified and collaborated within a musical modality that in turn transformed mood and conduct. This action was, quite literally, in concert (for a detailed discussion of this example, see DeNora 2013a).

New technologies (personal computers, iPads, phones, mobile music devices) continue to have an impact upon relations in public in ways that drive privatization and gating. Simultaneously, they may be preventing minute and often split-second opportunities for mutual aid. The increasingly blurred area between virtual and real (people who are present but absent in physical space because they are connected, or tethered, to displaced others through smart phones and personal entertainment systems) grows. It is further fed by the ever-increasing forms of personless processes (automatic or electronic check-in at airports, automatic scanning devices, automatic check-out services in supermarkets). Artefacts, as Langdon Winner put it, 'have politics' in the (ecological) sense that their presence and use may imply and be associated with socio-political arrangements (1980). In the case of mobile music devices, those arrangements are double-edged. As with removal activities in general, as I discussed in Chapter 3, on the one hand, they offer amelioration, on the other, they offer alienation.

Again, these politics are not inflexible, not inherent. Even privatizing technologies do not necessarily need to be used in the ways for which they were designed and, because most research on the use of personal stereos has focused on the over-18s, certain key points have been overlooked. When we consider younger people, the picture changes. It is possible to see personal listening in terms of its more social role as part of the furnishing of spaces for action.

For example, in a study of young people's use of private music listening devices, Arild Bergh, his 15-year-old daughter, Maia, and I found that young people reconfigured, adapted and tinkered with iPods in ways that shifted the iPod's social implications. Through shared earbuds and more use of docking stations for MP3 and iPod players, young teens used music to consolidate friendship groups and to debate issues relevant to/constitutive of their function as a micro-public sphere. As part of this constitution, shared iPod listening afforded new communicative modes and new categories of meaning and experience (Bergh, DeNora and Bergh forthcoming), including folksonomy understandings of musical genres and their relation to aspects, realms and activities in everyday life. In particular, music sharing afforded opportunities for discussing value and for 'claiming' styles and genres in ways that appropriated them as emblematic of particular values, groups or action styles, rather in the ways that Roy has described genres are claimed by actors in the public sphere of music criticism and the media (his case study [2010] examines the reconstruction of the meaning of folk music in the USA between 1930 and 1980).

In the study by Bergh, DeNora and Bergh (forthcoming), respondents classified music in terms of social activities ('The perfect music for a sunny afternoon'). These grounded classifications highlighted how, for these young music listeners, music was expressly linked to aesthetic ecology and its formation, to moods or vibes, styles of action, emotional requirements and sensibilities associated with, different places, spaces, activities and temporal locations (riding a bike, summer versus winter, night versus morning, getting ready for a party). These classifications were, for these young people, part of the equipment necessary for their production of themselves as aesthetic agents, reflexively, in relation to these classifications and thus how music, along with its understandings are part of the furnishing of social ecology, linked both to forms of action and action's times and possible territories (summer, late night, cycling, early morning and so on).

These alternative understandings of music's place and meaning are empowering, because they arise from and validate personal and local, collective experience. They are thus part of these young people's informal, situated learning about music (Green 2002, 2008), which is nothing less than learning how to use music to articulate values and realities in the world, to consolidate patterns of action in and on that world. Music that is thick for example, is allied with other concepts and patterns of action, it firms up or musically frames that action and thus empowers the actor by enhancing the sense of rightness or fit between action and environment. At the same time, the coupling of music with experience enables these young people to assert (homegrown) understandings of things other than music and to test general assertions about reality against personal experience. Discussions about music then become ethically charged as discussions about those worlds, what is in them, what should be in them and what should not be in them. In this way, music is a medium of world-making that binds. As one respondent put it, music 'can make you feel less alone if you're like part of all the people who listen to this music and stuff' (Bergh, DeNora and Bergh forthcoming).

So privatized forms of music listening are, for the generation who were born into the era of the mobile music device, a tool for sociability and a medium of world furnishing. Of course, taste is, as Hennion has described, one of those 'things that hold us together' (2007), but mobile music extends music's flexible role as a medium of world-maintenance because of the physical, exploratory and storage conveniences of mobile music devices.

Similarly, other studies have highlighted some of the potentially numerous ways in which technologies of private music listening can be adapted for public sharing, for example, flash mobs (Bergh and DeNora 2009). Further possibilities offered by computer supported distribution technologies blend private and public modes of music consumption in ways that offer new opportunities for control over the public or quasi-public musical space (O'Hara and Brown 2006).

In short, personal music listening is undoubtedly a medium for self-care. It is a form of asylum, in particular a removal activity. Personal music listening offers a room in which to recharge one's batteries, avoid noxious stimuli in the immediate environment and dream, play and otherwise engage with an alternate world. Sometimes, as with the example of young teenagers and the ways they adapt personal listening technologies, that room may be shared and thus provide a platform for a micro-public sphere.

However, as I have just described, personal music technologies have limits and disadvantages. Additionally, there may be times when escape into music, whether on one's own or with one's clique or circle of friends, is not enough. For example, individuals and groups may wish to feel engulfed by music coming in, as it were, from the outside, to hear the surround sound of music in and reverberating against one's wider environment, to feel as well as hear the music (such distinctions raise questions about what it means to hear). So too, there may be occasions when one actually desired to share, broadcast or extend musically configured territory, when one feels the need or desire or takes pleasure from introducing particular sounds into the world.

Personal Broadcasts and Discreet Music

Music broadcast or quasi-broadcast in liminal spaces – the loud speakers in a car, the mobile phone ring-tone, the music that leaks from iPod earbuds or the teenager/ student who blasts her or his music to the rest of the household, neighbourhood or hall of residence – highlights how private forms of musical asylum (removals) can shift into more public attempts at musical engagement. These examples highlight musical sharing as a strategy of refurnishing and thus a technology of self and thus wellbeing that is different from but overlaps with the asylum pod as just described. A few examples are in order.

For *Music in Everyday Life* (DeNora 2000), I interviewed a softly spoken 20-year-old woman 'Beatrice' who had a strong interest in music (she took pleasure in playing Bach's *Well-Tempered Clavier* at home). She described how, as she put it, 'whenever anyone gets angry we all tend to go to our rooms and turn on the music really loud' (DeNora 2000: 56). Here Beatrice describes a musical practice that is akin to the use of the asylum pod (entering a self-chosen musical environment as a way of coping with a hostile environment), but in this case that music is simultaneously forced upon the environment much as is the case when people play their iPods or DVDs without the headphones in public. In these cases music is both a removal or retreat into a medium of choice and it is an imposition, and attempt to refurnish the environment. Similarly, 21-year-old 'Monica' described how, when living with her partner's parents one summer she sometimes played Radiohead's 'We Hope You Choke' at full volume as an attempt to send them a message. In a third example, 'Lesley' describes how her home-listening habits were initially curtailed by her husband ('Within nine months I was listening to Radio 4 rather than Radio 1, because he just didn't like Radio 1 at all. ... During the '80s I didn't really bother with music because I thought it would cause friction. ... The later '80s I started listening to Beehive and the Thompson Twins, which of course my husband didn't identify with at all' [DeNora 2000: 126]). Later, music became a subject of contention within the marriage and later still Lesley began to broadcast music as a sonic message of her impulse to leave the relationship, using a particular song ('Say Hello, Wave Goodbye') at full volume ('It was a hint really').

In all three of these cases people can be seen retreating into music and yet, all three of these retreats involve musically fostered communicative engagement with others – in each example, those making the broadcast are intervening and thus refurnishing their aural surroundings. That intervention may be about nothing more than a need to lash out, to inflict one's music on others simply by making a noise, as in Beatrice's case ('I am angry!'). But it may be about much more, a narrative showing of more than musical taste.

For example, musical broadcast can be, as in Monica's case, a hostile message, passively conveyed (as if saying nothing) through musical lyrics ('we hope you choke'), but it may be yet more of an intervention and in ways that simultaneously provide building blocks for effecting change, as in Lesley's case where musical broadcast of prohibited songs was simultaneously a message about growing independence and a way of working up courage/motivation to make a move out of the relationship and family home. No wonder Lesley's husband feared her music – in the domestic environment, that music was associated with aspects of her past and present tendencies that were antithetical to the relationship he felt capable of and wished to have with her. In all these cases, the message is discreet: one might choose not to hear, it might be unspoken. The discreetness of the message, its liminal status, in turn affords user-discretion: what one hears may be sculpted in various ways and the meaning is at once clear and unclear in the dappled light and wavering sound world that is, par excellence, the world of play.

Music for Hire

In the examples of young teens' publicization of private listening technologies and those of respondents who broadcast music to reconfigure the environment, it is possible to see music mediating self and group identity and thus also providing cues to self/others about the environment as well as how that environment related to future and potential action orientations. To put this in more explicit ecological terms, music was appropriated in ways that afforded the further appropriation of the environment, allowing its users, individually and collectively, to inhabit a territory or social niche that was not removed from but very much in the world, indeed, that contributed to making that world user-friendly. This appropriation was achieved through what music and/or repertoires of music were understood to signify about self and thus, implicitly, also about environment, through the sonic placement of self, through how music allowed these actors to feel and through how music fostered possibilities for action and experience. Music, and more broadly organized sound, is a way of framing, furnishing or removal from the sphere of action and thus a way of creating asylum in or away from a social world.

In this sense, music is a form of aesthetic output that signifies or promises ways of being in and acting on the world. Music and/or organized sound is used not merely to signify (to be meaningful): indeed, thinking of any cultural material in this way tends to downplay what it means to speak of meaningful forms. Music, as a meaningful and aesthetic form, affords the creation of pathways toward or away from desirable and undesirable environmental matters. Music is simultaneously meaningful and functional. So, for example, Beatrice, the young woman who vents by blasting her music to the household, is someone who has effectively issued a warning and a statement of intent ('Engage with me at your peril!') but who simultaneously understands that the music she uses for this purpose is not random. On the contrary, it is genre-sensitive, albeit in ways that are mediated by her personal understandings of what genres might mean (she does not blast the household with Bach's *Well-Tempered Clavier*). Monica, who broadcasts 'We Hope You Choke' to her boyfriend's parents in their home, is someone who is using music to send a message that says something to the effect of 'Stop bothering me'. Lesley, meanwhile, uses music to prepare herself emotionally, come to terms with, but also hold and enhance motivation for, the decisive action of leaving her husband and family. As part of this task, Lesley uses music to inflect the household and reconfigure it aesthetically as a kind of launch pad out and a platform – following the song lyrics:

> You and I
> It had to be
> The standing joke of the year
>
> We tried to make it work
>
> Take a look at my face for the last time
> I never knew you, you never knew me
> Say hello, goodbye
> Say hello, wave goodbye

In this last case, one might argue, Lesley used the domestic broadcast of a song as a virtual performance – the record 'sang the message and displayed the stance' on her behalf. Simultaneously, the song got into her, nourishing her intent and providing a road map of where her action would take her next. This, perhaps unwanted, sharing of a musical world was, simultaneously, the crafting of a shared or perhaps imposed definition of the situation. Once we appreciate how musical assertion is simultaneously a means for social assertion (that the musical and the social are not separate realms but mediate and constitute each other), then it is possible to appreciate with fresh eyes and ears why young people so assiduously listen to music while sharing earbuds and why their ethno-classifications and folksonomies of what music is, what it is not and what is good are so essential to the question of who they are and why. Once again, the distinction between aesthetic value and functionality dissolves in the medium of lived experience and social action.

Music and Meaning: One More Time

In all of these cases, private music listening melds into collective musical participation where music is both being manipulated and is manipulating. In all of these cases, music's semiotic force is inextricable from its situated uses and from the reactions and responses to it, and this point underlines yet again the ways in which culture and agency mutually constitute each other, the ways in which, in this case, the music itself did nothing but rather came to afford certain acts according to how it was connected to and disconnected from other things. For example, in Lesley's use of 'Say Hello, Wave Goodbye', we see her choosing a song whose lyrics and performative features (the melody is somewhat monotonous, the singer's stance in video renditions somewhat listless) are arguably appropriate, furnishing her domestic environment with discourses and aesthetic materials that could render the environment into a launch pad for her imminent departure. In this case music offers a platform for subsequent narrative elaboration: it cues scenarios of leaving and thus can be said to prime that leaving. Yet, the music itself did not do these things. To take a hypothetical example, imagine this scenario: Lesley's children come into her room and begin to sing along, perhaps humorously, to the music. Or: her husband uses the earliest of Lesley's musical broadcasts of this song to instigate a conversation. He tells her he is concerned that they have grown apart, indeed, perhaps about how hearing that song made him aware of this concern. In either of these cases what the music made possible, or afforded, would have been quite different.

The point here is two-fold. First, within the domestic environment, the song had a moral career: it was an object that afforded Lesley whatever depth or level of conviction/involvement she wished or felt comfortable with maintaining. Second, and related to this point, that what the music meant (its connotations about Lesley's intentions) was by no means unequivocal. On the contrary, it was possible to maintain competing definitions of the situation through this musical message. This is because music can be understood as a boundary object (Star and Greismar

1989) or, as I describe in Chapter 7, a mutable, immutable mobile (Law and Mol 2002). There were two (or more) contradictory positions present in the title of the song: she could 'Say hello' (again) to her family and/or she could 'Wave goodbye' to them, both at the same time or either at different times. Music's flexibility – both in terms of its semiotic force and in terms of how adamant Lesley's broadcasting of it became – afforded latitude in the social environment: Lesley could take the stance that the musical broadcast was just a bluff or an aberrant emotional phase or moment, or, conversely, she could take the a more hardline stance, that this music showed her intent to leave home. As a medium from within which to take stances, music is thus a rich resource, a way of engaging in extra-musical action, musically transposed, such that, at any time it is possible to slip back out of a stance, an implication or a promissory line of conduct. Music's slipperiness is linked to its liminal status within social ecologies, its not quite meaning and its flexibility, and this is one reason, well known and well discussed by music therapists but increasingly discussed by others in relation to music and change (Bergh 2007; Hagen with DeNora 2011), that musicking is an often-preferred medium for social movement activity and for social protest and dissent. There, music can function as a proxy or alternative medium for political action, and, unlike more overt forms of political action, radicalization through music affords gradual immersion, gradual conversion to one or another stance. For example, in his detailed study of the making of underground culture in Eastern Europe and the importance of music as a medium for radicalization, Hagen observes that:

> Musical experience, then, is understood as the intersection of sounds, music, technologies, and places. Music, in this understanding, is a flexible medium – a liminal space – one in which all of the fine shades of the actors' lifeworld can be displayed. This display, we suggest, permitted music listeners to pursue – to varying degrees – alternative or independent ways of being and feeling, from dipping a toe in nonofficial waters to plunging in and never resurfacing. (Hagen with DeNora 2011: 441)

Whether or not one dipped in to ankle, hip or eyebrow was connected to situated and temporal circumstances:

> Reconfiguring the space through active listening during radio and LP playback and collective listening connected actors to networks of feeling, being, and thinking and thus enabled actors to distance themselves from official society and to dip more than a toe into nonofficial culture. How far individuals dipped in and how long they stayed immersed was, of course, dependent on a web of other social and familial ties. (Hagen with DeNora 2011: 627)

In short, what began, perhaps tentatively (as a message or a threat or even as the first little dissociative steps toward separation, perhaps such small steps that, at any time Lesley could have turned back) became, over time, much more firmly embedded as, through the accumulation of the music's associations over time, Lesley's pathway came to be laid down through repeated broadcasts. Through these repetitions, learning occurred – the whole family came to understand what this song signified in increasingly regularized ways ('Mom is planning to leave us'). Thus, attempts to specify what music means, what it signifies or represents or what it might or can afford are doomed. They are doomed for three reasons: misplaced isomorphism, failure to appreciate music's flexibility as a material for play (world-making) and failure to appreciate the importance of situated learning as the means by which music's powers are made manifest. I will, briefly, consider each of these in turn.

First, attempts to decode, definitively, what music means are theoretically suspect, because they take the theoretical shortcut of presuming isomorphism between the knower and the known, in this case, the analyst's readings or reactions, the music and other people's readings or reactions, instead of attempting to validate those reactions through at least some form of empirical enquiry. They integrate their own readings with the potential readings of others when these matters should – if they are to be better understood – be understood in terms of the mechanisms and processes that produce the effects of integration.

Second, and the reason why isomorphism is wrong, decoding attempts do not consider the ways in which phenomena, music included, take their meanings in relational, situated and thus emergent ways that cannot be deduced in advance since their reality does not exist in advance. This empirical uncertainty, the degree of ambiguity and the polysemic potential of music allow it to be something with which people play (in interaction and in tandem with other materials such as texts or objects). People play with music both through performance, through setting up situations of musical consumption and encounter, and through discussion about music. Music is an ideal plaything, because its properties and connotations are potentially flexible: it could have done other things, a point routinely demonstrated in music therapy sessions where musical forms are cleverly and creatively re-appropriated in ways that allow them to do different things in varying socio-musical contexts (playing with music).

Third, and most notably, decoding attempts sidestep the critical role of learning, relearning and remembering, particularly social learning and socially negotiated remembering, and their role in world-making and, thus, in the distribution of opportunities for action. In this respect, situated and social learning is the missing link between culture and agency, and it is ironic, therefore, that studies of education and learning (arguably too often linked to the study of educational institutions rather than processes) are not appreciated for their rich, and potentially even richer, contributions to how we understand what culture does and how it is made. Learning how to read, how to do, how to respond and what to do next, whether by indirect observation, attempts at imitation (of interest for how, in remaining imperfect they create new conventions) and more overt instruction are of fundamental interest to virtually every aspect of human (and indeed, animal) being. Lesley's family learned how to read this music, and, with it, they allowed a new relationship to develop between them and a new aesthetic ambience to take shape within the home, one full of trajectories of future parting and new arrangements in this case. Coming to know those things took shape and was negotiated over time, and the first musical broadcast was not necessarily heard in the same way as the second, the third, the fourth and so on. As Howard S. Becker described in 'Becoming a Marihuana User', being able to associate one thing (in this case a drug or substance imbibed) with another thing (the drug's effects) is linked to, as he puts it,

> a sequence of changes in attitude and experiences during which the person acquires a conception of the meaning of the behavior, and perceptions and judgments of objects and situations, all of which make the activity possible and desirable. Thus, the motivation or disposition to engage in the activity is built up in the course of learning to engage in it and does not antedate this learning process. For such a view it is not necessary to identify those 'traits' which 'cause' the behavior. Instead, the problem becomes one of describing the set of changes in the person's conception of the activity and of the experience it provides for him. (Becker 1953: 235)

This focus on learning, understood as 'changes in the person's conception' is critical to considering the topic of music and consciousness, and I will return to it in Chapter 6. For now, the point is that ascribed effects, motivations and practices, the things that achieve music's effects – as with marijuana according to Becker – develop, accumulate and emerge historically, in situ and in collaboration with others, with modes of instruction and pointers and with material–cultural objects and techniques. We learn (and learn to learn) what things mean, what they do and how they behave in ecological context, through incremental interactions with others across time and space, and this learning is nothing less than the way that we furnish and refurnish, simultaneously, our world and ourselves.

Chapter 5

Music Asylums, Part II: Making Musical Space Together, Furnishing and Refurnishing Worlds

As I have described in relation to the privatization of public space through mobile music practices, music's deployment can refurnish the perceived world, and thus (for the individual) the sphere of action, rendering that sphere fit for (and sustainable to) forms of self, identifications, fantasies and plans. Music is functional for individual wellbeing (Skånland 2011), but music is more: it is also a supra-individual medium, part of affiliative interaction. As an entry into this topic, consider the musical broadcasts described in Chapter 4, which can be understood as bids for collective, shared, intentionality, as examples of intentional action, 'where *I* am doing something only as part of *our* doing something. … If I am a violinist in an orchestra I play *my* part in *our* performance of the symphony' (Searle 1995: 23).

This form of collective intentionality is described well by Schutz, in his classic discussion of 'making music together' (which considers chamber music where there is no conductor). Schutz describes the ways in which musical performance involves mutual orientation to materials outside of – but created by – individuals. Thus Schutz's concept of attunement draws out the notion of collective intentionality and brings it into the realm of practical object relations and embodiment where, arguably, it belongs (and from where it can enrich our understanding of consciousness and intentionality, as I discuss in Chapter 6).

In his study of Kaluli musicking, ethno-musicologist Steven Feld described the supra-individual character of aesthetic environments and the ways that humans share the tendency of making aesthetic environments with other species. He points to the 'co-evolutionary tendencies for ecology and aesthetics' by which the Kaluli people not only take pleasure from the sounds of the rain forest, but become a part of the forest through their/its soundings in a virtuous spiral where sounding and sentiment are mutually enhanced and where sounding can be understood to be an active ingredient of – Durkheim's term – collective effervescence, those features of collective life that emerge or bubble up to create collective phenomena that are more than, and different in kind from, the sum of its parts (Feld 1982: 395).

I have considered how, at the level of the individual, materials outside individuals (music on an iPod) can transform, redirect or enhance individual experiences of the world, outlooks or orientations. Produced collectively, however, soundscape is not merely the sum of individuals' attempts to alter or improve upon the world, it is the world qua world and thus the subject of negotiation, contention and – potentially – ways of being together (and helping others to learn about potential ways of being together through musically mediated social learning). Whether musically mediated realities are produced (reduced) to the individual level or whether they are the result of joint practice and collective orientation, music is simultaneously functional and aesthetic – we do not need to draw a distinction between music's instrumental properties and its adaptive role, on the one hand, and its aesthetic features in human cultural life, on the other. In broaching this issue I am also anticipating matters that will be discussed in Chapter 7.

Why do Birds Sing?

The issue of music's functionality has been considered with at length by Ellen Dissanayake. For example, in a discussion of the adaptive features of music, Dissanayake points toward similarities between human musicking and the role of sonic culture across animal species. In highlighting music as a means of conveying and shaping emotion, Dissanayake points to 'suggestive similarities' between evolutionary processes in animal communication and the ritual uses of music in human societies. So for example, she considers the rhythmic scratching and pecking of pheasants in terms of how these soundings can be understood as ritualized display (Dissanayake 2006: 36–7) or, as she puts it elsewhere, 'making special' (later re-termed 'artifying' [Dissanayake 2008]), the hallmark for her of what art is. In this sense, rhythmic action is a medium through which pheasants (not unlike people) achieve focus, meaning and coordination, and through which they signal intent or, to make this concept less overtly cognitive, inclination. Here, musicking or sounding would appear to be part of a general strategy for calling up and conducting behaviour and for accomplishing tasks in concert.

Of course ornithologists have suggested that the birds sing so as to fulfill functions linked to their survival. Males sing, for example, to signal availability and, it is often suggested, demonstrate exceptional ability as a singer to attract mates. They also sing to mark out territory and – the Beau Geste hypothesis – some birds will sing a variety of calls so as to sound like more than one bird and thus discourage other birds from attempting to infringe on their territory. They sing to pass on important news, much as the talking drum was used in western Africa to communicate from village to village faster than anyone might be able to travel by horse (Carrington 1949; Gaines 1996; Ong 1977). Birds also sing in chorus (perhaps more accurately a coordinated call and response distributed over space) in ways that signal position and temporally specific activities (such as the twilight choruses associated with roosting). (Perhaps not dissimilar from hearing the bell of a religious centre in one's neighbourhood – it is a marker and a reminder that it is time to go to worship, for example.) Consider in this context, Goethe, describing the Venetian fisher-folk of pre-modern times and in a manner that precisely enfolds the human function of music with the question of how to assess music's aesthetic character, an aesthetic concern to which I will return in Chapter 7 and the Conclusion:

> My old manservant ... wanted me to hear the women on the Lido, especially those from Malamocco and Pellestrina. They too, he told me, sing verses by Tasso to the same or a similar melody, and added: 'It is their custom to sit on the seashore while their husbands are out sea-fishing, and sing these songs in penetrating tones until, from far out over the sea, their men reply, and in this way they converse with each other.' Is this not a beautiful custom? I dare say that, to someone standing close by, the sound of such voices, competing with the thunder of the waves, might not be very agreeable. But the motive behind such singing is so human and genuine that it makes the mere notes of the melody, over which scholars have racked their brains in vain, come to life. It is the cry of some lonely human being sent out into the wide world till it reaches the ears of another lonely human being who is moved to answer it. (Goethe 1962: 92–3)

Hearing these signs of a social world can comfort (restore ontological security) and, through that comfort, such sounds become beautiful. On the one hand, and for both birds and humans, singing establishes – for each and all – a kind of collective presence (thus perhaps also security – for both humans and birds perhaps a kind of audible, phatic, all is well, one in which the medium is the message). So too, singing signals group affiliation: it creates a sound world that sketches sonic–aesthetic repertoires. Again, this function seems to be shared by birds and humans, for example, some species of birds use songs as 'passwords and proclamations of group membership' (Brown and Farabaugh 1997: 118) and, when faced with new repertoires (for example through the proximity of new members of the species), some species begin to adopt and share new musical repertoires within a week of exposure (Brown and Farabaugh 1997: 113), thus highlighting birds' capacity, like humans, for social collaboration and musically mediated social learning in ways that are 'guided by affiliative interactions' (Brown and Farabaugh 1997: 118). So too, birds may use sound to call out warnings and otherwise convey information (for example, that food is on its way). In these descriptions, the ecological functions of sounding are linked to the conduct of survival tasks. On the other hand, birds also sing, or so some claim (Hartshorne 1973; Rothenberg 2005), because they can and because singing is a source of pleasure, an enjoyable occupation. If this is so, then singing is part of the birds' bird-ness, as much as flying (itself much more than a mode of transport, as exemplified in courtship and in what would appear on some occasions to be sheer enjoyment of air currents and gusts – gliding rather than travelling). Singing is a modality that birds can do. The birds sing, as Hartshorne puts it, because they are 'born to sing' (Hartshorne 1973): singing is part of their innate capacity for communicative musicality, the ability to coordinate and build up social worlds through sonic means.

So what one's physical and social situation afford, what one can do, is simultaneously functional for being and a creative, enjoyable and thus valued thing to do. Just as, for example, braying and talking are modalities used by donkeys and humans respectively for functional purposes, so too braying, talking, flying, walking and singing are media for aesthetic and expressive conduct. Thus the birds sing, perhaps, just as the Kaluli described by Feld sing, just as the teenagers described by Bergh, DeNora and Bergh play their iPods to themselves and others, just as Lesley, Monica and Beatrice blast their music to their respective households, because, to sing, or to emit or broadcast one's music is to be in, furnish and be at one with the environment (that one is furnishing). Singing is, itself, an end, something that one can and might wish to do and have within that environment.

Conceptualized in this way, music is much more than a form of communication, or at least more than communication understood as information processing, and much more than a merely adaptive modality. It is also much more than a means for stimulating the brain in ways that are linked to feelings of pleasure or other positive stimulation. Music and musicking in social relationships are constitutive ingredients of association. From simplistic statements about shared situation (sonic warnings such as alarm calls, whether made by birds or ambulance sirens) to ambient mood music (to sit in a tree to, for dining) to music that is done so as simply to show what kind of musicking can be done, humans and many other animals seem to musick as part of their social condition. Whether human or animal, then, music is part of world-making. Is this then why human beings also sing and what, psycho-sociologically, we need to note about the human singing voice?

The First Human Musical Instrument?

In the broadest sense, human music is patterned sound: pitch, volume, vibration and timbre, rhythm, pace, combinations. It is also sound to be performed and heard and sound that is associated with things that are not sound and with other patterns of sound. If we think about music in these basic ways, it is possible to consider the ways in which music overlaps with the sonic features of seemingly extra-musical matters, including how human beings make or emit sound as we do what we do in daily life. It is here that we can begin to consider music's role in relation to body regulation, for the body is itself a music producer, insofar as it produces rhythms (breath, heart beat, blood pressure, blood sugar, hormones, sleep, growth) and sounds (hands brushing, feet hitting the floor, various actions and bodily processes such as burps or gurgles and, the paramount human musical instrument, the voice).

In recent years, there has been a renewed focus on singing. Research has suggested that belonging to a choir enhances members' sense of wellbeing (Clift and Hancox 2001). The factors so far identified as active ingredients are that singing with a group builds social capital and thus a sense of belonging in the world (Bailey and Davidson 2003; Einarsdottir 2012) and that music aids memory and is thus stimulating for those with memory impairment (Hara 2011). Scholars have also suggested that singing enhances relaxation and thus the production of endorphins through the ways it calls for deep breathing, its impact on muscle tension and posture (Stacy, Brittain and Kerr 2002). Other work has suggested that singing releases emotional tension (stress levels) and facilitates self-actualization (Grape et al. 2003). So far, however, the focus has been upon what singing achieves not what it is about singing that achieves these cognitive, emotional and physiological ends. Is there anything specifically about singing per se, as opposed to, for example, card or board games or lawn bowling or even team sports, that lends itself to health promotion?

The answer to this question may be found by considering in more detail just what it means to sing. First, singing is a whole-body activity: the body (primarily the chest, neck and head) are resonant; the body is the musical instrument (Blacking 1971, 1973, 1977). Singing also involves, as just mentioned, deep breathing, and, because singing is using the body as a musical instrument, there is a unity of sound and sounder.

Moreover, this unity means that one feels one's body producing the sound. One is the instrument. Simultaneously, being that instrument involves synchronicity. Even singing solo, one needs to use one's body to produce sounds in time, and one can feel one's body in the act of producing this synchrony. Singing with others – such as in duets or choirs – further confirms this sense of embodied synchrony, which is nothing less than finding a place in (musical) things, being in time and being full, literally, of voice. Finally, singing builds upon the pro-musical activities of human bio-social being that can be seen at the very start of life in the synchronous vocal coordination of mother and infant (Malloch 1999/2000; Trevarthan 2002).

In addition, singing is, like speaking, the social and communicative use of the voice. Typically, when one sings, one is not merely vocalizing but singing words and singing to an implied or actual recipient. (And no other musical instrument can articulate sound (pitches) as words.) Singing is performance, the musical presentation of self and the reflexive furnishing of socio-musical space through that presentation. How then can singing be harnessed for mental/physical wellbeing, and how specifically does singing afford the asylum-seeking strategy of furnishing a social environment? Conversely, how might singing for oneself also offer a form of removal capable of eclipsing those things which cause disease?

Room for Music, Music as Room

From 2006 to 2011, Gary Ansdell and I explored these questions in context of a longitudinal study of community music therapy in a centre for mental health, BRIGHT (Borough Centre for Rehabilitation, Interaction, Group Activity, Hospitality and Training). We described this project in some detail elsewhere (Ansdell and DeNora 2012). The research side of the project examined mental health clients' creation and negotiation of shared musical-aesthetic space. In collaboration with music therapists and each other, and by drawing together musical performance and extra-musical acts, clients shaped this socio-musical space in ways that created opportunities for communicative action.

BRIGHT is housed in the basement of a building directly across a courtyard from a major urban mental health centre. The building's main use is as a public cafe, open 365 days a year. BRIGHT also offers career support, IT facilities and opportunities for employment through projects such as gardening, floristry and a packing/mailing service, and its service provision is expanding. In addition to its musical activities (the Tuesday afternoon group music/open mic, a rock band and a choir plus music theory lessons), BRIGHT also sponsors a range of social activities, from weekend and evening clubs to group holidays for up to 40 people a year. How then is it possible to see musical play making room for selves in a collaborative way that furnishes the BRIGHT space with opportunities for individual and collective socio-musical agency? How, in other words, does BRIGHT afford opportunities for the asylum-seeking strategy of furnishing/refurnishing?

A typical Tuesday music session involves between 20 and 30 people. Some are hospital residents from open wards, others, mental health clients who have returned to the community in different stages of recovery. A few others are members of the public, either regulars or, occasionally, people who simply happen upon the scene, drawn, in some cases, by the sound of music-making spilling out to the street. BRIGHT's catchment area includes one of the city's poorest housing estates as well as some lavish mansions and apartments. Participants come from a diverse range of ages, ethnic, racial, economic and social statuses. For most of these participants the mental health experience takes the form of a chronic mixture of good and bad times – not unlike, although more intense than, the experience of health-state in normal life with all its vicissitudes. The challenge for all participants (BRIGHT staff, hospital staff, music therapists and clients) is to provide an environment conducive to recognizing and building upon resources and thus to healing and development in the widest meaning of those terms.

Before a BRIGHT music session, we walk across to the hospital where the percussion instruments are kept. We pile maracas, tambourines, rhythm sticks, bells, rattles and bongo drums onto a trolley and carry a cymbal on a stand, a microphone, an electric guitar and song books, colour-coded (red, blue, yellow) across and down the stairs to the cafe. The instruments are placed on a side table and participants choose one or two that they tend to use throughout a session. At other times, they are offered around at the same time as the songbooks (compilations of lyrics from group favorites, pop, folk and standard classics). Some people have become associated with 'their' instrument, Hermione, for example, always selects the tambourine, while Billy, a professional musician, routinely takes one of the electric guitars. There is tacit respect for these regularities: I remember being gently warned off the tambourine the first time I arrived, since that was 'Hermione's instrument' (DeNora, field notes: July 2006).

If there is any sense within BRIGHT of a status-order built upon musical instrument choice, I have yet to detect it after visiting the centre for over 6 years.

As there might be elsewhere, there is no implied or explicit suggestion that playing, say, the electric guitar is any better or more advanced than playing the tambourine or maraca, despite their obvious differences in cost, size, melodic, harmonic and dynamic capacity. To the contrary, there seem to be tacit ground rules in BRIGHT culture that a gourd, a set of rhythm sticks, a triangle, castanets and an electric guitar take equal shares of importance as objects for playing. This egalitarian focus is linked to a participatory and grounded aesthetic that I will describe in more detail in Chapter 7. At the same time, participants nonetheless acknowledge and are quick to admire skill when it is displayed as mastery of an instrument or proficiency of singing. Where this BRIGHT aesthetic differs from music in the more mainstream and commercial/professional world is that skill is evaluated relative to personal features of the musical activity – who, how, when and what they have hitherto been able to do. The ethos of music as personal development and musical learning/education is a key component of aesthetic judgement at BRIGHT.

Since BRIGHT music sessions are held in the cafe, participants tend to cluster at tables, neatly arranged in rows with the piano and microphone up front. Individuals tend to occupy particular segments of the physical room from week to week. Sessions are organized around a mix of group sing-along, individual and small-group performances at the mic facing the audience and instrumental/vocal improvisations by the group as instigated by Gary, until 2008, and then Sarah, who took over and is still working at BRIGHT as a music therapist/facilitator. Each musical format affords certain activities. For example, the solo performances of (mainly pop) songs allow participants literally to present their musical selves to others in a format that mirrors being on stage and to do so for a relatively brief period – the length of a song (2–3 minutes). The group improvisations, on the other hand (which may last for much longer), allow for collective perception and collective soundings – the group hears itself being a group and can hear individual solo lines as they emerge from and return to that collective sonic ground. Group singing of pop songs offers a chance to collect individuals together into one musical form and one musical melody line. The individual musical performances (solo, improvisation, group singing) are in turn linked, often in seamless ways, to other features of the environment, for example, to the talk before and after, to people's appearances and to the ways that they position themselves and move about during the musical sessions and during the breaks.

Thus, performance at BRIGHT is the medium through which the group becomes not only a group, but a socially textured group, cohesive and differentiated as individuals, sub-groups and alliances shift from week to week, indeed, moment to moment as people position and reposition themselves in and through music. What, then, does it mean to speak of positioning self in and through music? To answer this question is also to describe how much is involved in performing a song and how performing a song is, simultaneously, furnishing BRIGHT's space with resources for future action and future identity claims (enhancing the territories of the self) and furnishing the self (the singer) with resources and capacities for future action in that space. Put differently, musical performance, which temporarily holds the floor, controls the musical space and projects into that space. To sing a song or otherwise take part in the musical activity at BRIGHT is an opportunity to furnish space in ways that offer, for next time, resources for the self-in-action and to offer potential resources to others – for identity and for interrelation. What then, in the fullest sense, does it mean to perform a song, in and outside of BRIGHT?

The Double Performance of Song and Self

Solo singing at BRIGHT or anywhere else is a double performance. It is the performance of a song and, through song, it is a performance of self, a rendition of either or both the singer (as a person through how they sing) and the implied speaker of the song. That self is itself the outcome of repeated alliances between repertoire, performance and reception, and the habitus exhibited/constructed through this performance is produced from within the event, contextually. Indeed, this contextual production is part of what allows music to be so situation-specific and thus so flexible and useful a medium of psycho-social change, as I describe below. The performing self is the outcome of a negotiation of (what comes to count as) successful performance and how it comes to furnish the space into which it is projected is part of what is musically negotiated. This point requires additional explanation.

All solo performers at BRIGHT are at least implicitly affiliated with song repertoires, although the scope of their individual repertoires varies. (For example, some participants perform the same song from week to week.) Taken collectively, as I will describe, these musical repertoires mediate social repertoires of affect and agency – the psycho-cultural and symbolic space of available ways of being within BRIGHT's socio-musical compass. They are thus means by which to occupy the social space and means by which to furnish that space in ways that render it hospitable to self over time. The double performance of song and self produces the BRIGHT music space as social topology, cultural geographical terrain. So musical performance, and the introduction of music into BRIGHT space, is much more than mere 'show and tell': it brings something in to the social space in ways that afford or demonstrate certain things. To sing a solo at BRIGHT, then, is to offer a strand of values and practices to live by and the social distribution of music in space is, simultaneously, the distribution of potential music asylum: here, a cozy corner (not too many sing this song, this style, this genre), and, there, a piazza or a place where musical modes (genre, song style, performance format [solo, group, duet] instruments, song title) are prominent, shared and popular. In Figure 5.1, how this topology appeared in 2006 is represented, with font size indicating how often a genre is performed.

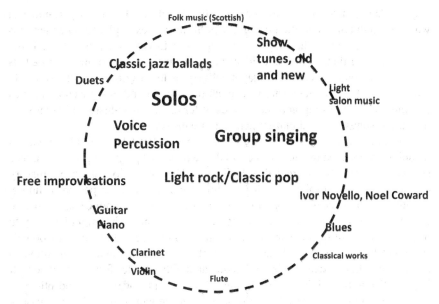

Figure 5.1   BRIGHT musical space, 2006

How the various sub-locations come to relate to each other is equally important to the social distribution of asylums and opportunities for asylum. At BRIGHT, music is combined in flexible ways, albeit with a few regularities. For example, a classical work or light salon song may precede and follow a light rock or pop number or improvised work. Similarly, how 'performing' is defined will vary and is flexibly determined. At a basic level, performing a song is about managing to get through the performance from start to finish and also about being associated with song repertoires. At a more complex level, it includes musical-delivery styles – timbres, rhythmic tendencies, embodied stance and gesture.

Moreover, and a point that highlights the interpenetration of public and private standards (an issue I will return to in Chapter 7), some of these stylistic patterns are unintended and linked to the physical features of participants' voices and/ or appearance. This 'collective un-intentionality' as I shall call it (in contrast to Searle's 'collective intentionality') allows for new sounds and musical handlings to emerge. Socio-politically – and thus vital for therapeutic and quasi-therapeutic purposes – it allows for a kind of bespoke aesthetic tailoring, a to-and-fro between what individuals can do or what their attempts produce, for example, a squawk in the voice (which shows potential vulnerability), and what we, their audiences, like or dislike, what we laud or laugh at, what makes us cry. For example, Tom's gravelly bass is highly distinctive and routinely causes comment. Others are para-musical, for example, Jane, who takes time to set herself up for a solo performance (arranging the sheet music, discussing interpretation). Indeed a number of the other singers also stretch their performances with an additional layer of para-musical work, through talk about the music they perform. For example, Robbie mentions in an off-hand way as he prepares to sing ('If I Loved You') that 'I am Billie Holiday', an affiliation that is evident in his manner of performing jazz ballads where he channels some of Holiday's delivery as his way of doing the song. So too, other participants take care to explain the background of their chosen songs and thus frame the song and themselves in terms of music-historical context or how those songs featured in their personal life histories.

Through these strategies, music performance at BRIGHT provides a way of inhabiting the shared musical space and thus a means of projecting self into music and music into self ('I am Billie Holiday'). This projection has a promissory character, it offers a token of what we might expect from the person in future, and thus it is a musical version of the social allocation of symbolic space – whose territory this song, and therefore this stance, is and is not, who might be likely to occupy this sort of musical space. By the term, promissory, I mean that Robbie's statement before he sings, 'I am Billie Holiday', calls his and our attention to a musical/extra-musical style and associated allusion to forms of action. It is part of how he builds, between himself and others, for himself and others, a sensibility and thus potential form of agency in the world. It is also promissory in its expectations and its claims upon that world, a kind of 'This is my way' or 'my stylistic bandwidth'. Finding, tuning in to that bandwidth involves a musical-spatial location, a declaration that 'This is where you will find me'.

Particular styles and forms of music are, or model, states and, by the authority of these states (the conditions of the music), music invests actors with agency, it authorizes actions and dispositions. Music is but one of the many aesthetic media that tacitly offer parameters, structures and modes for how to be and how to act and, thus, how to react and how to feel. Produced, as at BRIGHT, on a collective and shared basis, these states are also the means for creating and strengthening ties between individuals who invest (in) each other with shared and publicly negotiated musical forms in social time and socially negotiated space. This is nothing less than being-in-the-world, the very thing that is often problematic for people with enduring mental health conditions, understood as problems in living. It requires care and an eye (and ear) for balance, since making music is furnishing rooms for shared selves and forms of being (together) and securing this room for action seeks to avoid the twin dangers of over assertiveness and passivity.

The elements of performance style become proxies for identity, signs of embodied and tacit dispositions that shoot through and structure social action. Perhaps it is not, therefore, surprising that the question of how a song is to be rendered is potentially contentious (see Hennion 2007) since, as Cook and McCormick describe, performance instantiates social relations (Cook 2003; McCormick 2009). In this sense musical activity can be understood as an active ingredient of community formation: as McCormick put it, 'the context of musical performance is itself the result of an ongoing process of cultural construction' (2009: 7).

On one occasion at BRIGHT, for example, there was an overt struggle over how to render a standard jazz ballad. This struggle took the form of a musical-stylistic tug-of-war. While Gary (in the dual role of music therapist and accompanist) functioned as the rope, the audience (the rest of us in the role of listeners and chorus) were enlisted as further musical muscle by each of the vying parties. The participant who had initiated the performance began to sing it as a lyrical ballad, and Gary's musical introduction had announced it in this way. On hearing the opening notes, another participant went up to the mic to join the first singer because, as she put it, 'This is my song; I've got to sing this song.' Her rendition was musically different, however – it was a swing version. A musical debate then ensued, with each participant pulling the music in stylistically different directions.

As I have already described, Schutz has observed that musical interaction highlights social attunement, what it takes musically to be together in time (1964). At BRIGHT, it is possible to observe this attunement, as it is achieved from moment to moment and as it is simultaneously attunement to music-making and to the collaborative making of (space for, resources for) selves. It is yet something more, however, when the musical spills over into or is converted into something not, or not quite, musical – para-musical communication for example. We see actors engaging in musical activity as a (not necessarily intentional) means for furnishing, or aesthetically inflecting, the spaces into which musical acts are projected. These acts provide, as it were, statements and exemplars of how to be and of preferred versions of practice, aesthetic and social and this point now needs to be discussed at some length, again, courtesy of Goffman.

Projecting Self in Space and Time

For its existence, as Goffman observed (and as I discussed in Chapter 2), the self (and its perceived manifestation as self-identity, even if that self is multiple-stranded or fragmentary and variously known to different observers) has to be registered, if it is to be known to self and/or others. That registration takes shape through presentational and behavioural styles, devices, gambits and stances. Through how I hold my body and facial posture, through what I choose to say and how I say it (volume, pitch, accent), through what I can mobilize (humour, knowledge, experience, others), I come to be known as a type of person – quiet or aggressive, shy or shrill, halting or brisk (note the musical features here), stylish or dowdy, competent in some realms, incompetent in others. The self in these examples is thus a project: it involves a projection through various media in two directions that reciprocally affect each other: from self to others (who include one's own self, looking at self) and back from others to self in the form of attributions and orientations. This process of projection and introjection, and the identification work that it achieves, is, moreover, not only creating the individual self, but its performance simultaneously creates the environment and resources for self-formation. It highlights some of the links between ethnography and psychoanalysis (Bondi 2003).

This projection of self is especially interesting, sociologically, when it involves conscious or desired identity transformation. For example, as an inmate of some sphere of my everyday life, I might wish to be taken more seriously or to improve my standing with some social group, thought to be normal; or you, as my friend, teacher or therapist, might think that I would benefit from this improvement. In either of these cases, if I or we take steps to facilitate this movement, I will need to find a way of moving from A to B, and that way of moving can be understood, both prospectively and retrospectively, to consist of path-making activity.

Just how these ways of moving come about and how music provides resources for the forging of these pathways is the topic of further research on BRIGHT (Ansdell and DeNora 2012). So, for example, when Robbie performs himself musically, in the persona of Billie Holiday, and when, after the performance ends, he remains half in role, employing verbally an echo of Holiday's musical manner, he has found a modus operandi that transfers from making music to performing self through the medium of spoken interaction, a social vehicle for getting into and through a situation. When two or more participants coordinate their musical activities, they are entering into a shared temporal and spatial world and simultaneously developing skills that can be applied to extra-musical settings. Indeed, the very point of BRIGHT music is to provide yet another medium within which self may be projected and – outside of BRIGHT – converted into extra-musical resources with which to build bridges to the worlds and identities that lie outside BRIGHT's walls. So, for example, if I can acquire the knack of presenting myself musically, perhaps even forging a musical identity indexed by some regularity of style, repertoire and persona, I have developed my more general skill of sustaining a self through the mastery of competences in one form of medium. At the very least, as we have seen repeatedly at BRIGHT, this musical success will boost my confidence, which itself will serve as a resource for the way of moving I might be seeking to achieve somewhere else.

So musical performance is a means of resource generation, a way of generating materials for the sustenance and development of self. Thus, when I go to another social gathering tomorrow, I can talk about my musical hobby or interest and, if only to myself, recall that I did well there yesterday. In doing this, I am converting my musical activity into something extra-musical – a topic of conversation. By doing so, I have just projected or spread my self or presence across two days and two spaces. I have expanded my self by tapping the resource that I created for myself through my musical projection of self. Thus, like laying down pavement, in collaboration with others, I can pave the way to expanded and changed identities and associated health-states, paving block by paving block.

The Ethics of Identity: Taking a Stand

As Goffman suggested, it is through various cultural media that the self is registered, as an object for and in relation to others. For Goffman, the 'moral career of the mental patient' involved, as he put it, 'a standard sequence of changes in his way of conceiving of selves, including, importantly, his own'. Goffman continues in this vein by suggesting that this process consists of 'half buried lines of development [that] can be followed by studying ... happenings which mark a turning point in the way in which the person views the world'. The methodology Goffman implicitly advocates for illuminating these processes consists of a focus on the stands that individuals take 'before specifiable others, whatever the hidden and variable nature of his inward attachment to these presentations'. By noting these 'stands', Goffman suggests, it is possible to 'obtain a relatively objective tracing of relatively subjective matters' (1961: 168).

At BRIGHT, such stands are taken by mobilizing publicly available musical resources (repertoires, performance styles) in ways that illuminate the external materials through which apparently subjective or inner psychic space is constituted. Indeed, the expectation of stand taking is part of BRIGHT's tacit ethic. The solo slot in BRIGHT's structure can thus be understood as a non-therapeutic therapy, the creation of asylum through musical furnishing/refurnishing. The requirement for action that song performance poses is also a request for the performer to put him or herself in a situation where they must pull themselves together musically – they must perform and for real – in the shared, public, albeit safe, space of others. It is also an opportunity to stand outside the trappings of the therapeutic encounter, the sick role and the client–therapist relationship. The key issue here is that these community music therapy practices and the client–therapist roles they configure (deconstructing those roles in fact), highlight what all of us in the setting, irrespective of medical history, have in common: 'We are making music here today and will do next week', for example.

How participants manage the demands of performance varies. For example, Trevor, who typically strides in from the basement garden like a star, shouldering his way to the stage, sings one of what Gary calls 'the diva songs' (such as Elton John's 'Candle in the Wind') or an old group favourite (such as the Beatles' 'Hey Jude'). The custom is to applaud after each solo. While we do so, Trevor heads back to the garden, as if he is already late for another important engagement. We are still clapping after he has left the arena.

Other members, such as Lawrence, tend to be called upon once the session is in full swing and provide a kind of artistic peak in this socio-musical topology. A physically fit, trim and well-dressed pensioner, Lawrence offers one or two new songs that he has practised for the occasion. He hands Gary the chosen sheet music (mostly light salon classics or classic ballads and folk tunes – 'A Nightingale Sang in Berkeley Square' or 'Old Man River'). Lawrence's performances are quasi-choreographed, hand and arm gestures reminiscent of the recital stage, lieder performance and opera. His classical-music voice is splendid, and it is always greeted with enthusiastic applause.

Not everyone offers solo song performances: Hermione, for example, whom I have mentioned already, me (and not merely because I am a researcher, but also because I am an unskilled singer and uncomfortable singing in front of a mic) and, at age 87, gamine Maggie, a member of the public and friend of one of the clients, who comes because she enjoys these afternoons. Though we would be unlikely to sing solo, each of us contributes in our own way and in ways that are meaningful to us, however small or infrequent our act. In my own case, I feel I perform through a quiet and (so I like to think!) judicious use of the rhythm sticks (I happen to like their woody sound – a topic that could of course be explored) and through my attempts to be helpful and chatty (or a good listener) at tea time (which is by no means to say I am perceived this way by others). Hermione also has a role (as tambourinist, described above) and Maggie is a true sport: although she does not sing, she can be counted on to keep energy and motivation levels up – even dancing in the aisle on one occasion (to our collective cheers).

Then, there are those new or less secure performers (of which I would no doubt be one, if I were ever to venture forth into solo territory myself), whose musical activity needs considerable support, ever more so if a sense of self is to be built upon a musical foundation. Here is where we see the therapy of non-therapy. On these occasions, the concept of musical accompaniment is brought to the fore and it is possible to see Gary's considerable craft – both as a musician and music therapist – which enables him to move adroitly from musical foreground to background, to lend musical and social support when it is called for and to conceal the techniques which provide, as it were, a sheltered musical interaction. The appearance is, for all practical purposes, that nothing is happening except that people are making music and having fun. This juggling act is complex, virtuosic and self-effacing – as, to a much lesser extent, is our own as participant members of the audience, clapping, commenting, cheering, encouraging, with the promise of musical support (the chorus) always on tap. It is important to remember that the sheltering work performed by Gary is not a feature only of the community music therapy session: on the contrary, it is part of the everyday work of caring and is in no way linked to the specialism of mental health. As Goffman noted, this is all part of how demeanour is ceremonially constructed and conserved.

Andrew has to be gently coaxed up to sing and when he does, he almost always chooses the same song. His voice wavers and sometimes cracks in the upper register. Gary does what he can to help, singing along, playing the melodic line emphatically to keep Andrew on track when he falters, cueing the rest of us to join in and, when he excels, cueing the rest of us to drop out (so as to highlight Andrew's 'best practice' – to let him shine when and where he can). In addition, Gary modulates, if required to follow a singer's pitch shifts, makes use of shifts in tempo or dynamics, ornaments or rhythmic figures and does many other things as required in order to shepherd a singer, musically, from the start to the (successful) end of a complete performance. After Andrew finishes, we clap. I say to him, as he sits down next to me, that I enjoyed his performance (to me, and for whatever reasons, personal, professional, his voice is poignantly beautiful) and he flushes with obvious pleasure and smiles warmly. There is pleasure in shared accomplishment of making it come out all right but there is also beauty in being able to overcome the fear of appearing vulnerable – as measured according to some external (musical-aesthetic) standard. I will return to this topic in Chapter 7.

All of the participants at BRIGHT can be understood to occupy musical space in specific and overlapping ways. Some participants can cover a lot of ground, in terms of genre, style, repertoire and instruments – for example, David plays more than one instrument, sings, and can dip in to a wide range of songs, styles and genre. By contrast, Peter, whom we will meet again in Chapter 6, ploughs a narrower musical furrow, staying close to the comfort zone of old familiar songs and a more strictly delineated repertoire. Of interest here is how and when individuals can be drawn or venture out from the familiar and in ways that allow them to extend their musical territories and thus, the territories of themselves and with these territories, skills, capacities and identity stances for future use.

The Triple Time (and Multiple Spaces) of a Musical Event

To be able to explore this question from the inside of interaction over time, I use the schema of the musical event, developed in previous work (DeNora 2003). The musical event provides a schema for considering music's connection to change, for example affect management (Ansdell et al. 2010), perception, orientation and action.

The schema draws together three time phases, the first and third of which frame the second, which is the present moment (of musical engagement). Time 1 is the past. Things past include everything/anything associated by an individual with music prior to the present moment (Time 2). It is important to note that the past is both conceptual (embodied and cognitive memories of events and practices, for example: 'How we do/used to do this') and indicated through materials ('That is last season's dress') and their arrangements ('That is the group of records I never listen to anymore') which may also function as memory prompts (I remember aspects of my past life when I begin to listen to my old record collection). These materials evidence the past insofar as they show us how or where they were before they were here and now. Their physical properties and the relation of these properties to time's passing offer information of prior states, uses or acts – footprints or fingerprints, traces and temporal processes associated with materials. For example, I may not recall having taken the ice-cream out of the freezer or having gone out to feed the hens, but I must have done both, since the ice-cream is melting on the kitchen table and there are muddy footprints on the kitchen floor that are not yet dry.

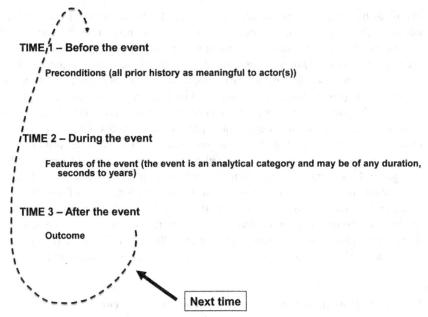

Figure 5.2   The musical event

Musically, the past may include personal associations and memories, tastes and musical practices and skills. For example, at BRIGHT, it includes prior involvement in one-on-one music therapy sessions. The past also includes impersonal, generic and conventional associations between music, action and reception such as the set of musical forms, genres and styles (as understood by actors) and the prior collective, organizational or institutional histories of the use of these forms, genres and styles.

Time 2 is the present, when people are performing, talking about, listening to or writing about music. What is paired with music and how, when and where is this pairing done and with reference to what other things? So, for example, as described above, how might a song be paired with a particular stylistic rendering and/or how might it also be paired with talk about that rendering, or talk about the song?

Time 3 is the future. At some later time (for example, in talk about a BRIGHT performance after a session, a follow-on performance or some situation outside of BRIGHT entirely) something happens that can be shown to be linked, in some way, to the musicking. To take a simple example, one hears a snippet of music in a shop, it evokes memories, one goes home and looks through an old photograph album which in turn leads one to write a letter to a distant relative.

Within the context of BRIGHT musical space, the musical event schema may be of service in tracing the ways in which the musical stands taken by individuals do or do not result in transformations (at Time 3) of the musical space, relations within that space and/or individuals' capacities for traversing space and converting musical into extra-musical resources. Thus, albeit heuristic (since exactly where does one event end and another begin and where is the boundary between present moment and past?), the musical event can be helpful in highlighting the mechanisms by which places (physical and social spaces and their personnel) and/ or psycho-cultural spaces (the internal geography of reminiscence, mood, reverie) may be health-promoting (or health-demoting), because they offer a method of tracing individual and group pathways over time as identities are developed and shifted, as new skills or social connections are forged and as new modes of accounting for self, health and social situation are forged in relation to music. We have now arrived at the gates of the public music asylum, decanted into everyday life and taking form as collaborative musical activity.

The Music Asylum as Collaboratively Furnished Space

BRIGHT is but one example of what people can do, together and for each other, with music. In *Musical Pathways for Mental Health* (forthcoming), the third volume in this book triptych, Gary Ansdell and I describe BRIGHT in more detail. BRIGHT offers a kind of natural laboratory for examining refurnishing activity and in a manner that permits us to see some of the ways that music can afford a health-promoting ambience, as well as how this ambience is achieved and constantly renewed through mutual work. There is not, at BRIGHT, any automatic connection between music, agency and affordance. Rather, affordances must be found and made manifest within a space. This activity is creative and collaborative. It is put together by BRIGHT's actors using BRIGHT's musical resources and supported by the music therapeutic team who work as musical mentors. BRIGHT is a space in which its participants can be seen to be engaged in paving pathways to and extending selves through a series of often minute 'happenings which mark a turning point' (Goffman 1961: 168). These happenings at BRIGHT in the form of musical stands – that is, the display of musical personae and musical affiliations – provide the building materials for moral careers.

The musical stands taken at BRIGHT are the traceable outward manifestations of an otherwise inaccessible process (though one that is by no means simply internal to the individual). They show us identification work: how selves are achieved (performed) through the couplings of individuals and materials, in this case, music (DeNora 1999; Hennion 2007), but they are by no means individual stances or creations. Rather, they are produced from the available stock of musical materials and practices known in and introduced to the scene and, simultaneously, mediated through performance. To observe how these stands come to be remembered or, perhaps more accurately, how they provide fragments or remnants of self, building materials that prompt and draw out stances and dispositions – embodied and conceptual – is to watch agency and culture being co-performed through the spectacle of performance reception. The former (agency or what we actually do in interaction at Time 2) taps the resources of the latter (culture, or, as it were, all the things there are to do and know at Time 1), and, in so doing, the latter comes to be constituted as the field or matrix for agency and self in situ. One musical event leads to others, and the collective field of musical events is what produces the musical space and its changes over time. This is not to say that the space is the result of nothing more than the accrual of individual acts. On the contrary, those acts take shape, are framed and made meaningful in relation to the supra-individual realm of the musical-public space as much as they determine it (the interpenetration of culture and agency, public and private).

In offering health-situations, BRIGHT also illustrates the interpenetration of public and private, as described in Chapter 4. To the extent that BRIGHT offers a shared, flexible socio-musical space, it also offers what might be thought of as a halfway house for refurnishing the world and for engaging with the world through the medium of music, a place for asserting and trying out values, stances, identities and ways of relating to others. In the sense that Bourdieu has described, BRIGHT offers a space in which individual and group stances and preferences can be asserted and developed (1985). Contra however to the zero-sum, game-based, hierarchical and economistic vision of space typically associated with Bourdieu, one in which spatial properties confer strength on their holders in relation to others who also occupy a space, BRIGHT's space is encomiastic: BRIGHT is a place where many varied – indeed, in other contexts, possibly contradictory – musical goods may be valued and respected, a place where aesthetic worth can be compounded rather than distributed according to some zero-sum game-based scheme. Honour, praise and applause, indeed the very concept of what is good, are all constantly under revision and configured with reference to their contexts and histories of production, such that even the shakiest of renditions can and is often beheld as a moment of beauty (see Chapter 7).

Despite music's importance within BRIGHT, the BRIGHT space highlights music as a fragile power, a power that is arguably all the more powerful because of its fragility, its dependence upon processes of local generation and regeneration, its role as a medium and also by-product of community activity. To behold the ways in which BRIGHT offers musical asylum is to see how the sociological study of identity and wellbeing, the therapeutic, collaborative crafting of self and other through music and the ordinary decencies of mutual respect, care and kindness are joined to the collective pursuit of (musical) skills and musical pleasures. How, then, are such things connected to outlooks on the world, self and other? In the next chapter I consider the topic of musical consciousness, understood as a situated, ecological and pragmatic affair.

Chapter 6

Musicalizing Consciousness:
Aesthetics and Anaesthetics

'Inner consciousness', said George Herbert Mead, 'is socially organized by the importation of the social organization of the outer world' (1912: 406). Mead's words, albeit slightly obscure, can be read as an epigraph to this chapter which is about how our awareness and orientation to the world is shaped by things outside the mind. In what follows therefore, I focus on how consciousness can be understood to take shape in relation to musical practice. This focus will in turn help to advance the idea of the music asylum by considering how music gets into and can shape our capacity to have emotional experience, to be functional in the world, to relate to others, and even to mediate bodily experience, to shape our very sensing of realities.

As an opening, I want to suggest that, in common with all creative work, producing consciousness is a 'systematic function' (Csikszentmihalyi 1996: 23; Sutherland and Acord 2007). By this I mean, in common with Mead, that consciousness does not reside and is not formed inside individuals and is not the property of individuals but is a collaborative achievement. As such, consciousness can be seen to emerge in relation to and from engagement with social and material-cultural settings, things, behaviours and situations that stand outside of individuals in ways that are often recognized and spoken about in commonsense terms as individual matters individually perceived, albeit in ways that often overlap. While the idea that consciousness can be studied in terms of its history, sociology and anthropology is not new, the focus on consciousness in relation to and mediated by music is new. Newer still is the focus on music, consciousness, health/illness and mental health/illness. The key aim of this chapter is to show how this theme is one that can and should be pursued through case studies and grounded examples. Those examples will, at times, further develop the discussion of removals and refurnishings from Chapters 3 to 5.

What I have to say here is organized into two main sections. First, after a review of issues in the philosophy of consciousness and the pragmatics of mind, I turn to the topic of music and governmentality (DeNora 2003: ch. 5; Foucault 1988; Rose 1996), with a specific focus on how musically embodied consciousness (physical orientation to environment) and musically mediated verbal conduct are linked to forms of social control, self-control and to the control or administration of selves and others by institutions and organizations. To develop this theme, I use examples of music's role in the workplace to consider how individuals are allocated to and come to experience themselves as exhibiting features of musicalized forms of identity, motivation and action orientations linked to different types of tasks. This consideration pushes some of the arguments developed in the previous chapter into the territory of how rooms for wellbeing include a psycho-dynamic or psycho-geographic dimension that is itself a resource for agency and wellbeing, understood as capacity for functioning and flourishing within situated worlds.

From there I return to the topic of mental health and thus, to the scene of BRIGHT, examined at the close of the previous chapter, and to one of its members, Peter. I will describe Peter's presence within BRIGHT and consider the interconnections between musicalized forms of awareness, understood as orientation, embodiment and disposition, and wellbeing, understood as opportunities for refurnishing the world, and thus, as I described in a more general way in the previous chapter, for creating connection to others through musical acts.

Overall, I shall argue that musical consciousness is a medium for social relation, regulation and self-presentation and that, if consciousness consists of dispositional orientations and selective sensitivity to the world, then consciousness is a vehicle for social contact and coordination. Music is truly 'imported' (Mead's term) and in ways that can be seen to structure consciousness, understood as an amalgam of orientation, mind, action, emotion and sensory experience. Where, then, does consciousness originate, how is it acquired, and in what ways is it possible to see music as a formative material of consciousness?

The Cultural Pragmatics of Consciousness in the Philosophy of Mind

Various philosophers have suggested that consciousness is characterized by degrees or levels, shared to some extent, though this is highly contended, with animals. These degrees range from pre-reflective awareness, to sentience, reflection and self-awareness (Zelazo 1999; Zelazo and Sommerville 2001). Some scholars, perhaps most notably Daniel Dennett (1992), have argued that consciousness should not be equated with perception or awareness, but reserved as a term referring to higher order forms of reflection that include awareness of self and of self as a knower. This distinction also resonates with the conventional philosophical categories of first- and second-order consciousness, the former (for example, tasting an apple) linked but not primarily concerned with accounts about experience which characterize second order consciousness (for example, reflecting upon the taste of the apple, preparatory to communicating to self and others about that taste).

In its higher, reflective or second-order form, consciousness is something more than sentience or awareness. It involves the social organization of perception as a form of representation – as 'consciousness of', 'consciousness for' and (since these are arguably inseparable in practice) 'consciousness in relation to' matters outside the individual. Understood in this sense, consciousness is cultural, coordinated and negotiated. It is a social phenomenon, in Durkheim's sense, 'a whole world of sentiments, ideas and images which, once born, obey laws all their own' (1961:

471). Moreover, if consciousness is a means by which realities (including the self as known to self and others) come to be registered publicly as objects in the world – objects to which one may be directed by others, then consciousness is also functional, it is a means for communal living.

Thus, at least in terms of its outcomes, higher order consciousness is a practical activity, part of what it takes to live and coordinate with others. Indeed, perception, or first-order consciousness, is also arguably quasi-social, and, although it is a challenge to explain precisely how perception is supra-individual (a challenge which the study of music can address through its role in mediating embodied awareness), I will attempt to address this issue below. The study of consciousness is the study of the means by which perception (and accounts about perception) is aligned with media external to individuals and the study of higher order consciousness is the study of how individuals come to be connected and contribute to what comes to count as their realities – realities in relation to themselves and to the world.

Understanding consciousness as a culturally constituted tool for living accords well with what some philosophers of mind have had to say about the history of consciousness in western culture. According to Jaynes, consciousness as we understand it emerged in the aftermath of the Trojan War as an artefact of new linguistic arrangements by which the construct – lynchpin of the modern self – the reflecting 'I' first emerged (1974). Prior to the linguistic innovation of internality, as displayed in Homer's *Odyssey*, individuals, Jaynes purports, 'heard voices' of the gods which told them what to do, rather in the manner that we speak of hallucination today. In both cases, the voices were heard as if they really existed, that is, without being accompanied by a corresponding reflexive understanding that the voices were imagined, the product of the hearer reflecting on – being conscious of – reality through the medium of language. The shift that Jaynes describes was also one that effected a shift from sacred to secular authority and thus to the possibility of negotiating the *polis* and the good through individual conscious reflection. This move was of course developed in the secular humanism of Plato and Aristotle's political theory. No longer god-given, the world and what was real and good, could be discussed, developed and maintained through seemingly democratic procedures.

While the historical evidence for Jayne's claim may be contended (and while the complete thesis extends well beyond this historical observation into the interaction between mind and brain), Jaynes offers much that is of heuristic value, as recent work in the sociology of the self has observed (Housley 2010). In particular Jaynes highlights consciousness as a cultural product (created by importing things from outside the mind, in this case language) and as a building block of the notion of the person, the individual and the self–other distinction. In this respect, his perspective on consciousness and the person overlaps with that of others who have considered how the sense of person is linked to language use (see Becker 2010: 133).

According to Jaynes, the components of consciousness are: (1) the metaphor of mind-space, constructed from further metaphors, such as distance, proximity, clarity and light. (2) an 'I' who inhabits that space and employs it as a grid from which to be aware of the world and express that awareness in the form of (3) narratives about the world, narratives that in fact bring that world into the realm of consciousness, the mind-space, as an assembly of consciousness. Examining each of these components, in terms of their socially located production lays the groundwork for thinking about the externality of consciousness, that is, its culturally extended character and, thus, for thinking about consciousness' musically extended character.

This externality (consciousness as extended) is most obvious in the case of Jayne's third component, narration, understood as the practice of reporting on what has become available to consciousness. Narration is storytelling. As such, it mobilizes conventional resources – grammars, plot devices, stock characters, imageries and tropes. It is discursive practice and as such performs the world. It is not neutral or merely descriptive but provides candidate grids with which to formulate or organize the world. Thus consciousness performs itself through its discursive practices (narrations about itself / the world) or, rather, the discursive practices of consciousness perform the narrating subject, or 'I', who is consciousness.

That narrator (Jaynes' second component of consciousness) is both the spokesperson of consciousness and, by virtue of the narrative act, an 'I' or person in, through and for the telling. While Jaynes makes it clear that the 'I' is not a 'self', the 'I' inevitably asserts a putative identity, at least for the duration of a narrative account. The 'I' is, in other words, the effect of a stance from which the account is offered which is (albeit fleetingly) a potential self and this conception of the 'I' and having consciousness or being a conscious I (or of being a vehicle that has consciousness) is produced through narratively afforded stance-taking.

Finally, how a subject comes to be an 'I' (potential narrator) and, thus, the sorts of things that are brought to her or his consciousness will itself depend upon how Jaynes' first component of consciousness (the mental space) is furnished; that is, upon the cultural products that organize and produce consciousness. On this topic, there is a venerable tradition of work that focuses upon the role of metaphor as constitutive of reality, as an orientation device (Lakoff and Johnson 1980), although Jaynes only briefly touched upon this issue. True, Jaynes describes how mind can be conceived of as a mind-space in which features of physical space are projected on to mental space (distance, light), but he does not, however, go on to describe how there are many other cultural products (metaphors and other forms of cultural material) that affect mind-space and thus orientation to the environment. (Again, Lakoff and Johnson explored this theme: in addition to metaphors of light and distance, consciousness is also built upon the foundation of less abstract, more substantive metaphors such as 'the world is a stage', 'love is a journey', 'social life is a game', 'nature is war'.)

Moving beyond metaphor, other cultural materials that condition consciousness include incorrigible assumptions about what is out there to find (no flying pigs, for example) and certain ways of attending to the out there that filter information in particular ways. Through these cultural materials, consciousness manifests itself as predispositions, forms of affect, sensibilities and predilections. Cultural materials, as I will argue throughout the rest of this chapter, offer the pre-optive (tacit and pre-conscious) resources by which consciousness is formed, and, as such, they mediate consciousness. We have now come back to the definition of consciousness as selective sensitivity and a practical ability to adopt and deploy the cultural materials from which public consciousness is produced. While these points may seem somewhat removed from the focus on music and the music asylum, they help illuminate the question of how music can be understood to structure consciousness and, more fundamentally, perception. That topic is linked to a concern with health/illness ecologies. How, in other words, does music structure consciousness, and in what ways that can be harnessed to promote wellbeing?

To address this question is to ask about consciousness in action. It is one thing to speak, in general terms, about how consciousness can be understood to take shape in relation to things external to individuals. It is quite a different thing to examine this question in situ, and in real time. Thus, while Jaynes' work addresses the question of consciousness in a general way, it does not provide a method by which particular, situated forms of consciousness arise nor an understanding of how the mechanisms can lead to changing consciousness over time and space. There is no attempt to theorize the history of consciousness in terms of its mechanisms of change over time and space. Additionally, Jaynes' work does not include a theory of the subject as an emotional and embodied being (a theme to which Lakoff and Johnson returned in later work [1999]); it provides no mechanism for how the lower (first order) forms of consciousness (embodied awareness, feeling) might connect with and indeed inform the higher (second order) levels.

Some of the ground for considering these issues has been prepared by another philosopher of mind, Giovanna Colombetti in her work on the links between language (poetics), the plastic arts and emotional experience (2009). Her work returns us to a more empirically oriented focus on how things from the outer world get imported into and thus construct what we take to be our internal consciousness.

Colombetti suggests that language individuates and scaffolds cognition and, importantly, that emotion, feeling and embodiment are themselves resources for cognition's production. By this she means that words, far from being neutral descriptors, may elicit and structure feelings (she makes specific comparison to music in this regard). Both words and music, as she puts it, with reference to mental health clients and their emotional experience, 'enhance patients' emotion experience, and [help] to entrain and thereby structure their expression and physiology' (Colombetti 2009: 13). (In passing, Colombetti also considers the plastic arts, specifically surrealist practices, and how they pulled experiences into being, shedding 'a particular light' on experience and, eventually, through that light, altering consciousness of reality.) Colombetti suggests that verbalization and musicalization provide external media that socialize or draw and shape experience. As she puts it (and her words chime with Mead's and Jaynes' perspectives), language is a device that 'pulls the mind "from outside", by signposting and recommending possibilities for experience' (Colombetti 2009: 23). Moreover, by labelling these feelings, language makes feelings conventional and publicly available (part of the social ecology as I described it in Chapters 2 and 3). Language thus affords the possibility of shared emotion. Moreover it can lead to the formation of ecological niches or specialist cultures where certain attitudes, modes of awareness or forms of experience are honed and reproduced. Such niches might include cultures with heightened knowledge/awareness of a natural phenomena (for example, the apocryphal idea of numerous words for snow in Inuit culture) or identity practices, as described by Hacking and discussed in Chapter 1.

In sum, philosophers of consciousness suggest that expressive (aesthetic) modalities and materials can be seen prospectively to structure, refine and channel experience. In so doing, expressive modes and expressive materials heighten our awareness (consciousness) of experience and of self, they sensitize us to being in the world (the original meaning of the term 'aesthetic'). The arts can enrich our capacity to narrate or, more generally, formulate experience as a conscious 'I', giving it inflection, new categories of experience and, depending on the materials, affective content. These inflections, affective states and categorical presumptions are, I would suggest, part of a dispositional arrangement of our orientation to the world. Thus the shape they take is formative of consciousness, of our selective sensitivity to environment. This consciousness is elicited by the media ('things outside us' in Mead's sense) through which we come to be aware of our surroundings and ourselves.

I will now develop this point specifically in relation to music, through examples of real life experience. I will begin by broaching what I shall describe as two forms of musical consciousness. Building upon the discussion above, of primary and secondary consciousness, I will use the heuristic of 'warm' versus 'cool' musical consciousness. (In practice these forms are not necessarily distinct – I am deliberately separating them so as to be able to describe different ways in which music conditions awareness.) By the term 'warm consciousness' I mean pre-reflective, embodied, perceptual awareness (feeling, sensing) that sidesteps verbal media and accounts (for example, categories of description often used in self-reports of subjective or physical states such as emotion or pain levels). By the term 'cool consciousness', I mean self-reflective forms of awareness (thinking, speaking about) that are shaped by and make reference to verbal accounts in the manner described in the discussion of Jaynes' and Colombetti's work above.

Warm and Cool Musical Consciousness: Aerobics

Warm consciousness involves a non-verbal, embodied way of being in and being aware of oneself in the world. It is experiential – what Dorothée Legrand calls, 'the "transparent body" (the pre-reflective bodily experience of the world)' (2007: 514). Thus my term, 'warm' could also mean unconsidered (I chose the term 'warm' to highlight the embodied character of unconsidered consciousness).

Warm musical consciousness involves, as I shall describe, connections or articulations between musical activity/experience and some form of physical action/experience, and it is a form of consciousness that is achieved without any significant degree of awareness of music's role as a shaper of action/experience and that is achieved through near-instantaneous connection with music (I am immediately entrained by the music – I walk to its pulse, I begin to move in orientation to its style or genre). Warm musical consciousness has a heat-of-the-moment quality. By contrast, cool musical consciousness takes shape more slowly. Here the music features as an object not only of perception but also of contemplation. Music here is an object that offers resources for knowledge production, for example through the ways it may provide a template or metaphor. Cool musical consciousness involves a relationship between music and action/cognition that is less visceral and more verbal.

My earlier work on aerobics exercise classes (DeNora 2000) highlighted music as a medium that could be used to draw participants in and out of self-conscious reflection (from cool to warm forms of musical consciousness and back again). Sometimes, music could be seen and experienced as a material that recalibrated the exercising person into a bodily mode of being-without-reflection – a moving being more than a thinking being. This is warm musical consciousness. At other times within aerobics activity, music was used to recall participants to a mode of conscious reflection, part of a cool-down and a shift into a highly conscious mode of exercise in which one needed to think about (be conscious of) what one was doing.

In each of these cases certain musical styles and genres were used to afford different temperatures of consciousness – fast-paced rhythmic dance music for warm, slower-paced, more sentimental ballads for cool. Most often, these musical materials were activated, augmented or harnessed through the ways they were coupled with other media and cultural practices such as talk about, or in rhythm to, the music.

For example, aerobics teachers were quick to emphasize how too much core music (music associated with the mindless mode of high energy exercise prior to cool-down) could be dangerous, since, when it was working correctly, it distracted exercisers from being conscious of their bodies (pain, fatigue) and thus could lead them on to the point of injury (more on pain management below). Core music was, typically, the loudest and fastest music used in the session and these properties were in turn framed through instructors' uses of their voices. During core, instructors would model vigorous activity through their own less verbal vocalizations – shouts, single syllable commands ('Go!') and forms of vocalization that mirrored the music, for example a tonal upsweep or the use of sheer volume as a way of performing high energy. Conversely, at the stage in the session where instructors wanted class members to think about how they were using their bodies (for example, during the precision-toning section nearer the end of the session), instructors used music that featured lyrics, that had a slower and more defined pulse, that was played at lower volume (so they could issue detailed instructions about how to execute a stomach crunch, for example) and thus that afforded higher order consciousness, the 'I am thinking about myself doing this' that was required for the task of toning exercise.

In sum, 'warmth' refers to forms of awareness where bodily self-perception does not involve conscious reflection and where there is an interaction between music perception and bodily perception that circumvents or has no need for language and thus also sidesteps or does not lead to higher order forms of cool consciousness. Cool musical consciousness by contrast enhances and is shaped by or accessed through verbal modalities, even if the words are heard only inside the head ('And two, and three', 'Strrrretch – and rest, strrrretch – and rest').

Circumstances

The concept of warm musical consciousness, understood as a form of embodied orientation that is not accompanied by verbal or cognitive forms of knowing, is not necessarily associated with fast or impulsive forms of action or bodily action, though in the case of aerobic exercise that was the case. To take a different example, one may not even realize, for example, that one has become suddenly very still and calm in relation to music. It would be a mistake, therefore, to jump to the conclusion that fast music leads to a loss of cognitive modes of consciousness (and, linked to this, for example, to suggest that only some forms of music will be effective as background soundtracks for study, contemplation, spatial reasoning or mathematics, as is often claimed in 'Mozart effect' research). While it does seem to be the case that faster music is associated with faster paced forms of bodily activity, such as eating, drinking or walking, that music and those behavioural correlates by no means automatically reduce the capacity for verbal and cognitive forms of awareness. To underline this point consider the question of what counts as good music for studying.

In 2011, just after the time of year when students in the UK sit their exams (university and secondary school), I did an online search using the term 'music to study to' (the term was suggested by Google after I had typed the words, 'music to study'). I listened to tracks on Last.fm's, 'Music to Study to Radio' (<http://www.last.fm/tag/music+to+study+to>) and also tracks offered for that search terminology by YouTube. The tracks were varied (Last.fm offered slow, often heartbeat-tempo tracks from Portishead, Death Cab for Cutie and other jazz, folk and quiet rock. YouTube offered options with titles such as 'Baroque Music for Concentration', 'Study Music (For Final Exam)' (classical guitar medley including an excerpt from the Rodriguez concerto for guitar and orchestra 2m 33s into the track, see comment below) and various forms of 'relaxing' music. On YouTube, listener comments abounded, as follows, all entered between two weeks to one hour earlier than my online search (conducted at 7.54 a.m. 14 June 2011) and linked to the Rodriguez concerto:

> what if where u study at is the computer?

> Waste of time :)

> What the? I thought this music is very useful for studying but i don't think it's helping me.

> nice music but what the heck am i doing here? i really should turn off the pc and go study

> had this on repeat for 5 hours before my exam and got an 88 on a course I can barely understand. this music is witchcraft

> this music just made me hungry, and i am procrastinating by writing this

> i guess romance. check it out

> I like this music. At 2.33 [minutes into the track] i was like zzzzzzz

> I like the last part of the song :] what is the name of the song? very nice, beautiful guitar

In short, there are many local factors that render music, and the accounts about music as good for or not good for tasks and cognitive modes (focus, concentration on a task, sleepiness or alertness, minded versus bodied, cool versus warm). These local factors frustrate attempts to predict the forms of music that will be most effective for different groups and individuals. (One of the two top-rated comments, drawn from ratings of all comments from all time by the site users, was 'the best way to study is to click on the off-button of your computer'.)

This casual glance at on-line commentary about music and its uses and benefits highlights some of the ways that our behavioural, emotional, embodied and cognitive responses to music are mediated by personal and situated factors, by the ways that music relates to things outside itself and is contextualized and activated by those things and, methodologically important, how our accounts about these issues are themselves socially framed. Music's circumstances of appropriation (Becker 2004, 2010; Herbert 2012), biography (Batt-Rawden 2006) and current physiological factors (Loewy et al. 2005) are all important components of musical affect and self-reports are not transparent windows into the topic of personal musical experience. We should not assume any simple one-to-one correspondence between musical genre, style or acoustical features and psycho-social or even physiological musical response.

Why, then, have so many 'music and mind' scholars repeatedly sought to find definite correlations between music and responses to music? In part perhaps because the romantic imagery of music's powers (Bergh 2007) is alive and well in the pseudo-science and science of music's purported powers in relation to brain activity, though the rhetoric is increasingly subject to critique in ways that challenge some of the more inflated claims made by neuro-science to reduce everyday forms of behaviour to brain activity (Tallis 2011). A consideration of what I call 'musicalized perception' helps highlight some of the things that brain science elides and thus also highlights (once again) the importance of an ecological perspective for music, health and wellbeing.

To that end, I now turn to the question of how embodied perception can be mediated through cultural techniques that, in effect, trick the brain (and in ways that can foreground or background bodily feelings). From there, I turn to the topic of music in medicine and the focus on pain perception. I suggest that this focus helps to clarify some of the ways in which warm consciousness can be musically mediated. I will begin with the question of how features outside the brain (and mind) can condition what ultimately happens inside – that is inside both the brain (neuro-processing of pain, for example) and the mind (one's sense of body position and thus bodily self-consciousness). For that purpose I begin with the famous 'rubber hand' illusion, a useful example for thinking about mind–body integration.

The Rubber Hand Illusion as an Introduction to What Culture Does

The rubber hand illusion refers to a series of experiments that produced phantom sensation and a misattribution of embodiment. The research subjects were positioned such that one of their hands was hidden by a drape, while a rubber hand was positioned both in sight and in such a way that it gave the appearance of being the subjects' own hand (the rubber hand was positioned in parallel to the subject's other hand on a table). Both hands, the subject's real hand and the rubber hand were then stroked and tapped in an identical and synchronized manner while subjects were instructed to look at the fake hand. Subjects reported the sense of believing that the fake hand was actually their real hand.

The rubber hand illusion illustrates how one sense modality (visual information) can be used to 'capture' (Legrand 2007: 495) another (tactile information) in ways that significantly alter aspects of self-consciousness and orientation. As such it also highlights the interconnection between the senses of sight and touch and the production of proprioception (the sense of one's body position). Here, then, the circumstances of sensory information processing are thus capable of tricking the brain or, rather, tricking the ways that subjects' brains processed sensory stimulation/information. Key here, as an introduction to music and pain management, is that the rubber hand experiment highlights how matters external to the embodied and perceiving subject can structure the ways that this subject perceives seemingly internal sensations.

It is worth considering in more detail what is meant here by 'external matters', for the experimenters themselves have yet to appreciate these details and their significance for cultural theories of sensation and embodiment. In the case of the rubber hand, there are parallels to the craft of the conjurer, who summons or causes things to appear to the senses of her or his audience. The conjurer makes use of various resources for her or his tricks – devices, instructions and verbal frames, apparatuses and set-ups. These devices may be material – for example, the disappearing coin trick relies upon making the top of one hand sticky so the coin will adhere to it in a way that will be hidden from the audience's view. They may also involve misdirection or masking, whether explicit ('Now watch my hand' – when in fact the audience should be watching the other hand) or implicit (our attention as an audience is caught by the waving hand while in the background, out of our focus, the other hand is completing a vital action).

In all cases, conjuring will be produced by specific, unexpected and unnoticed practices, often apparently micro- or minor movements; for example, the quick flicking of a card into the conjurer's lap and thus out of sight, masked by the more elaborate and seemingly 'causal' circular waving of the arms over the table (the one arm hiding the flicked fingers and the moving card but not noticed because attention is focused on what the two arms are doing together). Note that the focus on the figure of 'two arms hovering over the table and going around in a circle three times' is a *gestalt*. As such, it functions like a metaphor or form of perceptual ordering device, drawing attention away from aspects of what can be perceived in the here and now of 'what that hand is doing at this moment'. The *gestalt* sets up expectations of what is (what must be) and what is not (what could not be) going on and these expectations are active in structuring perception (I do not look for what I do not expect to find). Similarly, the stuff of which whodunnits are made (consider, for example, Agatha Christie's *They Do It With Mirrors* [1952]) elaborates the point: a group of people may not hear a noise, because, in the framework that governs expectation, the noise seems insignificant or even absent, so intent are they upon the features that are apparently important ('Oh that?! We didn't pay attention to that! We were expecting to hear a shot much closer to hand'). In both of these examples, the card trick and the successful (fictional) murder, seeing or hearing one thing actually precludes seeing or hearing another. (A good example of this point can be found by considering optical illusions: try, for example, to see both the goblet and the two profiles simultaneously in the well-known example – the perceptual work required to see the one is precisely the perceptual work that blocks out the other.)

These examples highlight how perception does not occur in or by individuals alone but rather emerges in relation to culturally learned and culturally mobilized forms of apparatus or set-ups that, to varying extents, structure the typically tacit, pre-conscious anticipation of what there is to see and thus what is seen (or felt or heard or smelled). Proprioception is socio-culturally produced, sensing can be understood to be mediated through anticipation, and anticipation is itself mediated through culture. The power of framing and suggestion, then, can create sensory illusion. A specific form of this power lies in instances where we may experience sensations in sympathetic response with someone else who is being stimulated – even when we are not receiving the same stimulus. For example, my mouth may twist into a pucker as I watch someone else eat a lemon in ways that literally evoke the sensation.

Neuro-scientists account for these responses with reference to the 'mirror neuron system' (Asai Sugimori and Tanno 2008; Fabbri-Destro et al. 2008). The term 'mirror' refers to a sympathetic capacity where neural activity mirrors or simulates in a predictive way sensations felt by another. If I observe your sensation, I may empathize, bodily, in ways where I literally feel that sensation and where my neural activity is similar to (mirroring) your own ('activation in the observer of neurons that approximate the neurological activity of the person observed' [Asai et al. 2008: 1–2]). (I will return to this neuro-biological account of sympathy and predictive simulation below.) As with the example of the lemon, if I see a loved one being subject to a painful stimuli, I may actually experience pain, and my brain may register activity in the same locations as the brain of my loved one who is receiving the stimulus (Singer et al. 2004, cited in Asai et al. 2008: 3). To return to the rubber hand example, if I observe the rubber hand being touched, my own sensation of touch may be activated and in ways that suggest that I can sympathize with non-humans – objects (Botvinick and Cohen 1998). The example also highlights once again the cultural foundations of proprioception. We are now prepared to consider music's role in relation to pain management.

Neuro-scientific examples of our capacity for predictive simulation and its impact on sensation open up a rich seam for health humanities. The question, then, of when, how and if sensory illusions can become sensory realities is of immense importance in health humanities today. Even if such illusions provide only temporary respite from pain or anguish, the respite or room (to retain the asylum analogy) that is achieved may provide resources for further repair work – blood flowing back into muscles or the breaking of a vicious circle of mental depression such as getting out of the house again after a period of isolation, to take examples from the physical and mental health realms. The potential lines of investigation into this mind–body–culture area are numerous, and the surface has only been scratched, though the applications have, in many realms, been on-going (arts therapy, yogic breathing techniques for blood pressure and deliberate uses of placebo medications [see Chapter 1]).

How might individuals be trained or come to learn how to trick their perception in ways that translate sensation? How might these tricks be linked to cultural set-ups? How can such tricks be managed so that they can be pursued without endangering the patient/client (for example, under some circumstances feeling pain free is not a good thing, indeed it can be life threatening). Here, neuro-scientific accounts of how the anticipatory and sympathetic mirror responses work can benefit from dialogue with health–music studies and from current working knowledge in music therapy. I will now turn to key issues linked to this theme, beginning with a question about ontologies of the body.

Music and Pain

Accounts of the nature of perception and sensation typically make reference to the body and its capacities, but (as I have suggested in the previous chapters) this discourse may be too general to be of use to the cultural pragmatics of health promotion. Is this body here – in particular its capacities for sympathetic response – sufficiently equivalent (never mind the same) as that body there? Indeed, is this body here the same body from moment to moment, place to place? For, if the body and its sensations can be blocked, mediated, transposed and tricked, and if the apparatus that accomplishes these functions is human made, then we need to consider the interpenetration (mutual determination) of culture and physiology, culture and neurology. This is the 'body multiple' as Annemarie Mol puts it, in her description of how, within a hospital space, disease can be many things to many people (2003). So too, the experience of bodily conditions and bodily capacities and sensations can be understood to be multiple: what the body is, as a sensing and functioning organism, is arguably flexible and culturally bounded. If embodied phenomena – sensation, proprioception – vary according to cultural set-up, then embodied phenomena involve more than physiology, more than brain and more than mind–body interaction. That more is the social, technical and aesthetic apparatus and an ecological conception of consciousness (primary and secondary). We have thus returned to the place where practical experience (I respond sympathetically because I have been there and done that and experienced this), framing and informal social learning through interaction with others and modelling of how others do or experience things coalesce. This is also the place to recall the lessons from Howard Becker (discussed in Chapter 4) on the mutual determination of sensation, perception, learning, disposition, framing and milieu over time. Of additional interest is whether neural activity can be seen as the mechanism responsible for music's effects, or whether it is the byproduct of socio-cultural orientation. How much need we concern ourselves with neuroscience to understand and use music as a health technology and health-humanities media? To develop this theme it is useful to consider the realm of music and pain management.

The focus on the importance of apparatus (the framing of sensation) dovetails well with developments in music therapy on music and pain. It is worth noting by way of introduction that music has a venerable history in relation to psychic cures (Gouk 2000; Horden 2000). Music therapists have taken inspiration from recent reconceptualizations of pain as a phenomenon that is much more than a neuro-biological universal and more than physical sensations and reports to the brain's pain centre. By contrast, music therapists practising in the area of pain management conceptualize pain as cultural, emotional, personal and situated.

For example, Hanser describes how, 'a pin prick may elicit shrieks of distress in one person and hardly a notice in another individual. Remarkably, the response to a painful stimulus may be unrelated to its source' (2010: 857). She goes on to describe how the 'gate control theory of pain' (Dickenson 2002) conceptualizes pain signals journey to the cortex and other parts of the brain. Pain signals move through gates or dorsal columns, 'where they encounter inhibitory pathways that are descending from the brain. ... The gate opens or closes at the dorsal horn, where impulses are facilitated or inhibited' (Hanser 2010: 858). Hanser then describes how recent research in pain perception has pointed away from a notion of pain as a phenomenon produced, simply, by an injury, and toward a conception of pain as multi-dimensional, a 'neuro-matrix theory' of pain perception (Hanser 2010: 858, citing Melzack 2001: 1379). This multi-dimensional theory of pain perception allows for a much richer appreciation of mind–body interactions and as such seems to complement the multi-modal account used to explain sensory illusions and sympathetic sensation. The point, and a critical one for music therapy, is that cultural interventions – music but also other media – sculpt the mechanisms by which ascending pain signals travelling toward the brain are mediated and modified. How, then, should we account for this type of sculpture? There are many (and by no means mutually exclusive) accounts of how music ameliorates pain. According to the emphasis placed upon neuro-processing, these accounts heighten or suppress the importance of the external world, of social and cultural formations.

Beginning with accounts that diminish the social, some commentators describe music's role as a stimulus that speaks seemingly directly to, and thus requires processing by, the brain. As an example, in her summary, Hanser describes how musical stimuli, 'compete with incoming pain signals and contribute to the inhibitory effect' (2010: 858), and music may also stimulate certain neuro-transmitters (endorphins or other opioid peptides) that also modify and mollify pain signals to the brain. The perception of pain is modified through the distraction it poses to the neuro-processing of pain signals. Looked at this way, music is not so different from any other stimuli – it is merely a stimulus that disturbs pain signals. Other accounts, from music psychologists and cognitive scientists, emphasize the ways in which music's formal conventions enable it to mimic emotion and embodied experience. This musical mimicry in turn elicits mirror responses in its recipients. So, for example, slow or calming music may induce an embodied sympathetic response, one in which the body may be either foregrounded or backgrounded. This explanation makes space for thinking about how music's cultural properties are active ingredients in pain management. This line of accounting can contribute in important ways to perspectives in health humanities. But it requires, I suggest, yet further development linked to three key points: that music is an interpretively flexible medium, that music reception is temporally and spatially situated and that music reception involves formal and informal learning.

These three notions suggest that music can modify pain because of how it is linked to things outside of individuals and to things that individuals do in tandem with attending to / making music, including social connotations (forms of relationship and other people), physical movements or postures (I relax or roll my shoulders in time with the music and start to feel easier) and forms of activity (memory, eating, thinking, day-dreaming). All of these things are part of the apparatus of how music works. I use the term 'apparatus' here, as I used it earlier in this chapter when speaking of other forms of sensory illusion. The difference is that now the distinction between illusion and reality, the illusory and real bodies is more blurred.

In a striking case study that illustrates some of the ways in which music can be harnessed for medical and therapeutic purposes, Jane Edwards described the case of a 12-year old boy, 'Ivan', who was recovering from severe burns (1995). Ivan's treatment involved an excruciatingly painful process called debridement (the removal of dead skin in a bath). Ivan had continually resisted this therapy (having experienced its pain and thus coming to it primed to expect pain), and each time the treatment was conducted he had screamed and cried. In an attempt to intervene with music, Edwards (acting as medical music therapist) played guitar and sang to Ivan during the process (improvising lyrics to one of his favourite songs, 'With a Little Help From my Friends'). In relation to this musical environment and musical interaction, Ivan was better able to endure the treatment (assessed in terms of what he could tolerate during the procedure and his levels of distress as indicated by such things as his cries). Moreover, during the treatment, it was possible to see Ivan adopting a different role/identity, that is shifting out of being a patient in severe pain and shifting into being a participant (and critic of) a musical performance: he told Edwards at one stage, 'You are singing beautifully.' After the event, Ivan reported that he had felt little pain during the actual procedure. Moreover, as the nursing staff later reported to Edwards, the musical event / musicalized treatment provided a watershed moment in Ivan's recovery. After it, Ivan slept better, was more willing to submit to subsequent debridement procedures and more rapidly began to heal.

Ivan's story lets us consider an example where all three accounts of music and pain management presented above (from weaker to stronger ecological perspectives) can be seen to co-mingle. First, the music distracted Ivan from his pain (his brain processes were diverted) and the musical encounter may have triggered dopamine release. Second, the musical encounter may have primed Ivan's anticipatory stance to the event of debridement such that his perception of the event was recalibrated or translated by his expectancy – a musicalized event is a reframed event. As part of this reframing, and linked to the concept of sympathy described above, to the extent that Ivan (mind–body) was drawn into engagement with the music and came to sympathize with it, Ivan's mind–body was modulated and drawn into the music's tempi and its sonic parameters (potentially shifting body postures, blood pressure, heart rate, muscle tonicity). Third, these physiological and neurological functions may have been linked to the ways in which the provision of music was coupled with other factors that empowered the music to work for Ivan in these ways, such as his relationship with Edwards, opportunities to assume certain (pleasing) social roles (he assumed the role of music critic, for example, complimenting Edwards on the fact that she was 'singing beautifully') and – arguably vital in this context – the fact that people were devoting special, musical attention to him at his time of need. Equally significant, and a fourth factor, the addition of this musical relationship to the event of debridement refigured the negative / anticipated negative aspects of the event which now jostled for space in the social field with more pleasant features: the event – its form and content – was transformed in ways that the unpleasant and frightful aspects were now to some extent diluted by the new and larger, richer, more complex, social solution.

Moreover, the music that Edwards played had special biographical resonance for Ivan, and that it was therefore capable of drawing his attention and engagement was equally significant. The focus on how music's coupling with other factors and the importance of social learning to music's role as a medium of consciousness and health promotion has received increasing attention over the past decade in the area of lay music use and community musicking. Research has described how people suffering from forms of chronic illness use music as part of their everyday circumstances for managing pain and to achieve the clusters of activities associated with being pain free – relaxation, sleep or other forms of embodied reorientation. How music comes to be framed through narrative and expectation ('This music always helps me sleep') is critical here and highlights how music's recipients themselves act in ways that couple music with the things that come to frame music perception and musical response (DeNora 2000; Hennion 2001, 2007). It is the coupling of music and narrative and the ways in which music affords or offers opportunities for narrative that renders music (or rather the use and engagement with music) into a health technology (Batt-Rawden 2006; Batt-Rawden, DeNora and Ruud 2005). This is far removed from any simple behaviourist account of how music works to promote health and wellbeing.

Thus, it is possible to see how, musically contextualized, Ivan became not only a person in less pain, but a person better able to cope with pain – his identity was both transformed and enriched in ways that enhanced his agency as a hospital patient and burn victim. What happened with Ivan was not something that the music itself caused. Rather, music was paired with many other factors that in turn enhanced its utility for pain modification, and this enhancement had as much to do with the music's aesthetic and social meanings – and specifically for Ivan – as it did with the fact that it was music per se. Here, then, we see music humanly applied and humanly accepted in ways that highlight music's mechanisms of operation on behalf of health promotion as involving an intermix of biology and cultural praxis. Getting out of a situation of pain was simultaneously about getting into a situation of shared musical action and in ways that shifted pre-reflective (warm) consciousness away from negative sensations. Pain modification was simultaneously the configuration of self into an alternative social role and that configuration involved a shift in body nexus, or pre-reflective bodily orientation, in ways that predisposed Ivan to play the role of strong patient during the debridement operation. Music is a medium that can instil courage and with it a different attitude to pain. The physical and the social, the embodied and the cognitive preparation for action and/or endurance are thus intermixed in this example of music's use in modulating a form of warm consciousness – the embodied, proprioceptive awareness of pain.

Fighting Fit?

Just as music may recalibrate consciousness in ways that elide the perception of pain, so too it can recalibrate consciousness in ways that elide other perceptions, including perceptions of matters outside of our bodies but linked to bodily conduct. For example, music may help to deflect perception from situational features and definitions, along lines that might reconfigure actors' orientations and even abilities to act in certain ways. One of the most striking, and publicly available, examples of this type of perceptual deflection and calibration for action can be found in George Gittoes' 2004 documentary, *Sountrack to War*. Gittoes' film features interviews with American soldiers during the Iraq War, describing their music listening while on a mission in an Abrams tank (the technology of the tank can be adapted to enable the soldiers to use their MP3 players).

As Gittoes' interviewees described it, their music of choice was heavy metal (for example, Drowning Pool's 'Bodies'). In part, the soldiers' selections for music at work reflected the ways that these soldiers perceived there to be a fit between the music's sonic features and sonic features in the environment caused by the task (drums sounding like bombs and so on). In equal part, the soldiers described how they found this music to be suited to the destructive business of warfare because it psyched them up in occupationally appropriate ways. Gittoes shows us how music was one of the materials to which soldiers turned as they prepared to engage in potentially and actually violent conduct.

There are echoes, here, of Arlie Hochschild's research on how occupations often require individuals to engage in 'emotional work'; that is, to cooperate with an image and a feeling that the task requires (1983; see also DeNora 2000). While Hochschild's research focused on airline flight attendants, the concept of emotional work would seem equally appropriate here. As one soldier commented, when speaking of the heavy metal that he used in his work of soldiering, it 'gets you real fired up'. Gittoes' film shows how the soldiers themselves found the 'right music for the job', as it were: their fast-paced, blaring music of choice for battle suppressed a mode of consciousness that would have interfered with their work requirements. Whereas in the context of an aerobic exercise session, slower and more sentimental music was employed at a certain point as part of cool-down, so as to avoid injury, here, at work in battle, sentimental consciousness (reflection on current activity, self-awareness) is anathema. As one soldier commented, when discussing the music of the jazz crooner Diana Krall: 'We support you [Krall], but we can't listen to you while we roll.'

In short, Gittoes documents twenty-first-century 'battle music'. His film shows us soldiers as their consciousness is musically configured to afford a high level of arousal and a low level of distanced reflection on the meaning of what they are doing – they are musically pumped up for their work. In a manner not dissimilar from the ways in which music has been seen to work in relation to the tasks of eating and drinking (fast music causes fast eating and drinking), here music can be seen to draw actors into a specific form of fast conduct (rapid reaction) commensurate with the mode of conduct known as battle.

In these examples of music in medicine and music in war, it is possible to glimpse music's role as a medium in which an existing form of consciousness (understood as orientation to action scenarios and trajectories and thus experience in time) is transformed or transfigured. This transformation occurs in part when attention comes to be mediated through music (attention is diverted in the example of pain management) or structured through music's properties (when action's pace quickens or emotional orientation shifts). In such cases, it is possible to speak of how sensory orientation and sensory processing is captured by music in ways that are analogous to the process by which visual information captured sensory information in the rubber hand example. When we are captured by music, we are musically recalibrated, removed from one cognitive and/or sensory domain/ orientation into another, facilitating a dispositional shift that does not entail deliberation about how or when to shift.

The example from Gittoes film illustrates a warm form of musical consciousness, one wherein a behavioural and emotional modulation occurs but is not remarked upon or embarked upon with deliberation. By contrast, at times individuals use music deliberately to formulate knowledge about the world and so enhance or enrich consciousness; for example, in relation to problem solving. These are examples of cool consciousness, and they involve music as a candidate structure for formulating thought and/or talk about features of experience and for formulating knowledge of the world – in ways that then come to frame the perception of that world, that become part of the conceptual apparatus that frames the world as we know and engage with it. I will illustrate these points with a brief discussion of Guided Imagery and Music (GIM).

Sonic Imaging and Sonic Imagining

Guided Imagery and Music is a technique of music therapy developed by Helen Bonny (2002; Summer 2002). It provides one of the clearest examples of music's role as a tool for thinking, and one that examines that topic in real time as a client's consciousness of her- or himself and environment is articulated through on-going narrative. In a GIM session, the client is given a relaxation technique and an image to begin the music listening experience. While listening to a 30-minute programme of evocative classical music, the client responds with a variety of sensory imagery, feelings and body sensations which he or she relates to the therapist as they occur.

GIM casts music as a material that can offer structuring properties (such as metaphor) against which extra-musical matters can become known, be explored and be resolved (Summer 2002: 44; see also Bonde 2005: 137). It echoes Claude Lévi-Strauss's view of music as 'myth coded in sounds instead of words [which] offers an interpretive grid, a matrix of relations which filters and organizes lived experience, and acts as a substitute for it and provides the comforting illusion that contradictions can be overcome and differences resolved' (1981: 659). In this sense, music provides a space in which thought and imagination can be elaborated or developed in relation to various issues, problems or tasks (see also DeNora 1986). Like a Rorschach inkblot, music offers a template that can be used as a guide for actors' imaginative process as they set to work on a problem or to elaborate meaning (see DeNora 1986). So, as in the work by Colombetti described at the outset of this chapter that considers language to be a scaffolding for the elaboration of feeling, music may provide structure for the shaping of issues, concerns, images or concepts that might otherwise remain repressed or unnoticed. The things that we then elaborate can thus be understood to be musically led to the extent that our projections take on some of music's properties, which in turn help to shape what is then taken away from the process of musical engagement. Thus, for the socio-music scholar interested in musical consciousness, GIM is an excellent natural laboratory, a place in which to see how agents transfer musical properties to extra-musical properties and how they come to understand those extra-musical matters through the sonic structure of music and in real time, that is, in direct correlation with the unfolding musical event.

GIM also highlights issues that are relevant to the study of collective consciousness and thus illuminates how ecologies of action (the room discussed in Chapter 3) come to be furnished. By no means equivalent to a coincidence of individuals' consciousness, collective consciousness should also rather be explored in terms of its emergence in relation to things outside individuals, in terms of the scaffolding through which it is articulated. Collective consciousness may be understood to be built from public or shared affordances, recursively modified through copious micro-adjustments over time. So, for example, as individuals A, B, C, and D hear music X, A begins to react to the music with interpretation 1, possibly drawing upon earlier articulation work by herself and/or others – these might be other individuals or other sources of information/interpretation, including media sources. She may say something like, 'Music X reminds me of a flock of geese in flight.' Next, B, who had been responding to the music in light of interpretation 2 ('Music X is noble and free') can now, having been exposed to A's reaction, pair 'geese' with 'noble and free' and let these terms refine both each other and the music. B can say as much to A, who in turn might find yet another way of responding ('It is like being able to own the open skies'). Upon hearing this conversation (or reading about it or being told about it or even imagining it), C and/or D may join in ('It is like a hang-glider over the ocean'). (Thus it is possible to trace the modulations of a particular piece of music's meanings or connotations over time: for example, when a religious hymn is converted into a protest song or vice versa.) The result, constantly subject to further elaboration and revision, is an exponentially expanding set of permutations that depend only upon the recognition (identification work) and uptake of new responses to music X. Each time a further interpretive moment is added, the more the field of music X's affordances is expanded and the richer and thicker becomes the culture or set of meanings and practices anchored by music X. The making of associations, and their existence as resources for future making, is more than mere accumulation, since how things are added, by whom and in what order in turn modifies the ways that they refract upon each other and through that make themselves available for appropriation by next-users. As this process of refraction and development continues, culture is elaborated and with it possibilities for collective consciousness.

Over time, then, looking back on this music, to the extent that it was initially or retrospectively paired with some experience, event or thing, can afford collective remembering. In this way, music X offers itself as a technology of memory (Tota 2005; Wagner-Pacifici 1996); it is, not a material that merely aids recall but actually structures what is recalled and how. So too, collective action in a present moment may involve orienting to musical scaffolding in ways where music can be seen, coolly, to lead consciousness and motivation.

In short, GIM demonstrates how music and music-making can provide transferable resources for engagement with the social world. In these cases, music can be seen to provide a template, grid, myth, metaphor, model or mnemonic for elaborating thought – as when we turn to a musical model to show or lead us to the development of a social arrangement or use music as a mnemonic structure / technology of memory. In both of these cases, consciousness is composed through reference to music. Music provides materials with which to model the perception and narration of the environment and thus orientation, and – as I will now seek to demonstrate – participation in the world.

Music, Consciousness and Mental Health: The Case of BRIGHT

In their chapter on collaborative musicality, Mercédès Pavlicevic and Gary Ansdell summarize recent developments in music psychology as it has shifted from cognitive (individualized) to ecological (social) perspectives and to a focus on music in naturalistic settings of use (2008). Invoking the work of Charles Keil, they speak of music as a source of 'participatory consciousness'; that is, as having the 'capacity not just to model but maybe to enact some ideal communities' (Keil and Feld 1994, quoted in Pavlicevic and Ansdell 2008). Speaking of participatory consciousness returns the focus to music's role as a resource for the emergence of collective consciousness described above. Collective musical consciousness is a process that is articulated in and through the making of a shared cultural space, through inhabiting, making, and remaking cultural resources, among them, music. In the final section of this chapter, I will reflect on this theme, using examples from an on-going case study in the area of music and mental health. I will highlight mental health as the capacity to adopt and adapt participatory consciousness in daily life.

As I described in the previous chapter, for the past two years, I have had the opportunity to watch Ansdell in action in his work as a community music therapist in and around the BRIGHT centre for mental health. Over time it has been possible to map the emergence of collective musical culture within BRIGHT and with it to see how features of this culture permit participatory consciousness or the ability to enact community. Within this collective endeavour, it is also possible to see individuals experiencing consciousness shifts – in particular, forms of broadening out from private to public sensitivities and modes of expression within and beyond the BRIGHT world.

Insofar as they are associated with the occupation of varying parts of the musical space at BRIGHT (some participants, for example, tend to stick to some parts of the musical terrain and never venture into others), participants' musical acts can be diagrammed as trails in musical space, patterns of movement across the space that cover portions of the space with varying degrees of frequency and intensity. Trails highlight clients' musical pathways or progressions over time and their traversals of musical forms within a space. For example, the three trails depicted in Figure 6.1 are associated with the musical activity of three participants: Peter, of whom we shall hear more momentarily, Robbie, introduced in the previous chapter ('I am Billie Holiday') and myself (note that I do not dwell in the part of the space associated with solo singing, instruments or folk music and that my footprint is lighter than those of Robbie and Peter).

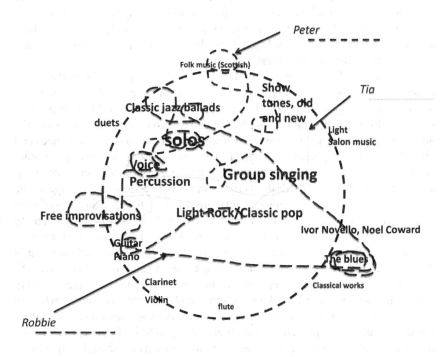

Figure 6.1　Three individuals' musical trails through BRIGHT musical space, 2006

Within BRIGHT, this inhabitation of a part of the musical space is not unusual. Some members never touch some features of the space: indeed, some leave the room for various purposes (to smoke, to use the toilet) when certain types of music are performed, while others do not participate in the group singing of some numbers. Others inhabit only a small part of the whole space. Still others will seek to personalize a part of the space (make it habitable) through talking about the type of music there and attempts to configure, performatively, how the music in that place should sound.

'Peter' (I have altered identifying details so as to preserve his anonymity and also altered his musical preferences) is in his mid-40s, has been in and out of hospital and is now a regular participant in the BRIGHT music sessions where he routinely brings his favourite songs which he performs at the mic. These are Scottish folk songs and he cherishes them. Peter is the only one at BRIGHT to perform this repertoire. In the early stages of our research, Peter participated only minimally in the sing-along sessions and hardly at all in the group improvisations. He typically did not join in when the group sang more modern songs. At that time, Peter described in an interview how the songs he sings remind him of his happy holidays in the Scottish Highlands. He also told of how he uses these songs to cope at times when he feels he is beginning to slip into illness again. In common with the respondents in *Music in Everyday Life* (DeNora 2000), he described how these songs provided him with (what I have termed) a technology of self and health and a medium for achieving and sustaining focus.

Music, I would suggest, provides Peter with a selective sensitivity to the world, a mode of consciousness. As such, it is a resource for his care of self (a source of ontological security through nostalgia and a tie to past identity). At the same time, however, this self-care and with it, Peter's musical consciousness, intensifies the gulf between Peter's musical consciousness, his occupation of musical space and others' musical occupation at BRIGHT. The musical trails of most of the other BRIGHT members do not overlap greatly with Peter's. In other words, Peter has a musical 'problem' at BRIGHT – how to make connections and engage in the remaking of his musical self and become more like the others and thus less of what he is at present. Peter is musically isolated, and the bulk of the work of maintaining the value of his music falls upon his own shoulders. The combination, then, of his music's position in the musical space and his own relative isolation within it limits the resources Peter has to articulate a shared musical world at BRIGHT (though he has other, social resources at his disposal, as do other participants). Although Peter's music affords him comfort and pleasure and a means by which to promote his sense of self identity and wellness, it does not simultaneously afford resources with which to align past with present so as to be in the current world, where musically associated sensibilities are only minimally shared. It functions, in other words, as a form of removal as discussed in Chapters 3 and 4, comforting and pleasing but also preventing Peter from more fully relating to BRIGHT's musical-social space. Paradoxically, Peter's music both provides what he needs in order to stay functional, but simultaneously restrains his capacities to function more flexibly over a wider socio-musical territory.

If Peter dwells within his preferred music exclusively, if he continues to function as, in Peterson and Kern's term, a musical 'univore' (1996), his opportunities for connection to others through music will remain dependent upon the degree to which others can be drawn onto his musical territory, his musical sensibility. In other words, Peter's musical habitus removes him from the shared reservoir of tastes and practices, musically speaking, and for this reason it is vulnerable to being ignored or derided (though this is something which does not in fact occur at BRIGHT). Simultaneously, other individuals, perhaps more able to marshal other social resources as well, can more readily inflect the BRIGHT space with their own music, and encourage further uptake of that music, reflexively repositioning themselves more closely in the core of the musical space.

It would be both dangerous and theoretically weak to say that there is anything wrong or pathological about Peter's values and practices or that there is anything about the music – its connotations and its aesthetic (however configured outside BRIGHT) – that in principle prevent it from taking a more central place in BRIGHT culture. If any custom or taste or practice is fully shared it becomes, in the sociological sense of the term, normal. We can only say that these values are in the minority at present. However, it is correct to acknowledge that Peter's musical values and practices are not able to afford rich participation in the musical world at BRIGHT as currently configured and that, because of this, his practices reinforce a mode of consciousness that directs him away from the opportunity for a greater shared musical and social world, and from sensibilities and orientations that are constantly emerging and shifting within that world.

More recently, developments instigated by the music therapists at BRIGHT have addressed Peter's musical situation, seeking to broaden his musical opportunities. It is at this stage that it becomes difficult to describe the nature of these changes without potentially compromising Peter's anonymity, and I will not therefore go further with this discussion, except to say that it has resulted in considerable musical development, both of his technical ability and of the repertoire that interests him. He has made a shift from a musically anchored preoccupation with private concerns to a musically engendered movement onto a shared terrain characterized by new expressive materials and topics. His horizons – musical and extra-musical – have expanded through his participation in a band, in which repertoire is negotiated and chosen by others and his musical habitus or comfort zone has been expanded, rendered more plastic (Lahire 2003). This expansion has not been entirely easy. The process of musical broadening has also involved Peter's attempt to reconcile involvement in a social group and an ever-widening musical terrain with a hitherto devout ploughing of a rather narrow musical furrow. With this widening, Peter's former self (in the form of a musical habitus) was not shed but took a step back to accommodate new ways of orienting and engaging, new outlooks on his social world. This musical broadening in turn has enabled Peter to engage in refurnishing, so that music becomes for him less a removal and more of a moving in (see Chapter 3).

In sum, the musical recalibrations described in this chapter – from Ivan in the burns unit to the soldiers interviewed by Gittoes to exercise class members to participants in GIM to Peter – illustrate how music is or can become integral to consciousness formation and in ways that are directly connected to health and wellbeing and how music is constitutive of both reflective (cool) and pre-reflective (warm) forms of consciousness. Music can offer an ally or template for new or emerging values or action plans. It can foster recalibrations of sensibility, and it can hold existing sensibilities in place. It can recalibrate the body in ways that call attention to the body or aspects of sensation (or, conversely, make bodily phenomena transparent). Thus, the study of musical consciousness not only helps to elucidate consciousness as an extended and aesthetic phenomenon – something that emerges in relation to social and cultural materials. It also highlights how those materials may be used – at times with deliberation – to heighten, suppress or alter consciousness, both individual and collective. Considering music's formative role in relation to consciousness elucidates the interpenetration and ecological bases of individual and collective forms of consciousness, which thus helps us to consider music's role in fostering mental health understood as the 'lack of a problem in living' (Szasz 1960: 113), namely, the ability to collaborate with others in furnishing the world with materials that afford asylum, that promote wellbeing.

Music is, often and insidiously, part of how, for better or for worse, we are drawn into social relations and made ready, in an aesthetic and pre-cognitive way, for courses of action about which we may be otherwise (verbally) unaware. By this I mean that the study of music and consciousness highlights the often subtle, often tacit, aesthetic bases of our selective sensitivity to the world. Music is therefore an important medium with which to furnish (or escape from) the world and thus discussions about which music is good or worthy of public commendation are simultaneously discussions about access to (musical) asylum. Thus, as an aesthetic medium, music is shot through with ethical implications since opportunities for musical experience are opportunities for care and health promotion. In the next chapter, I develop this theme, proposing an aesthetic of music's goodness that is linked to what music does, how, where and for whom. I shall argue that aesthetic judgements are themselves ecologically situated and that, in practice, the ethical and the aesthetic may be inseparable. What kind of good, then, is music and when is music good?

Chapter 7

Where is Good Music?

In the spring of 2008, the BRIGHT Singers gave a concert. Held in the atrium of a large metropolitan hospital, a venue renowned for the quality of its professional and semi-professional lunchtime concert series, the event would have been a cause for excitement and perhaps a few pre-concert nerves for any amateur group. For the BRIGHT Singers though a good deal more was also at stake. The atrium performance was, as the project's music therapist and choir director, Sarah Wilson, noted in her project diary a few days prior to the event, 'our first non-mental health venue performance – in a very public place'. (Sarah took over as convener of the BRIGHT sessions in 2007. She was then working half-time for BRIGHT and half-time for the NHS as a music therapist in the adjacent hospital. Because some of the BRIGHT personnel came over from the hospital and because Sarah had worked with others, since discharged, when they were hospital residents, Sarah and her activities bridged the two locations and networks.)

On the day, the singers arrived dressed in festive, colour-coordinated outfits. They gave a half-hour concert with an eclectic programme. As a musical event, the concert was a great success. Afterward, a number of audience members stayed on to mingle and several could be heard to comment favourably on the relaxed and rather personal presentation format and on the wide range of musical styles (from pop songs to classical to original material – a folksong by one of the clients).

After lunch, the group gave a series of short concerts in the actual hospital wards, during which time they were accompanied by the hospital's Arts and Culture Officer. I followed, carrying cameras, coats and bags. In the second ward we found two patients (and four empty beds), one of whom was very thin and gave me the impression of being near the end of his life.

Despite his physical appearance, however, this man was alert, cheerful and polite, and he gave all the usual indications of musical engagement and enjoyment. When the second piece ended, he made a request – did the group know 'Swing Low, Sweet Chariot':

> Swing low, sweet chariot
> Comin' for to carry me home
> If you get to heaven before I do
> Comin' for to carry me home
>
> Tell all my friends I'm comin' there too
> Comin' for to carry me home.

'Swing Low, Sweet Chariot' is a spiritual. As its lyrics make clear, it is a song about death, departure and the common human condition. (The song has also, since 1988, been the English Rugby anthem, a fact I did not know at the time.) Spontaneously, the BRIGHT Singers and the two men began to sing together, from memory.

As I looked around the room, I found I was by no means the only one with tears in their eyes. Something special was clearly happening, facilitated by this song. I believe that music, in this case the singing of this song together, inflected the situation, redrawing boundaries and social relationships. First, it put the singers in the spotlight and on the spot to perform this request (perhaps one of this man's last requests?) It called upon them to perform something important without preparation, in this ward at this time, and they rose to the occasion gracefully.

In rising to the challenge the singers' roles were transformed. They were no longer members of an amateur choir. Nor were they mental health clients. They were ministers and celebrants: the musical performance collected participants into a shared and emotionally charged occasion and an occasion that simultaneously transformed many features of the situation. The ward, for example, was temporarily no longer a ward but a place of communion. The patients in beds were no longer patients but collaborators in communal activity. The hospital staff members were no longer nurses and orderlies but co-participants. (Conversations afterwards with hospital staff, nurses, arts administrators and musicians touched, over and over again, upon how the was uplifting to staff as well as patients.) Performing music was catalytic, transcendent, forward-looking. It supplanted existing roles: in the instant of performing (music) well, all of these people, and in spite of their worldly cares, were well. (Which is not the same as saying that they were well forever after.) Performance, in other words, matters. By that I mean that the music, its lyrics, its format and its circumstances of production drew everyone together in and for a time and in ways that transcended the times associated with institutions and other obligations. This collaboration made, in short, asylum. The fact that there was risk involved in the production of this ritual (what if they had not been able to rise to this occasion?) only served to heighten the stakes, empower the achievement. At this moment, in these circumstances, the singing of 'Swing Low, Sweet Chariot', and indeed the concert writ large, was good, beautiful and true. Indeed, as I shall describe in this chapter, there could have been no better music anywhere.

Performance

A few days later, the feeling of exhilaration among the singers continued and permeated the BRIGHT space more generally. At the time, Sarah Wilson wrote in her project diary:

> Lovely atmosphere, everyone clearly pleased with themselves after the concert.

Comments made about the audience, their participation, how many there were etc. and how special it was on the ward, in particular the enthusiastic man who asked for 'Swing Low'. Lots of talk about musical achievement, not 'mental health' ones.

Sarah's final sentence highlights how, for the BRIGHT Singers, the occasion was one of musical achievement. It highlights how problems can often be resolved (or circumvented) by addressing them obliquely (see Ansdell and DeNora 2012). After the concert, but on the same day, as we ate our sandwiches in the courtyard area prior to the tour of the wards, the group's talk reflected that this musical achievement was extra special because it was won on musical terms: the singers had, in effect, passed; they were one more of the very many high calibre performing groups to have made music in this venue. Of course, this passing constituted a milestone in the career of the group (and thus a resource for future narratives) – it was a first public concert, a musical success. Achieving success on those terms made almost redundant the fact that the successful concert was also a mental health triumph. (Indeed, all performances, whether or not they involve music, are mental health triumphs and can be understood as ways of passing, which is another way of saying that there is no problem in living.) Thus, when, at one stage after the concert, a member of the audience asked some of the singers if they were a semi-professional choir drawn from the hospital's staff, the irony was richly appreciated, amusing and empowering, and this empowerment became compounded after the singing of 'Swing Low, Sweet Chariot', the musical ministering to another's need, the mutual celebration of being (in music) together.

Goodness in and Goodness from Music

There is no doubt in my mind that the music I have been describing did good. But the recognition that music does good is perhaps not contentious and an easy one to debate, since many different types of music may be equally good at doing good. The proposition, 'music does X, Y or Z' is open-ended. It is also one that underscores music's transformational capacity.

To restate the key question: the music of the BRIGHT Singers may have done good, but was it good? Does it conform to a canon of pre-established criteria of goodness? Answering 'Yes, this music was as good as, say, Beethoven's, as performed by the winner of, say, the Leeds' piano competition in 2012', is too often understood as saying that any form of music, performed to any standard anywhere and any time is equally good as any other. And this hands-up-in-the-air form of relativism is often linked to the idea that goodness is merely and only in the eye of the beholder, indeed that it is mere preference, a matter of personal taste ('I know what I like'). Such a position, I believe, belittles the importance of the arts and trivializes matters of judgement. I suggest that both the idea that there are a priori standards of goodness and the relativist notion that there are no standards both fail music in so far as neither take music seriously in terms of what it can do in particular contexts, times and places.

By contrast, I shall suggest a form of grounded, contextual aesthetics that links the question of what music is good for to the question of what music is good and that points to Wittgenstein's provocation that 'ethics and aesthetics are one and the same' (2001: 88). Such a vision is important because it helps to clarify why people value, and value the valuing of, aesthetic media and why aesthetic media are such an important part of asylum strategies, whether as forms of removal or as furnishing. It also poses an alternative way of evaluating art forms, one that allows for multiple and local understandings of goodness that nonetheless share a commitment to the idea that the recognition and appreciation of goodness is activity not observation.

To speak of what aesthetic media do is different from, but includes as a topic, forms of aesthetic valuation expressed through talk or writing about music. It understands the discursive acts of verbal evaluation as poetic acts that add meaning through the ways that they connect artworks to other things within the world. So, and sticking with Wittgenstein, we can examine how verbal attributions performatively define and refine artworks ('If I say of a piece of Schubert's that it is melancholy, that is like giving it a face' [Wittgenstein 2012: 4]). We can also explore valuation practices; that is, forms of valuation that take place non-verbally as aesthetic media are appropriated in and for contexts of use – through the ways that gestures and forms of activity are assembled around and in relation to aesthetic media. (Wittgenstein offers the example of showing that a suit is appreciated by wearing it not by talking about it [2012: 5]). We could go further, and look at how the wearing may in turn be linked to opportunities for action within a space, as I have already discussed in Chapter 3.)

Thus, valuation, whether as talk about, writing about or acting with or in relation to an aesthetic object, performs or attempts to perform, render or otherwise complete that object/media. It thus defines and places that object/media within a social world. Understood in this way, aesthetic valuation is not about knowing or attempting to articulate a correct answer about culture (what is objectively best or worst). It is making culture in and through the act of telling about, situating and using it. Thus valuation makes and takes away opportunities for action, forms of connection, identification and expression. It may impose meanings and forms of legitimacy that silence subversion (on the concept of symbolic violence, see Bourdieu and Passeron 1977: 4). It is for this reason that the opposite, relativist position is often proffered since it advocates a much more anodyne attitude to the question of value, though such an attitude is typically weak – while all aesthetic forms may have the potential to be or do equal good, how that potential is operationalized and clarified will vary according to situation, within ecologies of practice. A focus on this situated, contextualized production of value highlights aesthetic media as materials for living.

Classifying Music

Table 7.1 specifies four possible combinations of music that does and/or is good: music that is good and does good (A), music that is good but does no good (B), (C) music that is no good but does good and (D) music that is no good and does no good.

Table 7.1   Music that is good and music that does good

What music is What music does	Good	No Good
Good	A	C
No Good	B	D

Musicologists, music critics, aestheticians, friends, YouTube commentators (see Chapter 6) and popular music scholars have all at various times been concerned with just what should be put in each of these boxes. Where to locate Beethoven's Ninth (as opposed to his Seventh) or the feminist appropriation of death metal or the pre-electric Bob Dylan or Jimi Hendrix's rendition of the 'Star-Spangled Banner' or Frank Sinatra or a karaoke performance of 'I Did It My Way' or a community orchestra performance of Beethoven's Ninth? What about Ghanaian car-horn music or Evan Parker's saxophone improvisation or Mozart or Michael Barimo whistling the Queen of the Night's 'Vengeance Aria' from *The Magic Flute*? Such a list is potentially endless, or it is at least as long as differences (and willingness to make differences) between arbiters of taste might care to make it and certainly as long as an associated list of any differences between the arbiters involved. Such an exercise is routinely attempted by radio programmes such as *Building a Library*, *The Top Forty* on Radio 1, Classic FM's *Classic Countdown*, *The X Factor*, *American Idol*, and Last.fm's folksonomies and tag-charts, all of which highlight just how complex and contradictory definitions of good, better and best in music can be when one is seeking to form a right answer about musical worth.

This preoccupation with aesthetic taxonomy is of considerable interest to those who seek to explore how people do things with aesthetics, but, as a project in the world, it is both fraught and, as I will describe, wasteful of potential, conditional goodness. We need a more flexible understanding of taxonomy and thus of aesthetic classification, one that understands goodness as locally situated, grounded, property that is performed and emerges relationally in the same ways as does health/illness.

Music's Goodness is Relational and that Means a Focus on Identification Practice

If I point to something in the world and then describe it ('That house is red'), I am offering an example of a category descriptor, in this case a colour. What may be less obvious is that my act of matching the particular instance to the general category also defines, or attempts to define, the category to which the instance ('That house over there') is, in commonsense terms, thought to exemplify. My instantiation, how I flesh out this category (red), may have implications for how I, you and we think about and perceive both the instances I identify and the category as we know it and come to know it in future. Of course redness has physical properties (I may have difficulty persuading you that green is red) though of course my and your perceptual capacities will condition what we determine to be red as opposed to green. For example, I may be colour-blind in which case my red retinal receivers will lead me to different conclusions about what is and is not red or indeed if there is such a category as red. So too, other features of my environment may affect my and others' perceptions and the for-all-practical purposes conclusions that we reach. For example, if I engage in this classification while wearing rose-tinted glasses or under a red spotlight what counts as red may vary. Similarly, cultural prescriptions (codes, cues and situated practices) will guide and govern my/our perception, often tacitly, as conditions of reception.

To put the conclusion of the argument here at its start: all of these conditions need to be recognized, explored and unpicked ethnographically. They are all part of how we do the work of linking instances to categories. They highlight, moreover, the importance of perceptual and evaluative ecologies, recontextualizing the recognition of value and identity. To miss the ecological point, I shall argue, is to miss an attempt to illuminate, perhaps enumerate, the things that make good of music or anything else. This is why I said earlier that it could be considered wasteful to attempt to classify goodness in music in decontextualized ways: to do so is to miss opportunities to make and experience the multifarious character of musical goodness. Surely, finding more and novel ways to register or perceive and value music's goodness must be good? And would it not be bad to let the need to know the best be the enemy of that good?

Toward a Hyper-Contextual Aesthetic

John Cage once famously observed that, 'no two coca cola bottles are the same', by which he meant that the bottle is perceived in relation to qualities of light, differences in position in space and time and the interpretive and experiential orientations that we bring to the scene (Cage 1992). All of these things can render a seemingly identical object in individually differentiated and unique ways.

As it happens, what is on the inside of the Coke bottle also illustrates Cage's point and in a yet more grounded manner. Coca-Cola, the drink, is by no means everywhere and always the same. It varies by location, according to how its franchisers produce and bottle it. (Mexican bottlers add cane sugar rather than corn syrup, for example, and the taste and quality of the water varies markedly from region to region, country to country, even day to day, such that in some bottling locations, coke also contains DDT or other chemicals, and it was this that led to a complete ban on the sale of Coca-Cola in parts of India in 2004.) Even holding all of the above constant, within particular batches there are variations according to the way the drink is bottled (glass or plastic) or canned (more or less CO_2) and stored. (There are actually listserves and websites populated by Coca-Cola aficionados where these points are discussed in detail.) There is no one definitive version of 'the real thing': rather, there are different, indeed, competing, versions of that thing which appears unitary because its differences are effaced by global branding and by our complicit lack of attention to or concern with difference. Our culturally mediated consciousness (the prescription that each bottle is identical) desensitizes us to intra-categorical difference: each bottle passes as yet one more of the same thing. The reputation of Coca-Cola can and often does precede the reception of any one instance of Coca-Cola (a point that can be quickly verified at home with a randomized double blind taste test!).

This point can be further developed through reference to a paper by John Law and Anne Marie Mol and their concept of 'mutable, immutable mobiles' of which Coca-Cola is one. Law and Mol developed this concept using a different example, the Zimbabwean 'bush-pump', courtesy of a study by Marianne de Laet and Annemarie Mol (Law and Mol 2001). This device is composed of many parts. If the pump is to be deemed good (worth implementing in policy terms, helpful, effective), the relationship between those parts has to be aligned in such a way that the device can actually pump water that is clean enough to drink.

As Law and Mol observe (and faintly echoing Cage on the Coca-Cola bottle), however, there is no bush-pump per se. Rather, what counts as *the* pump physically mutates from site to site as it is variously configured. Rather like George Washington's infamous axe (first the handle was replaced, then the blade, then the material that connected the two), Law and Mol observe that, 'bits break off the device and are replaced with bits that don't seem to fit ... and other components ... are added to it ... which were not in the original design itself' (2001: 613). Yet the pump is recognized as *the* pump, from place to place, and it is hailed as a good thing (for example, as an aid to public health). This mutable immutability extends, as Law and Mol describe it, even to the question of whether or not it is actually producing clean water. As Law and Mol observe, 'the pump works if it produces clean water. But what counts as clean water? This, it turns out, is highly variable' (2001: 614).

Configuring the pump's effectiveness, its goodness (how it is assembled so that it pumps clean water), is simultaneously configuring our criteria of perception of the pump (What is clean enough water? What is enough water?) and the actions, people and policies connected to this pump. The goodness of the pump is thus a result of locally, contingently produced links between the pump's composition, criteria and technologies of assessment, and attribution. The pump – its mechanical form and the assessment of its value – is flexible; it mutates over time and place. However, when the pump is discussed in abstract terms, these contingencies are effaced and replaced with a fixed identity.

The point is that goodness or effectiveness in the case of the bush-pump is not self-evident. On the contrary, it is produced, time after time, from place to place, as both the bush-pump and its value-identity are realized in relation to contextual factors that are themselves realized and selectively mobilized as contextualizing factors. Context, in other words, is as much produced as producing. It is much more than a pre-existing set of constraints upon production or perception. As with the bush-pump, the colour red, Coca-Cola bottles (inside and out) so too, Mozart, car-horn symphonies, the BRIGHT Singers or the Rolling Stones.

Bush-Pumps, Colour Perception, Music and Other Identities

Vivaldi's concerto oeuvre, in particular the *Four Seasons*, is routinely broadcast in New York City transport hubs, such as the New York Port Authority Bus Terminal and Penn Station. There, this music that (it is claimed) is good (better than composer X, worse than composer Y), is used (it is claimed) to do good. The good it does in this case is to discourage 'vagrants' and 'hooligans' from 'loitering' (it is not longer their kind of space, or so the argument goes) while simultaneously raising the tone of the space.

I have used scare-quotes for 'vagrants', 'hooligans' and 'loitering' to highlight how whatever the goods music may do, these goods are relational, flexible entities – good for some things, good for some people. These forms of goodness are contextualized: their meaning takes shape in relation to a host of other (equally flexible) things that are tapped as conditions of perception and judgement – facts and features of the setting, ways of seeing, aims, beliefs, preferences, conditions of perception, discourses, and many other things.

Thus the recognition of the goodness that music can do is a topic in need of exploration. For example, Penn Station's programming practice, its use of muzak, is considered by some (the police, the mayor's office) to be good. For others, this practice is not doing good, in fact, it is doing bad, indeed, the music's goodness itself may not be good. Those groups might include, for instance, sub-groups of commuters themselves, the very people that the presence of Vivaldi supposedly improves the space for: those who cannot abide muzak (the hearing-impaired often find muzak disabling, the consumer activist movement Pipedown in the UK campaigns to have muzak abolished); those who cannot abide Vivaldi ('Nothing compared to J.S. Bach' or 'I actually prefer heavy metal') or for whom Vivaldi's music carries unpleasant, perhaps even distressing connotations (as was the case with my respondent 'Lucy' who was unable to listen to the music of some composers during a period of grieving following her father's death [DeNora 2000: 63]) or who find Vivaldi saturates the airways of classical music radio ('Oh God, not Vivaldi again!'); those who cannot abide what they take Vivaldi's music to connote ('This is such a pretentious attempt to seem posh!'); or those who cannot abide hearing this music in this context ('They ruin Vivaldi by playing it here in this way!').

Others whom Vivaldi has perhaps not helped include the homeless people attempting to take refuge in the transport terminal, perhaps to sleep in a corner or even just take shelter from the weather. For these people (and this is the intention of programming Vivaldi), the musical ambience may be discomforting, reminding them that this place is for more legitimate patrons and that sitting, or, worse, sleeping, on the floor in a corner is not a legitimate use of the space. This is precisely that to which the term symbolic violence refers: the recontextualizing of meanings as illegitimate and tenuous within a space. In this sense, music has done its (Penn Station's) good. But is that good itself good?

By contrast, consider Vivaldi played in a church: both the transport terminal and the church are public spaces, and both spaces are often used by homeless people. Depending on the church, both are spaces where one may encounter the sound of baroque music (for example, choir, concert or organ rehearsal through the day in churches). Does Vivaldi in church also dispel 'vagrants'? The very wording of this question highlights the impropriety of such a notion. Perhaps (this is mere speculation) in the church space, baroque music is not perceived as a form of sonic exclusion or policing because it is traditionally associated with some forms of churches and the churches are not seeking to encourage homeless people to stay away. The space inflects the music, just as the music inflects the space.

And so, again, 'Good for whom, where, when and how'? As scholars of organizational soundscape and setting have observed, music's distribution within space is characterized by a politics, especially, as in the case of the transport station, where audiences are, to varying degrees, captive (the same applies even more stringently to care homes [Hara 2011], prisons [Cusick 2008], schools [Bergh 2007], hospitals [Rice 2003]). In this case, there are assumptions (obvious to some, tacit to others) about what kind of (whose) good it is that music should serve which in turn beg questions about how individuals will respond to and experience the transport station's music policy which is unlikely to be one-size-fits-all.

This recognition of all the different kinds of difference, how they are elided, magnified, consolidated and collapsed (which version of the good prevails?) leads in turn to the point I have been developing in this section, namely, that the goodness music does is relational: it takes shape (its goodness is clarified) in relation to a range of contextual factors. If this goodness is relational, why not also the good that music is?

As told by Nancy Reich, Clara Schumann said of her own compositions that they were, 'women's work which always lacks force and occasionally invention' (2001). Why though should force or invention be valued over their opposites or over, presumably, less force or invention? Indeed, more fundamentally, when is / is not forcefulness or invention present or absent? These questions highlight the assembly and, in some cases, such as with Schumann, the institutionalization of aesthetic frameworks as selections, choices endorsed by some constituency, user group or community of practice. How could that process, and the ways in which it underwrites a selective social distribution of value, not also be a matter of ethical concern? For what is wrong (less good) with little music, quiet music, domestic music, music that is easy to play or understand? Under what conditions does such music also get recognized as great (Satie? Mozart? whistling?) Can we not argue that under some conditions it might be the best and, if so, what are those conditions? Moreover, and this takes us to the nub of the argument, what are the social implications and entailments of such an aesthetic stance? Our mode of valuing goodness in music is, in this sense, a component of our mode of valuing goodness from music. Who is it, then, that music pleases?

Otomo Yoshihide is hailed by many as Japan's premier improvisatory musician (officially therefore a claim to good music / aesthetic experience). When he collaborates with fellow musicians, who also happen to be a group of people with and without learning disabilities (Numata 2009), does the composition of this collaborative group affect the good we attribute to his work? Is it just as good, not as good, better?

Yoshihide pulls these amateurs' musical acts into the frame of his own work and, simultaneously, they pull him into the frame of what their acts create. This mutual determination of the music's goodness and the resulting sounds can be hailed as doing good (if one watches the video, it is obvious that many people were animated and enjoyed the experience and that many were proud: the music made a good day for them). Was the music itself good? It is if our evaluative accounts tap and feature conditions that clarify this music as good and doing good.

Yoshihide draws the sounds of amateur (or unconventional, untrained) musicians into the mainstream concert hall. He presents novel musical material, which, of course, in turn reconfigures our notion of the concert hall and its aims. The resultant sounds do not conform to preconceptions of good music (they might be considered different, strange, to defy expectations, to be too full of surprises [or, conversely, too repetitive], inharmonious or many other appellations we might connect with music that is not good). True, this music diverges from (perhaps is not able to stay within) conventional procedures such as functional tonality, even-pulsed rhythms, forms, formats, even styles of presentation, but much of what is classed as good music does the same thing, to varying degrees. (Where, for example, would we place Beethoven, Schoenberg and Stefan George's 'Rapture' ['I feel air from other planets'] or John Cage? Where to place extreme, free or experimental jazz?) Where would we place new performance or recorded performance techniques (crooning or electric guitars)? Where would we place new genres (the waltz, for example, was initially considered immoral and conducive to bad behaviour)?

The point is that in attributing new and different musical things with value, we redefine aesthetic priorities and with them music itself. In redefining aesthetic priorities, we allow for social transformation – new ways of attending to the world, of feeling, relating, perceiving, taking pleasure, new identities, statuses, appellations. When we get excited about something in music that we love, we are excited about what it affords, what it stands for, what it lets us be. Music is always, even at its most apparently neutral, social performance and ethically charged.

To say that goodness in music is a locally assembled entity (albeit often abstracted as a general account – as in 'This work/composer/genre is good') is to open up the topic of aesthetic value to a focus on the local, nuanced practice (craft) of making good with music: back, in other words, to the question: 'Goodness for whom, what, how, when, where, why and according to whom?' That practice, as with the bush-pump, involves tinkering or aligning the music we make, perceive and judge with the things that facilitate our judgement: for example, social roles, scenarios, discourses of musical value or genre, tastes, biographical histories, media representations, institutional practices or norms, materials and material practices, happenstance (the list could be extended). How these alignments or links are made is how to make good of the music in question. By contrast, this making good also involves a parallel process of deflecting or not noticing other connections that might detract from the making good, illustrated in the diagram above by the grey disconnected nodes.

These connections establish, as Erving Goffman puts it, the 'keyings' within which a thing (music's goodness) makes sense. Thus, to sum up, the study of musical value can be about much more than assigning music to boxes (scoring it as good, better, best). More powerfully, the study of music's goodness can be about examining how the ways in which people come to appropriate or grasp music's goodness, its aesthetic character, are simultaneously the ways they produce the goodness they appropriate.

Thus, to speak of music's goodness as fluid lends precision to the study of how goodness (in this case in relation to music) comes to be identified. This focus, the shift from a concern with identity to a concern with identification, in turn dissolves the distinction between 'goodness in' and 'goodness from' music because, in fixing the fluid identity of goodness in we refer to contextual features, including goodness from (think about exhortations to how beloved forms of music elevate or develop character or express / help us to recognize some value or lesson). This conflation of goodness in and goodness from comes with a price, namely, that we recognize music – even, and indeed especially, when at its most ineffable – as a profound medium of social ordering. That music orders (goodness from) is a lesson known well to J.S. Bach (the task of the musician was to organize the congregation), to the ancients, to various regimes seeking power and rule (on composers in Germany during the Third Reich, see Sutherland with DeNora 2011), as well as to everyday music lovers, musicians, music students and concert patrons.

Looked at from this angle, goodness in music is goodness from music, there is no difference between what is assigned to each of the quadrants. They are merely ways of appreciating music. When we discover a new way to love music, or a new music that we love, simultaneously we are adapting to and adopting a new sensibility, a new angle on how to hear, live and be. The question, then, is what and how many goods or aesthetic priorities we can sustain across situations of action so as to keep music's wealth actualized to its greatest capacity.

As various commentators have suggested, perhaps most notably Antoine Hennion (2001, 2007), in articulating our musical values, we are simultaneously articulating ourselves and our social priorities, for we are all, just like the clients at BRIGHT, fluid selves taking shape relationally within the ecological spaces we inhabit; and if we are, ourselves, flexible enough at perceiving/identifying goodness, that activity may well have implications for who may be associated with categories of social approval, such as musician, which, as we saw with the example of the BRIGHT Singers rendition of 'Swing Low, Sweet Chariot' may have yet further implications for how we identify people as well, able to be well, competent, skilled and so forth.

'The king can live as he pleases; I shall live as a Radziwil'

There is a perhaps apocryphal tale of a noble of the Radziwil family in the Grand Duchy of Lithuania who, when told he 'lived like the king', replied, 'the king can live as he pleases; I shall live as a Radziwil'. The story underlines the notion of deregulated, contextualized aesthetics. This is not so far removed from the argument I have been seeking to advance. From this perspective, goodness emerges as a way of life, linked to collective action and collaboratively, institutionally produced. Thus, within this view, goodness is a matter of identifying appropriate aesthetic criteria (for example, what counts as musical competence to perform and compose, what counts as beautiful sound). The key point is that identities and social relations follow from these aesthetics. How many aesthetics, or centers of gravity, can we manage? How many ways can we allow ourselves for conceptualizing and appreciating music? Just how aesthetically 'literate' might we be or, in Blackings words, 'how musical is man [*sic*]?' (1973).

In conclusion, to use Antoine Hennion's resonant phrase, music and the ability to hail some forms of music that we love is one of 'these things that hold us together' (2007). By this Hennion means that taste, identities (music's and our own) and performance of taste and music are all produced of a piece. Loving and caring about music is simultaneously loving and caring about each other, musically mediated: we hold each other dear in and through the ways that we hold our music dear. We love music because we know what it does, what it is about, what it takes and what it means (to us, for us, for its makers, for humanity). When we draw music into our environments, it is because we want to become what music can make us. Music is, in this sense, actualizing, transformative. When we modify music (slight changes in how we sing a song, the addition of a new song, the ousting of an old one from our repertoire), it is because we are tinkering, and not virtually, with our environment. Thus, the idea that there are many forms of musical goodness is not necessarily a problem once we begin to understand that our socio-musical forms of ordering are not in the music, but in what might be a basic human capacity to make and use music for ordering purposes, as a means of constituting our selves and our relations with each other. Once we realize these things, perhaps it is also possible to say that the example with which I began this chapter, the BRIGHT Singers' impromptu rendition of 'Swing Low, Sweet Chariot' was the finest music it is possible to make. By the time they finished singing, what could be classed as music (within BRIGHT, for me, for listeners, perhaps for readers of this chapter) had been changed. The change involved experiencing new ways to love music. I will take up this theme again in the Conclusion when I reconnect it to the question of how music helps to promote wellbeing and how it offers varied forms of asylum.

Conclusion

What Music Makes Us Well and When?
And How to Know How Music Helps?

Reprise

I began this book with key lessons from the sociology of health and illness (Chapter 1). These lessons, about the cultural and historical situation of what we define as illness and as health, helped to highlight health and illness as intertwined (health/ illness) and as emergent phenomena. To speak of health/illness as emergent is to say that health/illness takes shape and is experienced in relation to fluctuating configurations of people, meanings and material objects manifest in actual social settings. To speak of actuality, is to underline the temporal dimension of health/ illness, how the seemingly same condition, whether schizophrenia, cancer, depression or pain associated with an injury can be seen to vary over space and time depending upon its position in relation to other aspects of social ecology. I hope that I have been able to point out the considerable degree of freedom associated with what comes to count as particular forms of health/illness, namely that the compass of health/illness narrows in relation to specific material, social, symbolic and temporal arrangements.

After considering the development of personalized medicine, I began to define what I meant by an ecological perspective for health/illness. For that purpose, I used the case of mental health and the myth of mental illness as it was called in the 1960s (Szasz 1960, 1961), which I used as a case in point for health conditions more generally. As the World Health Organization puts it, 'there is no health without mental health', and my justification for using the case of mental health was that it underlines the co-configuration of culture, mind and body within social ecology. To illustrate this co-configuration, I turned to recent research on the placebo effect and suggested that to understand the placebo effect and mind–body interaction we need to consider more holistically the person in context of the environment, culture, social practices and others. I then turned to the complex and multi-dimensional phenomenon of health/illness. My point was that health/illness and ability/disability are not physical facts but rather conglomerates of inscription, performance and experience and that these things take shape in relation to culture, the built environment, practices and time – that is, ecologically.

In Chapters 2 and 3, I began to consider how the environment can be understood to afford wellbeing, and I used sociologist Erving Goffman's work as a springboard onto a theory of health ecologies and their making. After developing an understanding of agency that moves beyond Goffman's early notion of 'impression management' toward a notion of agency as cultural creation interactively conceived, I introduced a concept of asylum that was de-coupled from its conventional, institutional definition. My aim was to rehabilitate the concept of asylum, suggesting that asylum is not a place made of bricks and mortar, nor a set of clinical health practices or treatments, but rather a conceptual space, an anytime/anyplace of health promotion and maintenance and a set of practices for achieving (locating, maintaining, discovering, inhabiting) this place.

On the one hand, I suggested, asylum is a making of room – for creativity, expressivity, flow and flourishing; on the other hand, it is a way of gaining distance (space) from pathogenic factors that foster distress, pain or oppression. This idea of asylum as space for and space from led me to develop the further distinction between two forms of asylum, both understood as responses to the social environment. Asylum can be understood as activity oriented to furnishing the social environment with things (symbolic and material) that are conducive to, or afford, wellness, and it can also can be understood as a place that is removed from causes of distress that are otherwise present in the social environment, a way of buffering, alleviating, protecting or distancing the self from noxious environmental aspects, people or features (but in ways that do not alter that environment). Linked to this typology, I described how social ecologies, and opportunities for asylum within them, are political (in terms of the politics of representation but also in terms of the moral economy of entitlement and differentiation – who can do what when and where): social settings do not necessarily serve all participants equally well but may suppress opportunities for expression and flourishing, calling for actors to serve the plans, interests or, more subtly, styles and aesthetic orientations of others. Thus, examining the patterns of everyday asylum-seeking in relation to wellbeing is also a key to a critical examination of the politics of everyday existence: for whom, when, where and how does furnishing activity get done, and for whom, when, where and how is removal activity the easier, or perhaps only, option?

From Chapter 4 onward I turned to music, considering musical removals (Chapter 4) and refurnishing (Chapter 5). I described how music can be seen to heighten wellbeing by privatizing space (removing actors by dissociating them from the flux of real life) and how musical activity tinkers with other aspects of social ecology in ways that can alter the physical and symbolic spaces of action, making them more conducive to wellbeing. In Chapter 6, I examined music as it gets into or structures perception and consciousness (consciousness here understood in terms of minded forms of awareness but also more tacit and embodied orientation, understood also as readiness for action). I suggested that a theory of musical consciousness helps to highlight how music works in contexts of pain management, social adjustment, social control and mental health.

Finally, in examining what it is that music does, I suggested, it is also possible to understand what music is, or, more specifically, what kind of an object it is, namely, an emergent, flexible medium that, like health/illness, takes shape in relation to other things. Thinking about musical ontology in this way highlights new ways in which to conceptualize music's goodness, which I considered in Chapter 7. There, I suggested that the traditional aesthetic dichotomy of functional versus formal (or art) music needs to be rethought and I described how the idea of making general (acontextual and absolute) distinctions between different musical forms and formats is misguided and masks much of the good that music does and can be. By contrast, a flexible and emergent aesthetic, in which music that does good is good, makes it easier to perceive music's value and importance in human culture.

Not Idealist but Emergent: Toward a Realist–Constructivist Account of Health/Illness

To speak of health and illness as emergent and relational is not to take an idealist stance, it is not to deny the physicality of conditions, nor to deny that there might be preferable and better ways of going about healthcare and health promotion, given a set of aims. ('I am no longer flexible enough to stand on my head'; 'You can no longer eat fried food at night'; 'He needs to get that bone set and the wound stitched so it will heal and not lead to infection and an X-ray will assist in this process'.) There are, at any moment, certain facts and conditions – bleeding, pain, a broken bone, mental anguish, fibrillation, memory loss. But how these conditions come to be identified and experienced, how they are deemed to be best treated, how they are linked to social consequences and, indeed, how they come to emerge in the first place is always socially mediated.

Thus to say that health/illness is emergent and relational is to say that it is caused by things outside of individuals and that the causes of health/illness include cultural and social arrangements as well as physical, biological and physiological matters and events. How we account for and treat the conditions we wish to change can be greatly enriched if we consider the socio-cultural factors that contribute to aetiological accounts of what we deem to be illness.

It is here that the humanities and medical science can be most fruitfully integrated and in ways in which they are posed as equal partners with shared problems and concerns. For, if health/illness emerges in relation to ecologies of action and these ecologies work in ways that minimize, erase and augment aspects of what we come to recognize as the performed, inscribed and experiential features of 'health', then context matters. To say context matters is to say that we should not treat illness exclusively as a matter of individuals, whether in terms of their physical characteristics (genes, brain activity, traits) or what they do (smoking, drinking, poor diet, lack of exercise). At a much deeper level we need to examine how habits develop, how mind and body interact and how all of these things take shape and are fostered within worlds that are made by humans in partnership (collusion, conflict, cooperation) with each other and with aspects of the world, mobilized so as to do things together (for reasons, for pleasure, for duty, habit or at random) in time. We should be interested in how people manage to find asylum or respite from the things that distress them, however fleeting that asylum might be, whatever form it might take and how this can affect the tripartite phenomenon that is health/illness – inscribed, performed and experienced.

Into this picture, music enters: as an ecological material, a dynamic medium, a way to create, change and sustain the lifeworlds that are our health/ illness ecologies, flexible, potentially easy to add to an environment, linked to embodiment, emotion, memory and social roles, pleasure-giving, entraining, communicative and connecting. As I have described, music offers many ways to promote wellbeing. What I hope to have added to our understanding about music and health is an ecologically sensitive account of what music does in the actual social environments that we inhabit and an ecologically oriented theoretical account of how music helps. Within these environments, music is a medium for asylum-seeking, a medium for removal from and refurnishing of social environments so as to make existence habitable, hospitable, better. As part of this theoretical account I have also sought to show how music, like health, is not a straightforward object and thus is not a simple stimulus or even a uniform type of practice that lends itself to blanket recommendations ('We should all "sing for our health" by joining choirs or listen to Mozart to feel uplifted'). Rather music is an emergent, flexible object. Music's powers to help become activated only through the ways that we couple music with other things – postures and physical practices, expectations, beliefs and social relations to name but a few. There is nothing mechanical or recipe-like in this process; but, rather, craftwork is required and should be given its due. Music is not simply a medicine, object, treatment or technique to be taken (or practised) in a pre-specified, utilitarian way, in a way that fixes a particular problem (though as we have seen in the discussion of music and pain management, music can do work in this way too). Rather, and more importantly, music part of the fabric of human sociation.

Music On Trial and In Action

Increasingly, studies suggest that music can be used with great benefit in healthcare – both clinically and in everyday life. As I described elsewhere, randomized trials may show what music does, but they are rarely able to describe the mechanisms by which music is an active ingredient in relation to health/illness (DeNora 2006, 2007). Thus, at the outset of this book I posed the question: 'Music seems to work but how?'

> Music cannot be treated simply as a stimulus intended to provoke a predetermined behavioral response: above all, music making is social (and hence interpersonal). … Clinical trials inevitably focus on the outcomes of interventions rather than the process through which these outcomes may be achieved. Further research using mixed methods is needed if a better understanding of the active ingredients

of music therapy that enhance patient outcomes is to be reached. (Maratos, Crawford and Procter 2011: 93)

As Even Ruud suggested, 'what we need [is] some methodology to help in the understanding of how music, therapy and social contexts work together' (2010: 2). As I described when I presented the schema of the musical event, one route into this topic is to focus on what actually happens during musical engagement and this means opening up the black box of how music helps. In contrast to the randomized trial, which examines the before and after of musical engagement, the musical event focuses upon the middle period, the time when people are actually engaged in musical activity and the time after that activity when it is possible to see evidence of change, grounded in the activities and ecological settings inhabited by actors. It is here that we can focus on what elsewhere I describe as 'music in action' (DeNora 2011).

Thus, within the RCT, musical engagement remains – as it did in the various and highly mysterious discussions and customs of musical healing in bygone times – black boxed. How music works there remains a great, unanswered question. It is here that ethnographic, qualitative, audio-visual and autobiographical methods come into their own for socio-musical studies of music and wellbeing, as I have described in the previous chapters. In particular, the concern with ecological validity and with participants' experiences is central. If health/illness is relational and flexible, then both music and more mainstream forms of healthcare intervention need to be examined in terms of the ways they work in tandem with contexts of practical engagement.

Music, Magic, Transformation

As I described in the previous chapter through the case of 'Swing Low Sweet Chariot', people who come together through musical activity are people who, potentially, can be transformed. The BRIGHT Singers, in the hospital ward, responding to a request from a dying man, were – at that moment – not mental health clients but (musical) carers, celebrants, skilled musicians. Brought together in mutual performance, they were no longer part of a situation about some mental health clients and their concertizing success any more than they were part of one about some men in a ward for the terminally ill. Both of those stories (narratives) were yesterday's news. In the new now, the story was about these people and what they were doing together, the creation of meanings, possibilities and transfigurations rendered through joint activity. It was here, in the very middle of the music, right inside the otherwise black box, that music was effecting change.

To better theorize this phenomenon, it is perhaps useful to begin by remembering that music is always collective: it implies a 'we'. Irrespective of what music is deemed to mean or what it might imply about things apart from itself, music is socially cohesive: to engage with music is to engage with others and with things outside the self (even in passive music consumption, one must imagine music in one's head, turn on the radio or iPod and then spend time with music). When musical engagement involves active music production it can generate, as Simon Procter has put it, a form of proto-social, expressly musical, capital (2011). In the case of singing 'Swing Low, Sweet Chariot' in the hospital ward, we can see this proto-social capital taking shape as participants musically drew themselves together and as together they collectively created the song. While terminal illness and distress did not go away, they were for some period of musical time replaced by musical engagement, drawn into a form of musical asylum. This drawing in is what, in relation to the musical event schema, I have called Time 2.

After the song (Time 3), no one did a follow up survey to ask the BRIGHT Singers or the men in the ward if their quality of life had been improved and no information is available on what happened afterward in the ward. (Unlike Jane Edwards study of Ivan, which I described in Chapter 6, there were no reports from nurses about how these men were later on, though there is information about the BRIGHT Singers from Sarah's diary data, my field notes and informal conversations, all of which suggests that for the BRIGHT Singers life was indeed enriched, as I described in Chapter 7.) Indeed, there are dangers associated with questionnaires and their too literal focus on utility. First, questionnaires risk over-simplifying complex phenomena through multiple choice or Likert scale forms of measurement (for example, wellbeing surveys that require a client to say whether or not they are more or less happy than some time previously or whether they feel anxious 'never', 'occasionally', 'often', always'). Second, because questionnaires are administered outside the flux of everyday life (decontextualized), they may elicit accounts about wellbeing that may or may not be ecologically valid and that may not be aligned with what actually happens and with what people actually do and experience and are often linked to what respondents may feel obliged to offer or to what they think must be the right answer. Third, attempts to measure music's utility risk trivializing what transpires when musical engagement occurs. As such they reduce the convivial and musically caring, musically specific features of this moment of wellbeing (this song, not some other song, not, for example, the more upbeat, 'When the Saints Go Marching In') to mere technique: these human matters become but a means to an end. Fourth, as Simon Procter has observed, the focus on how people are at Time 3 can be over-played: equally importantly is whether, at Time 2 respite can be found (2009; on the importance of the present moment in health and end-of-life care, see also Hartley 2009). Finally, measures taken from questionnaires return us to the situation in which the 'how' of how music helps is evaded, is black-boxed.

By contrast, from within the middle of music, music (musicking activity), action and the experience of self/other and situation converge and interact. To speak of dependent and independent variables here is misleading. So, as I have described in the case of 'Swing Low, Sweet Chariot', in the moment of shared performance much was changed – at least in the short term: who, where and what music and the participants were at Time 1 was resounded at Time 2 (the time in the middle) through musical activity and in ways that, at Time 3, after the music stopped, after we left the ward, reconfigured (for the BRIGHT Singers) or may have reconfigured (for the men in the ward) music and people (for example, at BRIGHT 'Swing Low, Sweet Chariot' became a core part of the repertoire and the occasion in the ward became part of the BRIGHT Singers history, offering them a collective occasion that reminded them of achievement, connection, caring and something special). It is thus the complexity and potential flexibility of both music and illness/wellness that offers resources for wellbeing and that resourcefulness is produced, literally, in concert. Music is not simply a stimulus and health is not a static state: both these things, inextricably connected, are performed, created and recreated in action in ways that are situated and situate action in and over time. They are, rather than do, work and are perhaps better understood as *opera*, namely, ways of working and ways of being (Abrams 2011).

Understanding music as a way of being returns us, as Abrams (2011) describes, to the medieval (Boethian) concept of *musica humana*, or the harmony of the body and spirit for which *musica instrumentalis* or audible music – what we think of as music today – is but a means. Thinking about music as human *opera* (Abrams 2011), or works, returns us to the ways in which music is not an adjunct to, or means for, other things but an end in itself. As such, this way of thinking returns us to the specific focus in music therapy on music-centered or music-led music therapy (Aigen 2005), the idea that music is itself a way of being (Ansdell 1995; Pavlicevic 1997) or that music is a mode of communicative action, a way of sharing time and space. Within this perspective, music does not cause things to happen. Rather, music is itself a transformative practice: in the musicking, we become what it is that we are doing. I become, to take a simple example, a singer when I sing, I also become a part of a larger musical whole when I sing in concert with others. In that doing, active participation, whether through planning situations for listening and talk about music or through playing with others is central (Pitts 2005, 2012).

The focus on musical transformation is a focus on the ways in which musical *opera* transmute and transfigure, on how music replaces what has come before it and thus offers asylum, possibly in ways that will offer new inroads or pathways that also sidestep the situations, sensations, experiences, habits and identities otherwise associated with being ill. This focus is emphatically not a return to the mysterious rhetoric of music-as-magic of times bygone. Rather it opens the door for serious and thorough-going explorations of what transpires in the situations where music helps. At the same time, however, this focus opens the door to a revised notion of music as magic, in particular what might be termed a 'magic realist' theory of how music helps, a focus on how music can convert us from one state of being or mode of consciousness to another, in ways that are produced through concrete and practical actions and on craft, a focus expressly devoted to what people do with and attribute to music in specific settings. This programme of research is devoted to the scholarly and lay examination of the collective practices that draw together materials, modes of perception and action and beliefs in real time and with transformative consequences for what came before and for possibilities of what might happen next.

Music's Future Perfect?

Perhaps the best way to explain this transformative dimension is through a reference to a grammatical tense, the future perfect. In English and, more rarely, German grammar, the future perfect is used to refer to an act that is completed (perfected) before something else in the future happens. Consider the sentence: 'By the time I get to Phoenix, my sister will have left town.' Here, the past is the time before the speaker set out on his or her journey, the present has the sister in Phoenix and the speaker in transit, the future is the estimated time of arrival in Phoenix when the sister 'will have left town'. Key in this formulation is the unspecified moment at which the sister actually leaves town. In the future perfect tense, however, the actual moment of when the change occurs is elided: it happens somewhere between the speaker's utterance and his or her actual arrival in Phoenix. This tense and the temporal structure and temporal imprecision it conveys seem especially apt for conceptualizing the ways that music helps and for thinking about what counts as the therapeutic moment(s) or where, to use the language of the RCT, the intervention began and ended.

The metaphor of future perfect highlights some of the ways in which musical acts and their consequences for wellbeing are fluid objects, located and specified in terms of their meaning, value and efficacy only in retrospect and only in relation to (how they are coupled with) other things. The 'will have left town' is, for example related to time of day – that is an easy example. More difficult is the question of when is it that music makes a difference in, say, one's sense of wellbeing? In both cases, the change may come to be acknowledged but only retrospectively. But, and more confusingly, the change may have happened before it is acknowledged and, conversely, it may be acknowledged but never have happened (for example, I believe my sister left town, because that is what I thought, in advance, would happen, but in fact she never did; however, because I believed her departure to be true, I never actually phoned to see if she was still in town).

The question, then of when music helps is essential if we are to understand and theorize how music helps. I suggest that this is established performatively in action and in ways that can recover and reformulate events, occasions and relations (for example, Pam's increasing focus and coordination in her interaction with Ansdell in the example I presented in the Introduction, her additional mini-narrative of 'That's better', which adds yet a further frame and, in this example, consolidates the changes that were already evident in her embodied musical action). To explore this performative activity, there is nothing for it but to examine music in action; that is, to examine the ways in which music is coupled to many other things as part of a musical event. Those connections highlight the interconnections between the three time frames of the musical event drawing past into present and future. They also project possible and actual futures back onto the past in ways that reconstruct the past. This triple time is both the where and when of how music works: what we do together musically, in relation to each other and our environment (even if what is done is a removal activity) reconstructs us and repositions us for future action and identities. How this process actually transpires is a question for ethnography, for discussion between participants, and self-reflection: 'We are different now, but how did this change occur?' we ask one another.

To think of music as something that can be administered like a dose of medication (whether one-off or over time) so as to become better is, in short, perhaps as silly as asking which specific incident in my life over the previous 55 years or the previous 5 minutes led me to feel the way I do today as I enjoy smelling the roses in my garden. Instead, and I think more useful, is a focus on the processes and passages (socio-musical, socio-biological translations) whereby I become that something else, the passages by which I am transfigured into, for a moment, someone appreciating flowers, the process of attunement as I stoop to smell the rose and rise back up again having breathed perhaps more deeply, perhaps remembering the rose, other roses, and gathering together a veritable nosegay of associated experience, memories and thoughts which may or may not be shared at the time with others.

Thus there is an immediate history that galvanizes all earlier histories here, that joins past with current practice in the here and now. It is possible to explore this here and now: how, for example, is music is drawn into the frame of interaction along with other, para-musical things such as talking, people, settings, objects and embodied conduct as a part of situated, temporal, mundane activity? How does music and music-making inflect situations in ways that are transformative? How does music and musical activity offer new frameworks, skills and identities that can be transferred to para- and extra-musical situations, how does music affect what happens after music? To the extent that these questions signal a more gentle mode of enquiry focused on the microscopy of actual musical engagement (Ansdell and Pavlicevic 2010), they are also aimed at the changes that take place in, through and around music as they are put together through collaborative forms of action.

Music's reality and its potential as an instrument of change thus varies according to how it is coupled with many other things that inform the social processes between individuals. So too with health/illness – it is temporally variegated, fluid; it can be affected by our symbolic frames; and it can be made manifest, augmented and diminished in relation to things outside individuals. One challenge, then, for future research on the topic of music and wellbeing is to document the ethnomethods (mundane and often hidden practices) of how music is drawn into the performative activity by which the future perfect of wellbeing (for any duration of time) is achieved. If this understanding of wellbeing through music in everyday life points once again to a quasi-magical conception of music's powers, there is however a difference: this time, music's magic can be seen to involve concrete, careful and caring human practices. These practices are in the deepest sense the things that render health and illness as aesthetic and ethical matters to be shared.

References

Aasgaard, T., 2002. 'Song Creations with Children Who Have Cancer: Process and Meaning' (PhD Thesis, Aalborg University), <www.mt-phd.aau.dk/./6/6502_trygve_aasgaard_thesis_150909.pdf> (accessed 29 Apr. 2013).

Abbott, Andrew, 1988. *The System of Professions* (Chicago: University of Chicago Press).

Abraham, John, 2008. 'Sociology of Pharmaceuticals Development and Regulation: A Realist Empirical Research Programme', *Sociology of Health and Illness* 30/6: 869–85.

Abrams, Brian, 2011. 'Understanding Music as a Temporal-Aesthetic Way of Being: Implications for a General Theory of Music Therapy', *The Arts in Psychotherapy* 38/2: 114–19.

—— 2012. 'Does it Really Work?', *Voices: A World Forum for Music Therapy*, <http://www.voices.no/?q=fortnightly-columns/2012-does-it-really-work> (accessed 28 Aug. 2012).

Adam, Barbara, 1990. *Time and Social Theory* (Cambridge: Polity Press).

Aigen, Kenneth, 2005. *Music-Centered Music Therapy* (Gilsum, NH: Barcelona Publishers).

Alloy, L.B., et al., 2005. 'The Psychosocial Context of Bipolar Disorder: Environmental, Cognitive, and Developmental Risk Factors', *Clinical Psychology Review* 25/8: 1043–75.

American Psychiatric Association 2000. *Diagnostic and Statistical Manual of Mental Disorders, Fourth Edition, Text Revision (DSM-IV-TR)* (Arlington, VA: American Psychiatric Association).

—— 2010. *First Draft of Revised DSM-5*, <http://www.dsm5.org/Pages/Default.aspx> (accessed 24 Aug. 2012).

Anderson, Robert, and Wes Sharrock 1993. 'Can Organizations Afford Knowledge?', *Computer Supported Cooperative Work (CSCW)* 1: 143–61.

Ansdell, Gary, 1995. *Music For Life: Aspects of Creative Music Therapy with Adult Clients* (London: Jessica Kingsley Publications).

—— forthcoming. *How Music Helps* (Farnham: Ashgate).

—— and Tia DeNora 2012. 'Musical Flourishing: Community Music Therapy, Controversy, and the Cultivation of Wellbeing', in R. MacDonald, G. Kreutz and L. Mitchell (eds), *Music, Health and Wellbeing* (Oxford: Oxford University Press), pp. 97–112.

—— and J. Meehan 2010. '"Some light at the end of the tunnel": Exploring Users' Evidence for the Effectiveness of Music Therapy in Adult Mental Health Settings', *Music and Medicine* 2/1: 41–7.

—— and Mercédès Pavlicevic 2010. 'Practising "Gentle Empiricism": The Nordoff–Robbins Research Heritage', *Music Therapy Perspectives* 28/2: 131–9.

—— et al., 2010. 'From "This f***ing life" to "That's better" … in Four Minutes: An Interdisciplinary Study of Music Therapy's "Present Moments" and Their Potential for Affect Modulation', *Nordic Journal of Music Therapy* 19/1: 3–28.

Antonovsky, Aaron, 1979. *Health, Stress and Coping* (San Francisco: Jossey-Bass).

—— 1987. *Unraveling the Mystery of Health: How People Manage Stress and Stay Well* (San Francisco: Jossey-Bass).

Areni, C.S., and D. Kim 1993. 'The Influence of Background Music on Shopping Behaviour: Classical versus Top-Forty Music in a Wine Store', *Advances in Consumer Research* 20: 336–40.

Asai, Tomohisa, Eriko Sugimori and Yoshihiko Tanno 2008. 'A Secret of Hypnosis: A Dynamic Rubber Hand Illusion', *Nature Precedings*, <http://hdl.handle.net/10101/npre.2008.2276.1> (accessed 24 Aug. 2012).

Atkinson, Paul, 2010. 'Making Opera Work: Bricolage and the Management of Dramaturgy', *Music and Arts in Action* 3/1: 3–19.

Avdeeff, Melissa Kay, 2010. 'Finding Meaning in the Masses: Issues of Taste, Identity and Sociability in Digitality' (PhD thesis, University of Edinburgh).

Bailey, Betty A., and Jane W. Davidson 2003. 'Amateur Group Singing as a Therapeutic Instrument', *Nordic Journal of Music Therapy* 12/: 18–32.

Ball, Donald, 1967. 'Toward a Sociology of Toys: Inanimate Objects, Socialization and the Demography of the Doll World', *Sociological Quarterly* 8/4: 447–58.

Batt-Rawden, K., 2006. 'Music: A Strategy to Promote Health in Rehabilitation? An Evaluation of Participation in a "Music and Health Promotion Project"', *International Journal of Rehabilitation Research* 29/2: 171–3.

—— Tia DeNora and E. Ruud 2005. 'Music Listening and Empowerment in Health Promotion: A Study of the Role and Significance of Music in Everyday Life of the Long-Term Ill', *Nordic Journal of Music Therapy* 14/2: 120–36.

—— S. Trythall and Tia DeNora 2007. 'Health Musicking as Cultural Inclusion', in J. Edwards (ed.), *Music: Promoting Health and Creating Community in Healthcare* (Cambridge: Scholars Press), pp. 64–83.

Becker, Howard S., 1953. 'Becoming a Marihuana User', *American Journal of Sociology* 59/3: 235–42.

Becker, Judith, 2004. *Deep Listeners: Music, Emotion, and Trancing* (Bloomington: Indiana University Press).

—— 2010. 'Exploring the Habitus of Listening: Anthropological Perspectives', in P. Juslin and J. Sloboda (eds), *Oxford Handbook of Music and Emotions* (Oxford: Oxford University Press), pp. 12–57.

Bergh, Arild, 2007. '"I'd like to teach the world to sing": Music and Conflict Transformation', *Performance Matters*, special issue of *Musicae Scientiae*, pp. 141–57.

—— and Tia DeNora 2009. 'From Windup to iPod: Techno-Cultures of Listening', in N. Cook and D. Leech-Wilkinson (eds), *Cambridge Companion to Recorded Music* (Cambridge: Cambridge University Press), pp. 102–15.

——, —— and Maia Bergh forthcoming. 'Flexibility and (Dis)engagement: Mobile Music and the Politics of Everyday Life', in Sumanth Gopinath and Jason Stanyek (eds), *The Oxford Handbook of Mobile Music Studies* (Oxford: Oxford University Press).

Bijsterveld, K., and T. Pinch, 2011. *Oxford Handbook of Sound Studies* (Oxford: Oxford University Press).

Birke, Lynda, 1992. 'Transforming Biology', in H. Crowley and S. Himmelweit (eds), *Knowing Women: Feminism and Knowledge* (Cambridge: Polity), pp. 66–77.

Blacking, J., 1971. 'The Value of Music in Human Experience', *Yearbook of the International Folk Music Council* 1: 33–71.

—— 1973. *How Musical is Man?* (Seattle: University of Washington Press).

—— 1977. *The Anthropology of the Body*, ASA Monograph 15 (London: Academic Press).

Blaxter, Mildred, 2003. 'Biology, Social Class and Inequalities in Health: Their Synthesis in "Health Capital"', in S. Williams, L. Birke and G. Bendelow (eds), *Debating Biology: Sociological Reflections on Health, Medicine and Society* (London: Routledge), pp. 69–83.

Bonde, L.O., 2005. '"Finding a new place ...": Metaphor and Narrative in One Cancer Survivor's BMGIM Therapy', *Nordic Journal of Music Therapy* 14/2: 137–54.

Bondi, L., 2003. 'Empathy and Identification', *ACME* 2/1: 64–76.

Bonny, Helen, 2002. *Music and Consciousness: The Evolution of Guided Imagery and Music*, ed. Lisa Summer (Gilsum, NH: Barcelona Publishers).

Born, G., 2012. *Music, Sound, and Space: Transformations of Public and Private Experience* (Cambridge: Cambridge University Press).

Borus, J.F., 1981. 'Sounding Board: Deinstitutionalization of the Chronically Mentally Ill', *New England Journal of Medicine* 305/6: 339–42.

Botvinick, M., and J. Cohen 1998. 'Rubber Hands "Feel" Touch that Eyes See', *Nature* 391: 782–3.

Bourdieu, Pierre, 1985. 'Social Space and the Genesis of Groups', *Theory and Society* 14/6: 723–44.

—— 1990. *The Logic of Practice* (Cambridge: Polity).

—— and J.C. Passeron 1977. *Reproduction in Education, Society, and Culture* (London: Sage).

Branaman, Anne, 1997. 'Goffman's Social Theory', in C. Lemert and Anne Branaman (eds), *The Goffman Reader* (Oxford: Blackwell), pp. xiv–xliii.

Breggin, Peter R., 1994. *Talking Back to Prozac: What Doctors Aren't Telling You About Today's Most Controversial Drug* (New York: St Martin's Press).

Brown, Eleanor, and Susan Farabaugh 1997. 'What Birds with Complex Relations Can Tell Us about Vocal Learning: Vocal Sharing in Avian Groups', in

Charles Snowden and Martine Hausberger (eds), *Social Influences on Vocal Development* (Cambridge: Cambridge University Press), pp. 98–127.

Bull, Michael, 2000. *Sounding Out the City* (London: Bergh).

—— 2007. *Sound Moves: iPod Culture and Urban Experience* (London: Routledge).

Burns, Tom, 2002. *Erving Goffman* (London: Routledge).

Butler, Lisa, 2006. 'Normative Dissociation', *Psychiatric Clinics of North America* 29: 45–62.

Cage, John, 1992. Interview in *Écoute* [documentary], dir. Miroslav Sebestik, <http://hearingvoices.com/news/2009/09/cage-silence/> (accessed 3 Feb. 2013).

Caillois, Roger, 1961. *Man, Play and Games*, trans. Meyer Barash (Glencoe, IL: Free Press).

Carrington, John F., 1949. *The Talking Drums of Africa* (London: Carey Kingsgate Press).

Chambliss, Daniel, 1989. 'The Mundanity of Excellence', *Sociological Theory* 7/1: 70–86.

Charmaz, Kathy, 1993. *Good Days, Bad Days: The Self in Chronic Illness* (New Brunswick: Rutgers University Press).

Chew, Robert H., Robert E. Hales and Stuart C. Yudofsky 2009. *What Your Patients Need to Know about Psychiatric Medications* (2nd edn, Arlington, VA: American Psychiatric Publications).

Chodoff, P., 1982. 'Hysteria and Women', *American Journal of Psychiatry* 139: 545–51.

Chriss, James J., 1995. 'Habermas, Goffman and Communicative Action: Implications for Professional Action', *American Sociological Review* 60/4: 545–65.

Christie, Agatha, 1952. *They Do It With Mirrors* (London: Collins).

Clarke, Adele, 2005. *Situational Analysis: Grounded Theory After the Postmodern Turn* (Thousand Oaks, CA: Sage).

Clarke, Adele, Laura Mamo, Jennifer Ruth Fosket, Jennifer R. Fishman, and Janet K. Shim, (eds), 2010. *Biomedicalization: Technoscience, Health, and Illness in the U. S.* (Durham, NC: Duke University Press).

Clarke, David, and Eric Clarke (eds) 2011. *Music and Consciousness: Philosophical, Psychological, and Cultural Perspectives* (Oxford: Oxford University Press).

Clarke, Eric, 2011. 'Music Perception and Musical Consciousness', in David Clarke and Eric Clarke (eds), *Music and Consciousness: Philosophical, Psychological, and Cultural Perspectives* (Oxford: Oxford University Press), pp. 193–214.

Classen, Constanze, 1994. *Aroma: The Cultural History of Smell* (London: Routledge).

Clift, Stephen, and G. Hancox 2001. 'The Perceived Benefits of Singing: Findings from Preliminary Surveys of a University College Choral Society', *Journal of the Royal Society for the Promotion of Health* 121/4: 248–56.

Collins, Randall, 2004. *Interaction Ritual Chains* (Princeton, NJ: Princeton University Press).

Colombetti, Giovana, 2009. 'What Language does to Feeling', *Journal of Consciousness Studies* 16/9: 4–26.

Conrad, Peter, 1987. 'The Experience of Illness', *Research in the Sociology of Health Care* 1/6: 1–31.

—— 2007. *The Medicalization of Society: On the Transformation of Human Conditions into Treatable Disorders* (Baltimore: Johns Hopkins University Press).

Cook, Nicholas, 2003. 'Music as Social Performance', in M. Clayton, T. Herbert and R. Middleton (eds), *The Cultural Study of Music: A Critical Introduction* (London: Routledge), pp. 204–14.

—— et al. (eds), 2009. *The Cambridge Companion to Recorded Music* (Cambridge: Cambridge University Press).

Cooper, Clive, 2012. 'Games Leave Medical Research Legacy', *Financial Times* (1 Aug.), <http://www.ft.com/cms/s/0/526a200e-db15-11e1-8074-00144feab49a.html#axzz22HMeQ0bb> (accessed 1 Aug. 2012).

Cusick, Susanne, 2008. '"You are in a place that is out of the world ...": Music in the Detention Camps of the "Global War on Terror"', *Journal of the Society for American Music* 2/1: 1–26.

Csikszentmihalyi, Mihaly, 1990. *Flow: The Psychology of Optimal Experience* (New York: HarperCollins).

—— 1996. *Creativity: Flow and the Psychology of Discovery and Invention* (New York: Perennial).

—— and S.E. Csikszentmihaly 1988. *Optimal Experience: Psychological Studies of Flow in Consciousness* (Cambridge: Cambridge University Press).

Daykin, Norma, and Leslie Bunt 2009. 'Music as a Resource for Health and Wellbeing', in I Söderback (ed.), *International Handbook of Occupational Therapy Interventions* (New York: Springer), pp. 453–9.

Dennett, Daniel, 1992. *Consciousness Explained* (Boston: Little, Brown & Co).

DeNora, Tia, 1986. 'How is Extra-Musical Meaning Possible? Music as a Place and Space for "Work"', *Sociological Theory* 4/1: 84–94.

—— 1991. 'Fast, Faster, Fastest: Comment on Chambliss on Olympic Swimmers', *Sociological Theory* 10/1: 99–102.

—— 1997. 'Music and Erotic Agency: Sonic Resources and Social-Sexual Action', *Body and Society* 3/2: 43–65.

—— 1999. 'Music as a Technology of Self', *Poetics* 27: 31–56.

—— 2000. *Music in Everyday Life* (Cambridge: Cambridge University Press).

—— 2003. *After Adorno: Rethinking Music Sociology* (Cambridge: Cambridge University Press).

—— 2006. 'Evidence and Effectivenss in Music Therapy', *British Journal of Music Therapy* 20/2: 81–9.

—— 2007. 'Health and Music in Everyday Life: A Theory of Practice', *Psyke and Logos* 1/28: 271–87.

—— 2011. *Music-in-Action: Selected Essays in Sonic Ecology* (Farnham: Ashgate).

—— 2013a. 'Music and Talk in Tandem: The Production of Micro-Narratives in Real Time', in Even Ruud (ed.), *Music and Health Narratives* (Oslo: University of Oslo Press), pp. 321–30.

—— 2013b. 'Musicians Make Markets: Aestheticising Music Distribution in Beethoven's Vienna', *European Societies* 15/2: 212–28.

Diamandopoulus, G.T., 1996. 'Cancer: An Historical Perspective', *Anticancer Research* 16: 1595–1602.

Dickenson, A.H., 2002. 'Editorial I: Gate Control Theory of Pain Stands the Test of Time', *British Journal of Anaesthesia* 88/6: 755–7.

Dileo, Cheryl, and Joke Bradt, 2009. 'Medical Music Therapy: Evidence-Based Principles and Practice', in I Söderback (ed.), *International Handbook of Occupational Therapy Interventions* (New York: Springer), pp. 445–53.

Dissanayake, Ellen, 2006. 'Ritual and Ritualization: Musical Means of Conveying and Shaping Emotion in Humans and Other Animals', in S. Brown and U. Voglsten (eds), *Music and Manipulation: On the Social Uses and Social Control of Music* (Oxford and New York: Berghahn Books), pp. 31–56.

—— 2008. 'The Arts After Darwin: Does Art Have an Origin and Adaptive Function?', in K. Zijlmans and W. van Damme (eds), *World Art Studies: Exploring Concepts and Approaches* (Amsterdam: Valiz), pp. 241–63.

Durkheim, Emile, 1961. *The Rules of Sociological Method* (Glencoe, IL: Free Press).

Edwards, Jane, 1995. 'You are Singing Beautifully: Music Therapy and the Debridement Bath', *The Arts in Psychotherapy* 22/11: 53–5.

Einarsdottir, Sigrun Lilja, 2012. 'J. S. Bach in Everyday Life: The "Choral Identity" of an Amateur "Art Music" Bach Choir and the Concept of "Choral Capital"' (PhD thesis, University of Exeter).

Elias, N., 2000. *The Civilizing Process: Sociogenetic and Psychogenetic Investigations* (revd edn, Oxford: Blackwell).

Erkkilä, Jaakko, et al., 2011. 'Individual Music Therapy for Depression: Randomised Controlled Trial', *British Journal of Psychiatry* 199: 132–9.

Fabbri-Destro, M., and G. Rizzolatti 2008. 'Mirror Neurons and Mirror Systems in Monkeys and Humans', *Physiology* 23: 171–9.

Fausto-Sterling, Anne, 1985. *Myths of Gender: Biological Theories About Men and Women* (New York: Basic Books).

Feld, Steven, 1982. 'Sound Structure as Social Structure', *Ethnomusicology* 28/3: 383–409.

Feldhammer, George A., 2007. *Mammalogy: Adaptation, Diversity, Ecology* (Baltimore: Johns Hopkins University Press).

Fine, Gary Alan, 1979. 'Small Groups and Cultural Creation: The Idioculture of Little League Baseball Teams', *American Sociological Review* 44: 733–45.

—— 2010. 'The Sociology of the Local: Action and Its Publics', *Sociological Theory* 28/4: 356–76.

—— and Daniel D. Martin 1990. 'A Partisan View: Sarcasm, Satire, and Irony as Voices in Erving Goffman's Asylums', *Journal of Contemporary Ethnography* 19: 89–115.

Finness, D., et al., 2010. 'Biological, Clinical and Ethical Advances of Placebo Effects', *The Lancet* 375/9715: 686–95.

Foucault, Michel, 1988. 'Technologies of the Self', in L.H. Martin, H. Gutman and P.H. Hutton (eds), *Technologies of the Self* (Amherst: University of Massachusetts Press), pp. 16–49.

Freund, Peter E.S., 1982. *The Civilized Body: Social Domination, Control, and Health* (Philadelphia: Temple University Press).

Gaines, Joseph, 1996. 'The Talking Drum: Moving Toward a Psychology of Literary Transformation', *Journal of Black Psychology* 22/2: 202–22.

Garfinkel, Harold, 1967. *Studies in Ethnomethodology* (Englewood Cliffs, NJ: Prentice Hall).

Gayo-Cal, M., M. Savage and A. Warde 2006. 'A Cultural Map of the United Kingdom', *Cultural Trends* 15/2–3: 213–38.

Geertz, Clifford, 1983. 'Native's Point of View: Anthropological Understanding', in *Local Knowledge: Further Essays in Interpretive Anthropology* (New York: Basic Books), pp. 55–70.

Giddens, Anthony, 1991. *Modernity and Self Identity* (Cambridge: Polity Press).

Gittoes, George (dir), 2004. *Soundtrack to War* [DVD] (Beverly Hills, CA: Melee Entertainment).

Glenmullin, Joseph, 2001. *Prozac Backlash: Overcoming the Dangers of Prozac, Zoloft, Paxil, and Other Antidepressants with Safe, Effective Alternatives* (New York: Simon & Schuster).

Goethe, J.W. von, 1962. *Italian Journey, 1786–1788* (London: Penguin Classics).

Goffman, Erving, 1957a. 'Characteristics of Total Institutions', in *Symposium on Preventative and Social Psychiatry* (Washington DC: Government Printing Office), pp. 43–93.

—— 1957b. 'On Some Convergences of Sociology and Psychiatry: A Sociologist's View', *Psychiatry: Journal of Interpersonal Relations* 20/3: 201–3.

—— 1957c. 'Review of *Human Problems of a State Mental Hospital* by Ivan Belknap (New York: McGraw-Hill, 1956)', *Administrative Science Quarterly* 2/1: 120–21.

—— 1959. *The Presentation of Self in Everyday Life* (New York: Anchor Books).

—— 1961. *Asylums: On the Social Situation of Mental Patients and Other Inmates* (New York: Anchor Books).

—— 1963. *Stigma: Notes on the Management of Spoiled Identity* (Englewood Cliffs, NJ: Prentice-Hall).

—— 1967. *Interaction Ritual: Essays in Face-to-Face Behavior* (New Brunswick: Transaction Publishers, 2005).

—— 1971. *Relations in Public: Microstudies of the Public Order* (New York: Basic Books).

Goldfarb, J., 2006. *The Politics of Small Things: The Power of the Powerless in Dark Times* (Chicago: University of Chicago Press).

Gopinath, Sumanth, and Jason Stanyek (eds) forthcoming. *The Oxford Handbook of Mobile Music Studies* (Oxford: Oxford University Press).

Gouk, Penelope, 2000. *Musical Healing in Cultural Context* (Farnham: Ashgate).

Grape, C., et al., 2003. 'Does Singing Promote Well-Being? An Empirical Study of Professional and Amateur Singers During a Singing Lesson', *Integrative Physiological and Behavior Sciences* 38/1: 65–74.

Green, Lucy, 1997. *Music, Gender, Education* (Cambridge: Cambridge University Press).

—— 2002. *How Popular Musicians Learn* (Aldershot: Ashgate).

—— 2008. *Music, Informal Learning and the School* (Aldershot: Ashgate).

Greenberg, Gary, 2010. *Manufacturing Depression: The Secret History of a Modern Disease* (London: Bloomsbury).

Habermas, Jurgen, 1984. *The Theory of Communicative Action*, vol. 1 (Toronto: Beacon Press).

Hacking, Ian, 1995. 'The Looping Effect of Human Kinds', in D. Sperber et al. (eds), *Causal Cognition: An Interdisciplinary Approach* (Oxford: Oxford University Press), pp. 351–83.

Hagen, Trever, 2012. 'From Inhibition to Commitment: Politics in the Czech Underground', in Trever Hagen, Tamás Tófalvi and Gábor Vályi (eds), *Down to the Underground: Popular Music and Society in Eastern Europe*, special issue of *EastBound* (Jan.), <www.eastbound.eu/treverhagen> (accessed 24 Aug. 2012).

—— with Tia DeNora, 2011. 'From Listening to Distribution: Nonofficial Music Practices in Hungary and Czechoslovakia from the 1960s to the 1980s', in K. Bjikersfeld and T. Pinch (eds), *Oxford Handbook of Sound Studies* (Oxford: Oxford University Press), pp. 440–58.

Hanser, Suzanne B., 2010. 'Music, Health, and Well-Being', in P. Juslin and J. Sloboda (eds), *Handbook of Music and Emotion* (Oxford: Oxford University Press), pp. 849–77.

Hara, Mariko, 2011. 'Music in Dementia Care: Increased Understanding Through Mixed Methods Research', *Music and Arts in Action* 3/1: 34–58.

Hartley, Nigel, 2009. 'The Creative Arts in Palliative Care: The Art of Dying', in British Pain Society, *Consent and Deceit in Pain Medicine*, pp. 64–70, <http://www.britishpainsociety.org/members_sigs_philosophy_2009.pdf> (accessed 29 Apr. 2013).

Hartshorne, C., 1973. *Born to Sing: Interpretation and World Survey of Bird Song* (New York: Wiley, 1992).

Hauser, Gerard A., 1998. 'Civil Society and the Principle of the Public Sphere', *Philosophy and Rhetoric* 31/1: 19–40.

Hedgecoe, Adam, 2004. *The Politics of Personalized Medicine* (Cambridge: Cambridge University Press).

Hennion, Antoine, 2001. 'Taste as Performance', *Theory, Culture and Society* 18/5: 1–22.

—— 2007. 'These Things That Hold Us Together', *Cultural Sociology* 1/1: 97–114.

Herbert, Ruth, 2012. *Everyday Music Listening: Absorption, Dissociation, Trancing* (Farnham: Ashgate).

Herzberg, David, 2008. *Happy Pills: From Miltown to Prozac* (Baltimore: Johns Hopkins University Press).

Hiscock, Julia, 2007. 'Acquaintances, Friends and Strangers: Do They Matter to Medical Sociology? A Response to David Morgan', *Medical Sociology Online* 1/2 <http://www.medicalsociologyonline.org/oldsite/archives/issue21/afas_jh.html> (accessed 29 Apr. 2013).

Hobson, Katherine, 2009. 'The Era of Personalized Medicine', *US News and World Report*, <http://www.ihavenet.com/Health-Era-of-Personalized-Medicine-Edward-Abrahams.html> (accessed 14 Oct. 2010).

Hochschild, Arlie, 1983. *The Managed Heart* (Berkeley, Los Angeles and London: University of California Press).

Horden, Peregrine, 2000. *Music as Medicine* (Farnham: Ashgate).

Housley, William, 2010. *The Ordering of Relations: Jaynesian Psycho-History, Bicameralism and Post-Individual Digital Subjectivity*, Cardiff School of Social Sciences paper 129, <http://www.cardiff.ac.uk/socsi/resources/wp129.pdf> (accessed 29 Apr. 2013).

Howland, R.H., 2008a. 'Understanding the Placebo Effect, Part 1: Placebo Use in Clinical Trials', *Journal of Psychosocial Nursing and Mental Health* 46/5: 17–20.

—— 2008b. 'Understanding the Placebo Effect, Part 2: Underlying Psychological and Neurobiological Processes', *Journal of Psychosocial Nursing and Mental Health* 46/6: 15–18.

Huzinga, Johan, 1971. *Homo Ludens: A Study of the Play-Element in Culture* (Boston: Beacon Press).

Inglis, David, 2009. 'Cosmopolitan Sociology and the Classical Canon: Ferdinand Tönnies and the Emergence of Global *Gesellschaft*', *British Journal of Sociology* 60/4: 813–32.

Insel, Thomas, 2010. 'Re-Thinking Classification of Mental Disorders', *NIMH Director's Blog*, <http://www.nimh.nih.gov/about/director/2010/index-02-2010.shtml> (accessed 29 Apr. 2013).

Issa, Amalia M., 2007. 'Personalized Medicine and the Practice of Medicine in the 21st Century', *Mcgill Journal of Medicine* 10/1: 53–67.

Jaynes, J., 1974. *The Origins of Consciousness in the Breakdown of the Bicameral Mind* (Boston: Houghton Mifflin).

Kardinal, C., and J. Yarbro 1979. 'A Conceptual History of Cancer', *Seminars in Oncology* 6/4: 396–408.

Keane, John, 1998. *Civil Society: Old Images, New Visions* (Cambridge: Polity Press).

Keil, Charles, and Steven Feld, 1994. *Music Grooves: Essays and Dialogues* (Chicago: University of Chicago Press).

Kirsch, Irving, 2010. *The Emperor's New Drugs: Exploding the Antidepressent Myth* (New York: Basic Books).

—— and Guy Sapirstein, 1998. 'Listening to Prozac but Hearing Placebo: A Metaanalysis of Antidepression Medication', *Prevention and Treatment* 1, <http://psycnet.apa.org/journals/pre/1/2/2a/> (accessed 30 Aug. 2012).

Kivimälo, M., et al., 2012. 'Job Strain as a Risk Factor for Coronary Heart Disease: A Collaborative Meta-Analysis of Individual Participant Data', *The Lancet* (early online papers, 12 Sept. 2012), <http://www.thelancet.com/journals/lancet/article/PIIS0140-6736(12)60994-5/abstract> (accessed 29 Apr. 2013).

Korczsynski, Marek, 2011. 'Stayin' Alive on the Factory Floor: An Ethnography of the Dialectics of Music Use in the Routinized Workplace', *Poetics* 39: 87–106.

Kramer, Peter D., 1997. *Listening to Prozac: The Landmark Book About Antidepressants and the Remaking of the Self* (revd edn, New York: Penguin Books).

Kravitz, Richard L., et al., 2005. 'Influence of Patients' Requests for Direct-to-Consumer Advertised Antidepressants: A Randomized Controlled Trial', *Journal of the American Medical Association* 293: 1995–2002.

Lahire, Bernard, 2003. 'From the Habitus to an Individual Heritage of Dispositions: Towards a Sociology at the Level of the Individual', *Poetics* 31/5–6: 329–55.

Laing, R.D., 1969. *The Divided Self* (London: Tavistock).

Lakoff, George, and Mark Johnson 1999. *Philosophy in the Flesh: The Embodied Mind and Its Challenge to Western Thought* (New York: Basic Books).

—— and —— 1980. *Metaphors We Live By* (Chicago: University of Chicago Press).

Latour, B., 2006. *Assembling the Social* (Oxford: Oxford University Press).

Law, John, and Annemarie Mol 2001. 'Situating Technoscience: An Inquiry into Spatialities', *Society and Space* 19: 609–21.

—— and —— 2002. *Complexities: Social Studies of Knowledge Practices* (Durham, NC: Duke University Press).

Legrand, Dorothée, 2007. 'Pre-Reflective Self-Consciousness: On Being Bodily in the World', *Janus Head* 9/2: 493–519.

Lehrman, Nathaniel S., 2006. 'The Dangers of Mental Health Screening', *Journal of American Physicians and Surgeons* 11/3: 80–82.

Leucht, S., et al., 2012. 'Systematic Review and Meta-Analysis: Antipsychotic Drugs Versus Placebo for Relapse Prevention in Schizophrenia', *The Lancet* 379/9831: 2063–71.

Lévi-Strauss, Claude, 1981. *The Naked Man*, trans. John and Doreen Weightman (New York: Harper and Row).

Levinson, D.J., and E.B. Gallagher 1964. *Patienthood in the Mental Hospital* (Boston: Houghton-Mifflin).

Loewy, J., et al., 2005. 'Sleep/Sedation in Children Undergoing EEG Testing: A Comparison of Chloral Hydrate and Music Therapy', *Journal of PeriAnesthetic Nursing* 20/5: 323–32.

Mac Suibhne, Seamus, 2009. 'Asylums: Essays on the Social Situation of Mental Patients and Other Inmates', *British Medical Journal* 339: 1–2.

—— 2011. 'Erving Goffman's *Asylums* 50 Years On', *British Journal of Psychiatry* 198: 1–2.

McCallum, Richard, 2011. 'Micro Public Spheres and the Sociology of Religion', *Journal of Contemporary Religion* 26/2: 173–87.

McCormick, Lisa, 2009. 'Higher, Faster, Louder: Representations of the International Music Competition', *Cultural Sociology* 2009 3: 5–30.

MacDonald, Raymond, David Hargreaves and Dorothy Miell 2002. *Musical Identities* (Oxford: Oxford University Press).

McDonnell, Terence E., 2010. 'Cultural Objects as Objects: Materiality, Urban Space, and the Interpretation of AIDS Media in Accra, Ghana', *American Journal of Sociology* 115/6: 1800–1852.

McGuiness, Andy, and Katie Overy 2011. 'Music, Consciousness, and the Brain: Music as Shared Experience of an Embodied Present', in David Clarke and Eric Clarke (eds), *Music and Consciousness: Philosophical, Psychological, and Cultural Perspectives* (Oxford: Oxford University Press), pp. 245–62.

Malloch, Stephen, 1999/2000. 'Mothers and Infants and Communicative Musicality', *Rhythm, Musical Narrative, and Origins of Human Communication*, special issue of *Musiace Scientiae*: 29–58.

Manning, Peter, 1989. 'Goffman's Revisions', *Philosophy of the Social Sciences* 19: 341–3.

Maratos, A., M.J. Crawford and S. Procter 2011. 'Music for Depression: It Seems to Work, But How?', *British Journal of Psychiatry* 199/2: 92–3.

Marland, Hilary, 1999. 'At Home with Puerperal Mania: The Domestic Treatment of the Insanity of Childbirth in the Nineteenth Century', in Peter Bartlett and David Wright (eds), *Outside the Walls of the Asylum: The History of Care in the Community 1750–2000.* (London and New Brunswick, NJ: Athlone), pp. 45–65.

—— 2004. *Dangerous Motherhood: Insanity and Childbirth in Victorian Britain* (Basingstoke: Palgrave Macmillan).

Materson, Raymond, and Melanie Materson 2002. *Sins and Needles: A Story of Spiritual Mending* (Chapel Hill, NC: Algonquin Books).

Mead, George Herbert, 1912. 'The Mechanism of Social Consciousness', *Journal of Philosophy, Psychology and Scientific Methods* 9: 401–6.

Mehan, Hugh, 1989. 'Oracular Reasoning in a Psychiatric Exam', in Alan Grimshaw (ed.), *Conflict Talk: Sociolinguistic Investigations of Arguments in Conversations* (Cambridge: Cambridge University Press), pp. 160–76;

repr. in A. Jaworski and N. Coupland (eds), *The Discourse Reader* (London: Routledge, 1999), pp. 559–75.

Melucci, Alberto, 1996. *The Playing Self: Person and Meaning in the Planetary Society* (Cambridge: Cambridge University Press).

Melzack, R., 2001. 'Pain and the Neuromatrix in the Brain', *Journal of Dental Education* 65: 1378–82.

Menand, Louis, 2010. 'Head Case: Can Psychiatry be a Science?', *New Yorker* (Mar. 10), <http://www.newyorker.com/arts/critics/atlarge/2010/03/01/100301crat_atlarge_menand> (accessed 29 Apr. 2013).

Mendelssohn, Felix Bartholdy, *c.*1861. *Letters of Felix Mendelssohn Bartholdy from Italy and Switzerland*, trans. Lady Wallace (Boston: Oliver Ditson & Co.), <http://ia700306.us.archive.org/27/items/lettersoffelixme00mendiala/lettersoffelixme00mendiala.pdf> (accessed 29 Apr. 2013).

Mitchell, L.A., and R. MacDonald 2007. 'A Survey Investigation of the Effects of Music Listening on Chronic Pain', *Psychology of Music* 35/1: 37–57.

Mol, Annemarie, 2003. *The Body Multiple: Ontology in Medical Practice* (Durham, NC: Duke University Press).

Morgan, David, 2009. *Acquaintances: The Space Between Intimates and Strangers* (Maidenhead: McGraw Hill/Open University Press).

Moynihan, R., I. Health and D. Henry 2002. 'Selling Sickness: The Pharmaceutical Industry and Disease Mongering', *British Medical Journal* 324: 1.

NIMH 2008. *Mental Health Medications*, <http://www.nimh.nih.gov/health/publications/mental-health-medications-/mentalhealthmedications_ln.pdf> (accessed 29 Apr. 2013).

Newton, Tim, 2003. 'Truly Embodied Sociology: Marrying the Social and the Biological', *Sociological Review* 51/1: 20–42.

North, A., and D. Hargreaves 1997. 'Music and Consumer Behavior', in D. Hargreaves and A. North (eds), *The Social Psychology of Music* (Oxford: Oxford University Press), pp. 268–89.

Numata, Rii, 2009. 'Einscream! Possibilities of New Musical Ideas to Form a Community', *Voices: A World Forum for Music Therapy* 9/1, <https://normt.uib.no/index.php/voices/article/viewArticle/363/286> (accessed 29 Apr. 2013).

O'Hara, K., and B. Brown 2006. *Consuming Music Together: Social and Collaborative Aspects of Music Consumption* (Dordrecht: Springer).

Oliver, Jeffrie, 2006. 'The Myth of Thomas Szasz', *New Atlantis* (summer): 68–84, <http://www.thenewatlantis.com/publications/correspondence-fall-2006> (accessed 29 Apr. 2013).

Olfson, Mark, and Steven C. Marcus 2009. 'National Patterns in Antidepressant Medication Treatment', *Archives of General Psychiatry* 66/8: 848–56.

Ong, Walter, 1977. 'African Talking Drums and Oral Neotics', *New Literary History* 8/3: 411–29.

Pavlicevic, Mercédès, 1997. *Music Therapy in Context* (London: Jessica Kingsley).

—— and Gary Ansdell 2004. *Community Music Therapy* (London: Jessica Kingsley).

—— and —— 2008. 'Between Communicative Musicality and Collaborative Musicing: Perspectives from Community Music Therapy', in S. Malloch and C. Trevarthen (eds), *Communicative Musicality* (Oxford: Oxford University Press), pp. 357–76.

Peterson, Richard, and Roger M. Kern 1996. 'Changing Highbrow Taste: From Snob to Omnivore', *American Sociological Review* 61/5: 900–907.

Pieslak, Jonathan, 2009. *Sound Targets: American Soldiers and Music in the Iraq War* (Bloomington: Indiana University Press).

Pinch, Trevor, 2010. 'The Invisible Technologies of Goffman's Sociology: From the Merry-Go-Round to the Internet', *Technology and Culture* 51/2: 409–24.

Pitts, Stephanie, 2005. *Valuing Musical Participation* (Farnham: Ashgate).

—— 2012. *Chances and Choices: Exploring the Impact of Music Education* (Oxford: Oxford University Press).

PricewaterhouseCoopers LLP 2009. *The Science of Personalized Medicine: Translating the Promise into Practice*, <http://www.pwc.com/us/en/health-industries/publications/impact-of-personalized-medicine-today.jhtml> (accessed 29 Apr. 2013).

Procter, Simon, 2009. 'Improvisation with a Client Exhibiting Profound Psychosis' (paper presented at the symposium on improvisation, 'Flirting with Uncertainty', at Exeter University, Department of Sociology and Philosophy, May).

—— 2011. 'Reparative Musicing: Thinking on the Usefulness of Social Capital Theory within Music Therapy', *Nordic Journal of Music Therapy* 20/3: 242–62.

Putnam, Robert, 2000. *Bowling Alone: The Collapse and Revival of American Community* (New York: Simon & Schuster).

Rawls, Anne Warfield, 1987. 'The Interaction Order Sui Generis: Goffman's Contribution to Social Theory', *Sociological Theory* 5: 136–49.

Reich, Nancy, 2001. *Clara Schumann: The Artist and The Woman* (revd edn, Ithaca, NY: Cornell University Press).

Rice, Tom, 2003. 'Soundselves: An Acoustemology of Sound and Self in the Edinburgh Royal Infirmary', *Anthropology Today* 19/4: 4–9.

—— 2010. *Listening to Hearts in a London Hospital* (London: Sean Kingston Press).

Risse, G.B., 1988. 'Hysteria at the Edinburgh Infirmary: The Construction and Treatment of a Disease, 1770–1899', *Medical History*, 32: 1–22.

Rose, N., 1996. *Inventing Our Selves: Psychology, Power and Personhood* (New York: Cambridge University Press).

Rosenhan, David, 1973. 'On Being Sane in Insane Places', *Science* 179/4070: 250–58.

Rothenberg, David, 2005. *Why Birds Sing: A Journey into the Mystery of Bird Song* (New York: Basic Books).

Rothstein, Mark, 2003. *Pharmacogenomics: Social, Ethical and Clinical Dimensions* (Hoboken, NJ: Wiley-Liss).

Roy, William, 2010. *Reds, Whites, and Blues* (Princeton: Princeton University Press).

Russ, T., et al., 2012. 'Association between Psychological Distress and Mortality: Individual Participant Pooled Analysis of 10 Prospective Cohort Studies', *British Medical Journal* 345, <http://www.bmj.com/content/345/bmj.e4933> (accessed 29 Apr. 2013).

Ruud, Even, 2002. 'Music as a Cultural Immunogen: Three Narratives on the Use of Music as a Technology of Health', in I.M. Hanken, S.G. Nielsen and M. Nerland (eds), *Research in and for Higher Music Education: Festschrift for Harald Jrgensen* (Oslo: NMH-publikasjoner), pp. 2-12.

—— 2005. 'Music: A Salutogenic Way to Health Promotion?', in G. Tellnes (ed.), *Urbanisation and Health: New Challenges in Health Promotion and Prevention* (Oslo: Unipubforlag), pp. 143–50.

—— 2008. 'Music in Therapy: Increasing Possibilities for Action', *Music and Arts in Action* 1/1: 46–60.

—— 2010. *Music Therapy: A Perspective from the Humanities* (Gilsum, NH: Barcelona Publishers).

Sarjala, Jukka, 2001. *Music, Morals, and the Body: An Academic Issue in Turku, 1653–1808* (Helsinki: SKS/FLS).

Schutz, A., 1964. 'Making Music Together', in *Collected Papers*, vol. 2 (The Hague: Martinus Njhoff), pp. 159–79.

—— and Charles Thorpe 2006. 'The Sociological Imagination of R.D. Laing', *Sociological Theory* 24/4: 331–52.

Searle, John, 1995. *The Social Construction of Reality* (Cambridge: Cambridge University Press).

Sennett, Richard, 1974. *The Fall of Public Man* (Cambridge: Cambridge University Press).

Sharfstein, Steven S., 2005. 'Big Pharma and American Psychiatry: The Good, the Bad, and the Ugly', *Psychiatric News* 40/16: 3, <http://psychnews. psychiatryonline.org/newsarticle.aspx?articleid=109213> (accessed 30 Aug. 2012).

Simmel, Georg, 1903. *The Metropolis and Mental Life*, ed. Gary Bridge and Sophie Watson (Oxford and Malden, MA: Wiley-Blackwell, 2002).

—— 1949. 'The Sociology of Sociability', *American Journal of Sociology* 55/3: 254–61.

Singer, T., et al., 2004. 'Empathy for Pain Involves the Affective but not Sensory Components of Pain', *Science* 303: 1157–62.

Singh, I., and N. Rose 2008. 'Biomarkers in Psychiatry', *Nature* 460: 202–7.

Skånland, M., 2011. 'Use of MP3 Players as a Coping Resource', *Music and Arts in Action* 3/2: 15–32.

Smith, Dorothy E., 2005. 'K is Mentally Ill', in *Texts, Facts and Femininity: Exploring the Relations of Ruling* (London: Routledge), pp. 9–42.

Society for Neuroscience 2007. 'Depression: Brain Imaging Reveals Breakdown of Normal Emotional Processing', *Science Daily* (20 Aug.), <http://www. sciencedaily.com /releases/2007/08/070816111752.htm> (accessed 2 Nov. 2010).

Stacy, Rosie, Katie Brittain and Sandra Kerr 2002. 'Singing for Health: An Exploration of the Issues', *Health Education* 102/4: 156–62.

Star, Susan Leigh, and James Griesemer 1989. 'Institutional Ecology, "Translations" and Boundary Objects: Amateurs and Professionals in Berkeley's Museum of Vertebrate Zoology, 1907–39', *Social Studies of Science* 19/3: 387–420.

Stige, Brynjulf, et al., 2010. *Where Music Helps: Community Music Therapy in Action and Reflection* (Aldershot: Ashgate).

Streeck, Jurgen, 1996. 'How to do Things with Things', *Human Studies* 19: 365–84.

Stroman, Duane, 2003. *The Disability Rights Movement: From Deinstitutionalisation to Self-Determination* (Lanham, MD: University Press of America).

Summer, L., 2002. 'Group Music and Imagery Therapy: An Emergent Music Therapy', in K. Bruscia and D. Grocke (eds), *Guided Imagery and Music: The Bonny Method and Beyond* (Gilsum, NH: Barcelona Publishers), pp. 297–306.

Sutherland, Ian, and S. Acord 2007. 'Thinking with Art: From Situated Knowledge to Experiential Knowing', *Journal of Visual Art Practice* 6/2: 125–40.

—— with Tia DeNora 2011. 'Musical Creativity as Social Agency: Composer Paul Hindemith', in D. Hargreaves, D. Miell and R. MacDonald (eds), *Musical Imaginations: Multidisciplinary Perspectives on Creativity, Performance and Perception* (Oxford: Oxford University Press), pp. 73–86.

Sutton Smith, Brian, 2001. *The Ambiguity of Play* (Cambridge, MA: Harvard University Press).

Szasz, Thomas, 1960. 'The Myth of Mental Illness', *American Psychologist* 15: 113–18.

—— 1961. *The Myth of Mental Illness: Foundations of a Theory of Personal Conduct* (revd edn, New York: Harper Perennial, 1984).

Tallis, Raymond, 2011. *Aping Mankind: Neuromania, Darwinitis and the Misrepresentation of Humanity* (Durham: Acumen).

Talwar, N., et al., 2006. 'Music Therapy for In-Patients with Schizophrenia: Exploratory Randomised Controlled Trial', *British Journal of Psychiatry* 189: 405–9.

Taylor, Charles, 1989. *Sources of the Self: The Making of the Modern Identity* (Cambridge, MA: Harvard University Press).

Tolstoy, L.N., 2004. *Anna Karenina*, trans R. Pevear and L. Volokhonsky (New York: Penguin).

Tota, Anna Lisa, 2001. 'When Orff Meets Guinness: Music in Advertising as a Form of Cultural Hybrid', *Poetics* 29/2: 109–23.

—— 2005. 'Counter-Memories of Terror: Technologies of Remembering and Technologies of Forgetting', in M.D. Jacobs and N.W. Hanharan (eds), *The*

Blackwell Companion to the Sociology of Culture (Oxford: Blackwell), pp. 272–85.

Trevarthan, Colin, 2002. 'Origins of Musical Identity: Evidence from Infancy for Musical Social Awareness', in R. MacDonald, D. Hargreaves and D. Miell (eds), *Musical Identities* (Oxford: Oxford University Press), pp. 21–38.

Trythall, S., 2006. 'Live Music in Hospitals: A New Alternative Therapy', *Journal of the Royal Society for the Promotion of Health* 126/3: 113–14.

Tufts Center for the Study of Drug Development 2011. 'Lack of Clinically Useful Diagnostics Hinder Growth in Personalized Medicines', *Tufts Center for the Study of Drug Development Impact Reports* 13/4 (July–August), <http://csdd. tufts.edu/news/complete_story/pr_ir_jul-aug_201129> (accessed 29 Apr. 2013).

Wagner-Pacifici, R., 1996. 'Memories in the Making: The Shape of Things that Went', *Qualitative Sociology* 19/3: 301–21.

Wallace, P.G., 1991. 'Post-Viral Fatigue Syndrome: Epidemiology: A Critical Review', *British Medical Bulletin* 47/4: 942–51.

Weinstein, R.W., 1994. 'Goffman's Asylums and the Social Situation of Mental Patients', *Psychiatry* 57/4: 348–67.

WHO, 2004. *DALYs by Age Sex and Cause for the Year 2004*, <http://apps.who. int/ghodata/?vid=110001> (accessed 29 Apr. 2013).

—— 2010. 'Mental Health: Strengthening our Response', Fact Sheet no. 220 (Sept.), <http://www.who.int/mediacentre/factsheets/fs220/en/> (accessed 29 Apr. 2013).

Wilkinson, R.G., and K.E. Pickett, 2007. 'Income Inequality and Social Gradients in Mortality', *American Journal of Public Health* 98/4: 699–704.

Williams, Simon, 2003. 'Marrying the Social and the Biological? A Rejoinder to Newton', *Sociological Review* 51/4: 550–61.

Winkler, Amanda Eubanks, 2006. *O Let Us Howle Some Heavy Note: Music for Witches, the Melancholic, and the Mad on the Seventeenth Century English Stage* (Bloomington: Indiana University Press).

Winner, Langdon, 1980. 'Do Artifacts Have Politics?', *Daedalus* 109/1 (winter); repr. in D. MacKenzie and J. Wajcman (eds), *The Social Shaping of Technology* (London: Open University Press, 1985; 2nd edn, 1999), pp. 121–36.

Wittgenstein, Ludwig, 2001. *Tractatus Logico-Philosophicus* (London: Routledge).

—— 2012. *Lectures: Conversations on Aesthetics, Psychology and Religion* (Berkeley, Los Angeles and London: University of California Press).

Woolf, Virginia, 1929. *A Room of One's Own* (New York: Harcourt, 1981).

Zelazo, P.D., 1999. 'Language, Levels of Consciousness, and the Development of Intentional Action', in P.D. Zelazo, J.W. Astington and D.R. Olson (eds), *Developing Theories of Intention: Social Understanding and Self-Control* (Mahwah, NJ: Lawrence Erlbaum Associates), pp. 95–117.

—— and J. Sommerville (2001). Levels of Consciousness of the Self in Time', in C. Moore and K. Lemmon (eds), *The Self in Time: Developmental Issues* (Mahwah, NJ: Lawrence Erlbaum Associates), pp. 229–52.

Index

Page numbers in bold indicate tables, italics indicate figures.

9781472455987